KEITH WATERHOUSE
COLLECTED PLAYS

KEITH WATERHOUSE

OUR SONG
BILLY LIAR with Willis Hall
JEFFREY BERNARD IS UNWELL
GOOD GRIEF
MR AND MRS NOBODY

COLLECTED PLAYS

OBERON BOOKS
LONDON

WWW.OBERONBOOKS.COM

This collection first published in 2012 by Oberon Books Ltd
521 Caledonian Road, London N7 9RH
Tel: +44 (0) 20 7607 3637 / Fax: +44 (0) 20 7607 3629
e-mail: info@oberonbooks.com
www.oberonbooks.com

A catalogue record for this book is available from the British Library.

ISBN: 978-1-84943-121-7

Cover image by Mark Reeve; markreevecartoonz.webs.com

Contents

OUR SONG   7

BILLY LIAR   85

JEFFREY BERNARD IS UNWELL   178

GOOD GRIEF   239

MR AND MRS NOBODY   315

OUR SONG

ADAPTED FROM HIS OWN NOVEL

First performed at the Apollo Theatre, London, on 3rd
November 1992 with the following cast:

ROGER PIPER, Peter O'Toole
ANGELA CAXTON, Tara Fitzgerald
JUDITH PIPER, Lucy Fleming
BELLE PARSONS, Cara Konig
CHARLES PECK, Jack Watling
GUNBY T. GUNBY, Donald Pickering
MAITRE DE L'HOTEL, William Sleigh

Director, Ned Sherrin
Designer, Tim Goodchild

Characters

ROGER PIPER
An advertising executive, in his 50s

ANGELA CAXTON
His mistress, in her late 20s

JUDITH PIPER
His wife

CHARLES PECK
His partner

GUNBY T. GUNBY
Owner of a hotel guide

BELLE PARSONS
A friend of Angela's

MAITRE DE L'HOTEL

Act One

We discover ROGER pecking away on a portable typewriter at a small table. After some moments he addresses the absent ANGIE (to whom he will be talking constantly throughout the play.)

ROGER: She thinks I'm writing a novel. A splendid idea, she calls it – therapy. And so it is, but for a different trauma than the one she imagines I'm going through. At my age the experience is shattering, bruising and the ultimate disillusion – but it isn't terminal. I can tell, simply by putting our affair on the scales and comparing it with all the lightweight, short-weight, make-weight relationships I've had before, that you'll be with me now until my death. But you won't be the cause of it. Relax. This is the last and longest letter I'll ever write you, and you can take that pained little smile off your face – it's not what you used to call one of my whingeograms. It's a love letter, Angie. Therapy.

SCENE 1

The patio of ROGER's house in Ealing.

A christening party has spilled out on to the patio, where several guests are sipping champagne and chatting. A young woman dressed all in black, with a black veil, talks to another guest, her back to ROGER.

ROGER enters the scene, still addressing ANGIE.

ROGER: You were born, I once said – and you were not amused – with a silver cock in your mouth. My count on your ex-sleeping partners at Tim's christening party stands at half a dozen confirmed and two suspected, and none of them arrived in anything less than a Porsche. Was it by choice or chance that you set your sights at the advertising racket?

The young woman now turns, spots ROGER across the patio, raises her veil – and her glass – and favours him with a ravishing smile. As he responds, his wife JUDITH turns away from another guest and joins him.

JUDITH: Roger, who *is* that extraordinary creature dressed all in black?

ROGER: Angela Caxton? I suppose she's what you might call a freelance factotum.

JUDITH: Is that what they're known as these days? Who brought her?

ROGER: I don't think anybody did.

JUDITH: Did you invite her?

ROGER: Certainly not.

JUDITH: But she can't just have walked up the drive thinking, 'Hallo, there's a party, I'll just wiggle in on my stiletto heels and help myself to champagne.'

ROGER: From what I've heard, it's exactly the kind of thing she would do.

JUDITH: And you'd find that amusing, would you? What does she think this is – *Breakfast at Tiffany's?*

ROGER: *(As a narrative aside.)* To tell you the truth I was with Judith on that one. I hate, quote, 'characters'. But I was falling in love with you, wasn't I? Across an uncrowded patio.

JUDITH: In black from tip to toe and top to...bottom, I shouldn't wonder. Do you suppose she meant to gatecrash a funeral and came to the wrong house?

ROGER: *(As a narrative aside.)* I guessed that the black outfit was your only set of what you called your dressing-up clothes. My heart lurched in pity – the first constituent of my love. *(To JUDITH.)* When women dress to startle it's usually because they lack confidence.

JUDITH: It's more often because they lack taste. So come on, Roger – what does she want?

ROGER: *(As a narrative aside, looking across at ANGIE.)* Me, it's to be hoped... *(To JUDITH.)* I can only imagine she's meeting someone here.

JUDITH: It's Timothy's christening party, not a place of assignation. How does she come to know you anyway? Or you her?

ROGER: *(To himself.)* Luigi's... *(As a narrative aside.)* It should have been Our Restaurant by now, but we never had one, did we? Or an Our Pub or Our Wine Bar or Our Hotel. We did have an Our Song, though, but you didn't know the words. Did you, my dear?

JUDITH: Well?

ROGER: I hardly know her at all. We were introduced by Hugh Kitchener...

His partner CHARLES PECK, who has been hovering, joins in the conversation.

CHARLES: ...and Associates. When they were celebrating taking the Chepstow's Choccy-Mints account from under our noses.

ROGER: *(As a narrative aside.)* There were six of you, all moderately pissed by the time Charles and I came in for your late lunch. *(To CHARLES.)* I wasn't quite sure where she fitted in. Market research, I believe.

CHARLES: Summer temp, I'd say.

JUDITH: Office bicycle? *(She moves away to greet other guests.)*

ROGER: You were sitting between Hugh and that bearded Old Etonian in graphics – correction, young Etonian, sod him – whom you rather wittily characterized as –

ANGIE now turns from her conversation to provide – unheard by the others the remembered line –

ANGIE: Pont Streetwise.

ROGER: He struck me as the kind of man who would pee in your sink... And while you were giving me the eye he was trying, so you told me later, to touch you up under the tablecloth.

ANGIE: He was.

ROGER: Trying? Since you had a cigarette in one hand and a glass in the other you must have been fighting him off with your thigh muscles.

Taking offence, ANGIE turns her back on him. ROGER sits at a table, where CHARLES comes to join him. The party guests, including ANGIE, drift into the background during the following.

The first thing I noticed about you was the flattering fact that you were noticing me. And Charles said:

SCENE 2

A restaurant.

CHARLES: Roger, something tells me you're in with a very good chance of making a raging fool of yourself.

ROGER: Very possibly. *(As a narrative aside.)* You'd gone off to powder your nose. When you came back, it was not to Hugh's table and Oliver the Old Etonian groper but to ours.

ANGIE crosses boldly to their table. ROGER and CHARLES rise.

ANGIE: Please don't get up.

CHARLES: I'll get you a chair.

ANGIE: There isn't one. *(Gazing at ROGER, she kneels on the floor, her elbows on the table.)* There. Now I'm your apostle, kneeling at your feet.

ROGER: Disciple.

ANGIE: I thought they were the same thing.

CHARLES: *(Introducing.)* Piper and Peck.

ROGER: Of Peck and Piper.

ANGIE: I know. Since we've been pointed out to one another I thought I'd come over and say hallo. I hope you don't mind.

ROGER: *(Touching her hair.)* Lovely hair.

ANGIE: It needs washing.

Kneeling, she allows ROGER to trickle wine into her mouth from her glass during the following:

ROGER: *(As a narrative aside.)* The details I've forgotten from that first meeting, if they were grains of sand, wouldn't tip a horizontally-balanced egg-timer.

ANGIE: *(With wine dribbling down her face.)* Mmmmmm! Dribbling! Oh dear, Charlie doesn't approve!

ROGER: No one ever called Charles Charlie. Ice having formed, he tried his awkward best to break it.

CHARLES: We're told you're a freelance factotum. What does that mean exactly?

ANGIE: *(With a trilling laugh.)* Oh dear, I often ask myself the same question. Whatever it is, I really ought to go and do some more of it. *(She scrambles to her feet in a rather gauche manner. About to dash off, she takes an eyebrow pencil from her bag, and grasping ROGER's wrist, scribbles a telephone number on the back of his hand.)* But if you ever want any factotumizing done, that's my number. Bye!

She hurries away.

CHARLES: *(Laconically.)* And you'll never wash it.

ROGER: *(Regarding the number on his wrist.)* Not until I've transferred it to my Filofax... All right, Charles, what are you saying? Tears before bedtime?

CHARLES: Tears *after* bedtime. But that's your affair.

CHARLES rises and moves off.

ROGER rises and addresses the absent ANGIE.

ROGER: I made some enquiries about you – I would, wouldn't I? I found you went to the Corkscrew, our friendly neighbourhood wine bar, well-abbreviated as the Screw. It was never one of my haunts but that evening I went there, despite a command from Judith to be home –

JUDITH: Sober.

ROGER: – in time for supper with her friend – that trained freeloader Gunby J. Gunby, of the Good Living Guide.

GUNBY, who is present at the christening party, bows ironically.

I was entitled to ask myself what I thought I was up to. My love, I had no idea. I once asked you, long after I'd got to know you less, what you'd had in mind yourself.

ANGIE: I don't know. I never used to think as far ahead as tomorrow in those days. I daren't think beyond next week even now.

ROGER: The Screw was a sexual inferno, stinking of cheap scent and expensive aftershave, where the flotsam and jetsam of the advertising world danced to the music of their own voices. You were with the bearded young bugger you'd been sitting next to at lunch. Little realizing he was the future subject of an amusing anecdote revolving around his clumsy attempts to grope you under the tablecloth, he was confidently steering you towards the stairs. Your place or his? Quite suddenly I had a yearning to be home in Ealing, and I left, the only man in that place craving the clean taste of Ovaltine. The first time I ever took you to lunch you harked back, as I did, to that day, but neither of us to that evening. You were very funny about the bearded young Etonian, how he had contrived to sit next to you and yow you'd thwarted his under-the-table activities with the deflating remark –

ANGIE: I hadn't realized you were left-handed.

ROGER: The whole point of the story being that his strenuous advances came to nothing, you didn't spoil it by confessing that a few hours later they were to come to a good deal. Nor, since you didn't yet know me, was there any reason why you should. But I did wonder why you bothered to tell it... Wives get it wrong, you know. It's supposed to be sex alone that draws men like me into situations like this, but it isn't; it's the excitement. And it isn't the excitement of the chase, it's the excitement, when you feel like a dud battery, of having someone to be excited about...

He returns to:

SCENE 3

The christening party.

CHARLES approaches him.

CHARLES: Now that Judith's out of earshot – did you invite your little friend along as the spectre at the feast, or was it her own idea?

ROGER: She's doing some factotuming for me.

CHARLES: Oh yes, on teenage marketing trends.

ROGER: Did you see her report?

CHARLES: Yes – in *Marketing Week* six months ago. I will say she's copied it out very neatly...

GUNBY approaches with JUDITH, who bears a tray of canapés.

Hallo Gunby. How's the Good Living Guide?

GUNBY: It's a living. Roger, I've been trying to place your stunning guest.

JUDITH: Probably you met her at your step-daughter's wedding.

GUNBY: No – she wasn't invited.

JUDITH: What's that got to do with it?

JUDITH and CHARLES move away.

GUNBY: *(To ROGER.)* No, I've remembered where I've seen her. She dines at the World's End Brasserie quite a lot with young Ben Cheevers. Do you know it? Brilliant charcuterie.

ROGER: Ben Cheevers?

GUNBY: Complete shit – runs the Chelsea Auction Galleries. Now where's Judith gone with those delicious vol-au-vents...?

GUNBY moves off. ANGIE, carrying a glass of champagne, meanders out on to the patio, where she finds herself alone with ROGER.

ROGER: Angela, what a lovely surprise.

ANGIE: Surprise or shock? I knew I shouldn't have come. Shall I go?

ROGER: Of course you shan't go, you've only just arrived.

ANGIE: But quite obviously uninvited. Some of your friends have been looking daggers at me.

ROGER: They're admiring you or enjoying you, according to sex.

ANGIE: I really shouldn't have barged in on you like this but I've a friend who lives in Richmond which isn't all that far away, so I thought I'd kill two birds with one stone. I'm sorry.

ROGER: Please stop apologizing. I'm delighted to see you.

ANGIE: I was anxious to know what you thought of my research. On teenage marketing trends.

ROGER: Does it matter so much?

ANGIE: Very much.

ROGER: Our cheque is in the post.

ANGIE: I didn't mean that.

ROGER: So have you just come from Richmond or are you on your way there?

ANGIE: You mean you want me to go?

ROGER: I mean I want you to stay as long as you like and let me pour you some champagne, Angela.

ANGIE: Angie.

ROGER: Is that what your friends call you?

ANGIE: Only specially selected ones. You're only allowed to call me Angela when you're cross with me.

ROGER: Which I'm positively not. In fact on top of your fee I'm arranging to pay you a little bonus.

ANGIE: No, you mustn't do that.

ROGER: But it was damned hard work, Angela – Angie.

ANGIE: That's all right. I *like* doing things for you.

ROGER: Why?

ANGIE: You're appreciative. A lot of people aren't, you know.

ROGER: But as it's the first time you've ever worked for me, how could you tell whether I'd be appreciative or not?

ANGIE: Kind eyes.

ROGER notices JUDITH hovering and decides to neutralize the conversation.

ROGER: Champagne?

ANGIE: Just one more glass before I go.

ROGER: If you're going to Richmond I'm sure someone here could give you a lift.

ANGIE: No, I'm not going to Richmond – my friend's away.

ROGER: Oh – I thought you were on your way there.

ANGIE: Yes, I would have been, but when I rang her she was out. So I thought I'd drop in anyway.

ROGER: I'm very glad you did.

ANGIE: Also, I wanted you to invite me to lunch one day.

ROGER: Which day?

JUDITH now bears down on them.

JUDITH: Do you live here in Ealing, Miss Caxton?

ANGIE: No, Islington.

JUDITH: Oh good. Then you don't have far to go.

ANGIE: Even so, I must dash. *(Shaking hands with JUDITH.)* Thank you for having me. Goodbye.

ANGIE exits.

JUDITH, showing her out, turns back to ROGER.

JUDITH: *I* certainly haven't had her – how about you?

ROGER now addresses the now absent ANGIE.

ROGER: Later I found the christening present you'd left for Timothy on the hall table. We'd met only twice before but that early Victorian silver rattle must have cost your overdraft a good eighty to a hundred pounds. I was touched and exasperated. It was preposterous. At my time of life I was falling in love with you – and that was preposterous too...

The christening party scene is lost as ROGER steps into his London office at Peck and Piper.

SCENE 4

ROGER's office/ANGIE's dingy flat.

ROGER dials ANGIE's number. It rings for a moment, then we hear her answering machine.

ANGIE's voice: This is Angela Caxton and Belle Parsons. We're not taking calls at the moment but if you'd care to leave a message we'll get back to you. Speak after the bleep...

There's an electronic bleep.

ROGER: *(Into the phone.)* Angie, it's Roger – Roger Piper. About our lunch. I wonder if you could manage Wednesday at Le Bistro. Would you ring me back? Bye... Er – at my office number, that is. *(He hangs up.)* The bureaucracy involved in starting an affair is incredible. I rang you but you were out. Or rather you said you were out. I rang again. This time you'd forgotten to switch on your answering machine. Or you said you had. *(He picks up the phone and dials her number again.)*

The telephone rings several times.

ANGELA appears in her dressing gown. She looks impassively at the telephone until it stops ringing. She is petulant as she and ROGER launch into the subsequent conversation. She changes to go out for lunch during the following:

ANGIE: If I said I was out, how could I have been in?

ROGER: It's possible.

ANGIE: That I was in when I was out, or out when I was in?

ROGER: Don't be more confusing than you can help, Angie.

ANGIE: Angela, thank you *very* much. You're the one who's confusing. How do you make out I was out, when I was in to say I wasn't in?

ROGER: I'm talking about what you said later, *Angela*! You said you were out and you never got my message.

ANGIE: It's true – I didn't. My answering machine wasn't working.

ROGER: But I *spoke* to your answering machine. Several times!

ANGIE: It never passed on the message.

ROGER: *(With a great effort at patience.)* All right. I had your address. I sent you a note. Would you meet me at Le Bistro, and if you couldn't make it would you ring me?

ANGIE: I wasn't able to. I told you – my answering machine wasn't working.

ROGER: You don't make telephone calls with your answering machine! Anyway, that isn't the point. The point is that you didn't turn up.

ANGIE: Well, perhaps I had to see someone.

ROGER: Then why couldn't you just say so? *(Pause.)* Whom did you have to see?

ANGIE: It's ages ago. How can I possibly remember?

ROGER: By looking in your diary.

ANGIE: I don't always put things in my diary. If you really want to know, I think I had to have lunch with Ben Cheevers.

ROGER: Oh, him.

ANGIE: He's a friend. Or aren't I allowed to have friends?

ROGER: Of course you are, but why did you never call me back to make it another day? Why did I have to keep calling *you*?

ANGIE: There you go again – raking up the past.

ROGER: You can be so bloody exasperating.

ANGIE: Now you're raking up the present.

She exits. CHARLES enters ROGER's office carrying a file.

CHARLES: We ought to discuss the Penn's Shortbread Products account. How about lunch?

ROGER: Sorry, I have a lunch, Charles.

CHARLES: Entertaining a client?

ROGER: Prospective one, since you ask.

CHARLES: I hope she turns up this time. *(He tosses the file on ROGER's desk.)* None of my business, Roger, but if you take this with you, you won't be reduced to doing the *Evening Standard* word game.

CHARLES exits.

ROGER crosses to:

SCENE 5

A restaurant.

ROGER pours himself a glass of champagne.

ROGER: But turn up you did, eventually... I arrived half an hour early, like a teenager on his first date. And I wonder how many hours amounting to days, weeks, I've whiled away in souvenir boutiques and Hallmark card shops during that long, last haul between half-past twelve and one. And always you'd arrive half an hour late gushing apologies and within seconds you'd have the restaurant in turmoil.

ANGIE flurries in as anticipated, kisses him on both cheeks and knocks over the champagne bottle.

ANGIE: Sorry, sorry, sorry, sorry, sorry – I had to wait for Belle coming home – she's lost her key again – oh dear, did I do that? – how stupid of me – but it is quite a small table, isn't it? Not really a table for two at all.

ROGER: It has been a table for one in its time.

ANGIE: What's wrong with that nice big table over there?

ROGER: That's a table for six.

ANGIE: We could play musical chairs round it.

ROGER: And it's permanently reserved for Saatchi and Saatchi. Waiter – another bottle.

ANGIE: Do you always drink champagne?

ROGER: When I'm with effervescent company. That's a lovely dress.

ANGIE: Thank you. It was given to me.

ROGER: By?

ANGIE: Oh, just a friend. He found it among some stuff his wife had sorted out for Oxfam, and thought I'd like it.

ROGER: *(As a narrative aside.)* The mysterious Ben Cheevers, I had no doubt. For a long time after you told me that story I gleaned a good deal of comfort, on a juvenile, snickering level, out of thinking what a cheapskate he must be. *(To ANGIE.)* I hope you're hungry.

ANGIE: Starving. You must be too. I'm sorry to have kept you waiting – were you in a tizz?

ROGER: I might have been if your friend Belle had been a little later getting home.

ANGIE: I was furious. Usually when she loses her key she's back in time for breakfast.

ROGER: What does this night-owl do?

ANGIE: I've never been really sure.

ROGER: But you're flatmates.

ANGIE: I know. She *used* to work at the Chelsea Auction Galleries. That's where we first met. The only real job I've ever had.

ROGER: With Ben Cheevers.

ANGIE: *(Guardedly.)* Do you know him?

ROGER: Only by reputation.

ANGIE: Reputations aren't always what they're reputed to be.

ROGER: So when was this?

ANGIE: Six years ago. But then Belle was fired – for going to bed with one of the porters.

ROGER: Was that anybody's business but theirs?

ANGIE: In company time? On a Louis the sixteenth *chaise-longue*? In the firm's pantechnicon? On a double yellow line in the King's Road?

ROGER: Ah.

ANGIE: So perhaps you can work out for yourself what she's been doing since.

ROGER: She doesn't bounce up and down on beds for a living, does she?

ANGIE: I believe so.

ROGER: You mean she's a prostitute?

ANGIE: I think it's called being an escort. She's got a terrific collection of hotel bookmatches.

ROGER: *(As a narrative aside.)* And the subject was not so much dismissed as banished. I don't believe we ever had a single conversation we reached the end of. We did get one or two things settled, thought. *(To ANGIE.)* Background?

ANGIE: Daddy was a lieutenant-general.

ROGER: But your bedsitter accent demoted him to major. Education?

ANGIE: I ran away from all the best schools.

ROGER: CV?

ANGIE: I try to remain self-employed.

ROGER: Marital status?

ANGIE: The same.

ROGER: *(As a narrative aside.)* And then, over that last glass of champagne, and possibly influenced by the fact that it was the last of seven, not counting the intervening claret, you launched into a completely new scenario, the opening line being:

ANGIE: I think I'm in love.

ROGER: I thought at first you didn't mean me at all and I was to be your agony uncle. *(To ANGIE.)* I bet he's married.

ANGIE: Yes, he is, much to my annoyance.

ROGER: Are they always?

ANGIE: There's no always about it. I don't make a practice of falling in love.

ROGER: And are we allowed to know who is the lucky recipient of this exclusive affection?

ANGIE: It would be you, silly, if you weren't being so pompous.

ROGER: *(As a narrative aside.)* It was a good lunch we were having, the champagne was flowing, you were relaxed and happy, and you did feel a wave of love towards me... *(To ANGIE.)* I'm not really pompous, am I?

ANGIE: You can be. I don't mind, it's quite endearing.

ROGER: And how do I unpompously get you to repeat what you've just said?

ANGIE: That I'm in love?

ROGER: That you think you're in love.

ANGIE: I am. Madly.

ROGER: So what's to be done about it?

ANGIE: That's rather up to you.

ROGER: I wish it were. But you know my situation.

ANGIE: Yes, and you have an adorable baby boy with whom I'm even more in love, and I'm talking lots of nonsense. Thank you for a lovely lunch. Must dash. *(She gathers up her things and plants a big kiss on his cheek.)* Mmm – there!

She exits.

He contemplates for a moment and then crosses into:

SCENE 6

The patio of ROGER's house/ANGIE's flat.

GUNBY T. GUNBY is present, having drinks with JUDITH. Helping himself to a drink, ROGER joins them. GUNBY and JUDITH remain in conversation during the following narrative aside:

ROGER: That evening Gunby T. Gunby came in for drinks on his way back from slagging off a restaurant in Slough for the *Good Living Guide*. I was glad of the intrusion. You and I had only had lunch. But the deception had started, and I was already leading a double life. Forever after, for so long as it lasted, I should be two people, one going through the motions of domestic and business life, the other involved, on whatever level, with you. *(He reluctantly tries to come down to earth.)*

GUNBY: What do you think, Roger?

ROGER: About?

GUNBY: I was saying Judith ought to try her hand at television.

ROGER: Doing what?

JUDITH: Well – not reading the weather!

GUNBY: She *is* a cookery writer! Her own programme! I've some good contacts with daytime TV in the North. Worth exploring, wouldn't you say?

ROGER: *(As a narrative aside.)* And immediately I thought: the North, that means overnight, I could take you to a hotel. It was how I beginning to think and that was how it was to be for sixteen months. God forgive me, if Timothy had been rushed to hospital and Judith had gone along to hold his little hand, I should have thought that gives me more time

with Angie. *(To JUDITH and GUNBY.)* Well worth exploring.
Good idea.

JUDITH: *(To GUNBY.)* Would you like some more olives?

GUNBY: Oh, please...and some of those little salty bikkies!

JUDITH exits into the house. ANGIE enters her flat where she takes off her coat and begins brushing her hair.

(Confidentially.) I saw that mysterious young lady of yours a couple of nights ago.

ROGER: Angie.

GUNBY: With that little turd Ben Cheevers.

ROGER: Yes, it turns out she used to work for him. Where was this, then?

GUNBY: At Le Bistro.

ROGER: Two nights ago.

GUNBY: God, that chocolate soufflé!

JUDITH enters with a plate of canapés.

As JUDITH and GUNBY converse, ROGER enters into a future conversation with ANGIE.

ROGER: I wanted every scrap of news about you, anything that might be a piece of the jigsaw. I wish you'd said you knew Le Bistro almost as well as I did, Angie – that you'd been taken there so often it was a marvel we hadn't seen one another there.

ANGIE: I never said it was my first visit.

ROGER: You never said it wasn't. And why didn't you tell me you'd been there with Ben Cheevers a couple of nights earlier?

ANGIE: Why should I? It wasn't important.

ROGER: You could have said you'd forgotten.

ANGIE: I had, almost. And it *isn't* important, darling. Going to places with you makes them seem altogether different from going to them with him.

ROGER: What places? Which places?

ANGIE: Roger, you are not going to put me in the witness box! *(She turns her back on him.)*

ROGER: *(As a narrative aside.)* I just couldn't help myself, Angie. I didn't even want to know, that was the ridiculous thing. What the hell did it matter where you'd been with him? Then it came back to me that that wasn't what I'd asked. What I did want to know was why you were so cagey about telling me what you said was of no importance anyway.

JUDITH and GUNBY bring him back to the present.

JUDITH: Roger?

ROGER: Yes?

JUDITH: Gunby's leaving.

GUNBY: I have a table booked at the Ivy. An urgent appointment with the eggs Benedict.

ROGER: Give my regards to anyone I know...

JUDITH shows GUNBY out.

(In another future conversation.) Our third or was it our fourth lunch was at the Ivy, when with our ankles intertwined under the tablecloth I blurted out: Look, are we having an affair or not?

ANGIE: *(Demurely.)* It's not for me to say.

ROGER: We're not getting anywhere, are we?

ANGIE: You can always turn back if you want to.

ROGER: Do you want me to?

ANGIE: No, I should be very sad if you did.

ROGER: Then we are having an affair. Or we're about to.

ANGIE: We must be.

ROGER: *(As a narrative aside; returning to the patio scene.)* But you wouldn't say where we were going to have it.

JUDITH returns and clears away the glasses.

28

JUDITH: I wish you wouldn't come home with lipstick on your cheek, Roger. You know it doesn't suit you.

ROGER: Sorry. A gushing client.

JUDITH: You might at least invent a name for her. You're not having it off somewhere, are you?

ROGER: If I were, I'd very much like to know when.

JUDITH: Well, *I* don't know what you get up to when you're locked away in your creative sessions, do I? Or who you get up.

JUDITH goes back into the house.

ROGER moves to:

SCENE 7

A champagne bar/the patio of ROGER's house.

There are two full champagne glasses on the bar, and ANGIE's coat is draped over a bar stool. ROGER picks up his glass.

ROGER: We did get into one bad habit, though – staggering round to Freddy's Club for one more bottle of champagne after a long, long lunch... So it was that during all those sixteen months with you I was never entirely sober. If we didn't have an Our Restaurant, my darling, we certainly had an Our Drink. I bet we must have put away a good six hundred bottles of Lanson Black Label from the start to the finish of our loving. Three hundred magnums. Seventy-odd Methuselahs. Christ – if they gave you fivepence back on the bottle like they do with Newcastle Brown, we could have stayed legless for three days on the empties. I'm bleeding, Angie. Think of the good things, that's what you always said.

ANGIE appears from the Ladies' room and takes up her glass. She is sparky but on the verge of getting stroppy.

ANGIE: That really was a lovely lunch, darling.

ROGER: Pity Hugh Kitchener was sitting across the room. I wouldn't mind our being looked at like that if we'd done something to earn it.

ANGIE: Perhaps we look as if we have.

Their hands intertwine.

ROGER: I wish we had somewhere to go, Angie.

ANGIE: So do it.

ROGER: But haven't we?

ANGIE: Your place or mine?

ROGER: No, seriously, Angie.

ANGIE: You mean a hotel?

ROGER: I mean your flat.

ANGIE: So my place?

ROGER: Is there any reason why not?

ANGIE: Why not your place?

ROGER: Come on, Angie!

ANGIE makes a great show of getting ready to leave.

ANGIE: To your place? When? Now? Fine! How shall we get
there – tube or cab?

ROGER: Don't be silly. The house isn't unoccupied by day, as
you must perfectly well know.

ANGIE: Neither is my flat. As *you* perfectly well now.

ROGER: You mean Belle?

ANGIE: Who else? *I* haven't got a family tucked away, you
know.

ROGER: But she must go out sometimes?

ANGIE: Yes, I've told you – at night.

ROGER: So if I made myself available in the evening, we could
go round to your flat, is that what you're saying?

ANGIE: Made yourself available? You sound as if you were
putting time aside for a blood transfusion.

ROGER: Yes, I put that crudely. I'm sorry.

ANGIE: Besides, she isn't out each and every night of the week. What if you made elaborate arrangements to see me and then she stayed in?

ROGER: I'd still take you to dinner.

ANGIE: *(Softening.)* I'd like that.

ROGER leaves ANGIE drinking champagne.

He steps back to the patio of his home where he helps JUDITH into her coat. JUDITH carries an overnight bag.

ROGER: So dinner I took you to, at –

ANGIE: Mr Chow's?

ROGER: The Peking Experience. You ought to remember where we had our first dinner, Angie.

ANGIE: Does the place matter? It's the occasion that matters.

ROGER: There *was* no occasion – not for me. It was an occasion for Judith – her first television assignment. *(To JUDITH.)* Good luck, darling, and don't forget I'll be out this evening, so don't ring me, I'll ring you, because I'll be –

JUDITH: Entertaining a client? Rather a shop-soiled phrase, isn't it? That's why the Inland Revenue won't let you set it against tax.

They kiss lightly.

JUDITH exits.

ROGER: What a shit one feels at times like these – and what was it all in aid of anyway?

He rejoins ANGIE in the champagne bar and refills her glass.

I think I should have told you this earlier, but Judith's away from home tonight.

ANGIE: *(Stiffening.)* Oh?

ROGER: *(As a narrative aside.)* You'd arrived tense for dinner but you relaxed as what you thought was the Cinderella hour approached. Now you knew I wouldn't turn into a pumpkin if I missed the last train you were tense again. *(To ANGIE.)* She's making her television debut in Manchester.

ANGIE: So you must have known about this for some time.

ROGER: Yes. I didn't want to make a formal announcement because it would have sounded premeditated.

ANGIE: Premeditated what?

ROGER: That on such and such an ordained evening we would go back to your flat.

ANGIE: And my views don't count, I suppose? What if I don't want you to come back?

ROGER: Don't you?

ANGIE: Whether I do or not is beside the point, because Belle happens to be in bed –

ROGER: *(As a narrative aside.)* With what, or perhaps with whom, I forget.

ANGIE: The flu.

ROGER: No, it was the flu the second time Judith went up north. The first time it was her accursed curse. Not that it matters.

ANGIE: Why couldn't you have told me this earlier?

ROGER: Why? Would you have had her moved into hospital?

ANGIE: I'm sorry Roger – I know you're disappointed.

ROGER: But you're not?

ANGIE: Yes, I am!

ROGER: Can I ask you something, Angie? Have you taken other people back to your flat?

ANGIE: I may have done. What's that to do with us?

ROGER: How did you get rid of Belle?

ANGIE: I didn't have to. They weren't married men.

ROGER: Even if they were bigamists they don't appear to have fallen victim to her diplomatic menstruation.

ANGIE: I wish you'd stop being so bitter and twisted, Roger. Don't you understand it's because of them I'm so reluctant to have you round?

ROGER: No, I don't.

ANGIE: You don't understand you're special?

ROGER: What's so special about being refused your bed? I think I'd prefer to be run-of-the-mill.

ANGIE: Now listen to me, darling. Yes, I have had other people round to the flat but they were silly, pointless, aimless flings that didn't mean anything. I'm ashamed of them and I'm ashamed of my grotty flat and that's why I don't want you there.

ROGER: At all?

ANGIE: At all. Can't you accept that I'm paying you a huge compliment?

ROGER: A compliment. Look. You meet all these other characters and they seemingly have no difficulty in getting back to your flat and sleeping with you. I have been battering at your door to no effect for two months now and you tell me it's because I'm special!

ANGIE: I'm just afraid of us moving our relationship on to another plane.

ROGER: But you said you were in love with me.

ANGIE: I am, you know I am, but within that relationship.

ROGER: *(As a narrative aside.)* And I put you into a cab thinking: what a cock-teaser.

He helps ANGIE into her coat. They move out together, ROGER signalling for a taxi. He comes back without her and refills his glass.

I could have gone off you, Angie, in fact I did. To tell the truth the need to sleep with you wasn't all that desperate – no one can remain in a state of mental erection for weeks on end. Was I falling out of love with you? Had I ever really been in love with you? The answer seemed to be that whatever I felt for you was like a plant that needed water. It had to grow or wither.

ANGIE rejoins him in the limbo area.

ROGER: Angie, I'm afraid I can't see you on Friday. I have to go to Edinburgh.

ANGIE: Business?

ROGER: Penn's Shortbread Products. They're feeling neglected.

ANGIE: So am I.

ROGER: I haven't gone yet. I shall miss you.

ANGIE: I'll miss you too. Will you fly or go by train to Edinburgh?

ROGER: Fly.

ANGIE: I've never been in an aeroplane. Would you hold my hand very tightly if I came with you?

SCENE 8

A hotel bedroom.

ROGER and ANGIE enter. He carries an overnight bag and briefcase, she has a cheap little cardboard suitcase.

ROGER: *(As a narrative aside.)* I remember your first words as you saw the foil-wrapped after-dinner mint on the pillow.

ANGIE: Oo, look – they've left us a contraceptive.

ROGER: Then you sat on the bed and bounced up and down experimentally. It was all a bit matter-of-fact for me. It was as if you were testing the equipment in a gymnasium.

ANGIE, taking a silk kimono out of her suitcase, goes into the bathroom.

ANGIE: I'll just have a quick bath, darling, then I'm all yours.

ROGER: You screwed, and that's the word for it, like a promiscuous college girl grimly ploughing her way through *The Joy of Sex*. I'd never encountered the generation gap in bed before – making love to you, at first was like being a parent at a pop concert, tapping his foot and enjoying himself but being ever so self-conscious about where he is and the company he's in, and very, very careful not to make a fool of himself... You blithely and resolutely

34

went from one manoeuvre to another, from one position to another, as if ticking them off in a catalogue. I became gloomier and gloomier at the realization of how little my sexual vocabulary overlapped with yours. Once, when I tried some modest innovation of my own, you said quite sharply –

ANGIE, enters wearing her kimono.

ANGIE: *(Entering.)* No, I never like doing it like that. *(She stacks an armful of toilet requisites into her little suitcase.)*

During the following she takes the room service menu, picks up the telephone and punches out a number.

ROGER: You came out of the bathroom smelling like the perfume and toiletries department of Selfridges and wearing a kimono unknowingly bequeathed to you by the wife of bloody Ben Cheevers. You took a childish delight in the little grotto of soaps, shampoos, bath foam and other bathroom paraphernalia, and swept the lot into your suitcase. It was a cheap little suitcase and I made up my mind to buy you another one. I was afflicted with a desire to make you happy by giving you things – love, money, presents, new clothes, new friends, a new life if I could... Who are you ringing, kitten?

ANGIE: I don't think we should waste precious time going out for that late lunch you promised. *(Into the phone.)* This is room four-o-four. Could we please have smoked salmon sandwiches for two and a bottle of champagne? *(As an afterthought.)* Each. *(She hangs up.)*

ROGER: *(To ANGIE.)* That's a lovely idea, Angie, but in that case I insist on taking you out to dinner.

ANGIE: But you're having dinner with Penn's Shortbread Products.

ROGER: As they say up here, the best-laid schemes gang aft a-gley. I'll tell Mrs Penn I've got to get the night shuttle so I've only time for a cocktail.

ANGIE: So where does that leave me?

ROGER: It leaves you being treated to a three-course dinner instead of fending for yourself in a Pizza Hut.

ANGIE: This evening? But I have things to do.

ROGER: What things? You don't know Edinburgh.

ANGIE: No, but I like wandering about new places.

ROGER: Don't you want to wander around them with me?

ANGIE: Perhaps, but I want to be on my own sometimes.

ROGER: You're very often on your own, Angie. Come on – here's a chance to spend a whole day and night together for a change.

ANGIE: Yes, well, I don't like my arrangements being upset.

ROGER: But you don't have arrangements!

ANGIE: I have arrangements with myself.

ROGER: *(As a narrative aside.)* I could have shaken you. I could see you almost visibly deciding whether to go into a sulk or not. *(He snatches up the telephone and punches out a number furiously. Into the phone.)* Room Service?... This is room – what the hell is our room number, Angie?

ANGIE: *(Sulkily.)* It's on the telephone.

ROGER: *(Into the phone.)* Room four-o-four. Look, I ordered champagne and smoked salmon sandwiches hours ago... Thank you. *(He hangs up.)* They're on their way.

ANGIE: *(Softening.)* Now don't work yourself up into a tizz.

ROGER: *(As a narrative aside.)* All very well for you to talk – you'd less to lose. Like you I was no stranger to strange beds, but age catches up with you and this was it. You were having an affair, I was having *the* affair. When it was over, for me it would all be gone. For you, there'd be another along in a minute.

ANGIE: Come on, darling, we're going to have a lovely time. Promise.

They embrace.

ROGER: Are we going to do this again very soon, Angie?

ANGIE: We haven't done it the first time round, yet – why wish it away?

They sink on to the bed and begin to make love. There is a furious knocking at the door.

WAITER's voice: Room service!

ROGER: Fuck!

ANGIE: Let's!

Blackout.

SCENE 9

A champagne bar.

ROGER and ANGIE lurch in, the worse for drink.

ROGER: *(As a narrative aside.)* That should have been the beginning but it wasn't. You asked me to hurry back to you but you wouldn't be hurried back to, that was the trouble. Oh, we met as usual, for lunch as usual, but any hope I might have nurtured that I now possessed an open sesame to your flat, and therefore to your bed, was finally dashed one night when Judith was up in Manchester again and I took you to supper. I was emboldened to ask: *(To ANGIE.)* Why don't we have coffee at your place?

ANGIE: Oh, do put another record on!

ROGER: Don't you *want* us to make love again?

ANGIE: Of course I do, all the time, but you know about the flat situation. I've told you and told you.

ROGER: So I'm not just another notch on your bedpost?

ANGIE: You're being maudlin. Stop it.

ROGER: I'm entitled to be bloody maudlin! You've got me jumping through hoops, Angela! Here am I lavishing lunch on you twice a week, pouring champagne down your throat, bringing you presents, phoning you six times a day and for what? Just who the hell do you think you are?

ANGIE: *(Rising unsteadily.)* I'm going home, Roger.

ROGER: Bugger off, then.

ANGIE: I need some money for a taxi.

ROGER: Bloody walk.

ANGIE: It's raining.

ROGER: I bought you an umbrella – where its it?

ANGIE: *(Tearfully.)* I must have left it somewhere... Why are you being so horrible to me, Roger?

ROGER rises hurriedly as she turns away to leave.

ROGER: Hang on, Angie.

ANGIE: I've told you – I'm going. I feel sick.

ROGER: I'll take you home.

ANGIE: I don't want you to.

ROGER: I'm taking you home, Angie. Whether you let me through the door when we get there is entirely a matter for you.

With ROGER supporting ANGIE, who is now very drunk, they proceed to:

SCENE 10

ANGIE's flat.

It is in darkness as we hear ANGIE and ROGER stumbling in.

ANGIE: You can't come in, you know. Oh, shit!

ROGER: You've dropped your keys.

ANGIE: I know I've dropped my keys. I often drop my keys... thank you. Off you go – I did give you a fair warning.

ROGER: At least let me ring for a cab – it's pissing down.

ANGIE: No, I don't want you here. *(She switches on the light.)*

ROGER takes in the bare, bleak surroundings.

So now you know.

ROGER: *(As a narrative aside.)* It was the saddest room I'd ever come across. If I'd come by invitation and had brought

you flowers, there wasn't even a vase to put them in...
Where's your friend Belle?

ANGIE: Gone.

ROGER: Gone where?

ANGIE: Gone. Does it matter where?

ROGER: When did she go, Angie?

ANGIE: You keep asking that!

ROGER: No, I don't – but now that I *have* asked, Angie, what's
the answer?

ANGIE: *(With a resigned sigh.)* You obviously don't approve
of Belle or I would have told you. She's moved in with a
waiter in Soho.

ROGER: Of course she has. So your excuse that you couldn't
bring me back because of Belle no longer holds water.
Since when?

ANGIE: You're grilling me, Roger. Stop grilling me!

ROGER: I have to grill you, just to get a straight answer to a
simple question. I didn't ask why Belle left but quite simply
when did she go?

ANGIE: How do I know? I didn't ask her the date! Why do
you go on and on and on about everything? What does it
matter? *(Still in her coat, she slumps on to the sofa and goes into
a drunken stupor during the following.)*

ROGER: I go on about everything because it does matter. If
everything doesn't matter to us then nothing matters. Do
you comprehend that? Angela? Angela! *(He grabs her arms
and shakes her roughly.)*

ANGIE: *(Wrenching herself away angrily.)* Stop doing that! Let go
of me!

ROGER: I'm asking you a question, Angela!

ANGIE: I'm sick of your stupid questions and sick of you!
Leave, will you? Why don't you go!

ROGER: If I do go I shan't come back.

ANGIE: I don't want you back. I didn't want you here in the first place. *(She goes back into her stupor.)*

ROGER hesitates then moves out, switching off the light.

ROGER: Sweet dreams.

Outside the flat he hesitates.

(As a narrative aside.) I could have gone back and strangled you, you were so exasperating. I was sick of painting myself into humiliating corners. I was sick of your brick wall. It was all over...or would have been, had not Charles of all people come unknowingly to your rescue and to mine...

SCENE 11

ROGER's office/ANGIE's flat.

ANGIE remains slumped on her sofa. ROGER sits at his desk.

CHARLES enters.

CHARLES: I'm a fraction worried about the Penn's Shortbread Products account.

ROGER: I thought I'd sorted all that out.

CHARLES: Businesswise yes, but you don't seem to have sorted Mrs Penn out. She says you stood her up for dinner.

ROGER: I didn't stand her up – I was anxious not to miss the last shuttle.

CHARLES: But you didn't catch the last shuttle. You stayed at the *Caledonian*, remember?

ROGER: For Christ's sake, I was tired!

CHARLES: Be that as it may, Mrs Penn is miffed. She's going to be in London next week so I've made the supreme sacrifice and promised to take her to the opera.

ROGER: Very noble, but you have the Venice Luggage Fair next week.

CHARLES: *You* have the Venice Luggage Fair next week.

ROGER: But Benito Benotti's *your* client.

CHARLES: He's *our* client, Roger.

ROGER: *(To the absent ANGIE.)* I knew just how I'd break the news to you. 'Darling, you know that new suitcase I promised you. I know where there's rather a large selection...'

CHARLES, about to leave, hesitates and turns back.

CHARLES: By the way, I shouldn't get up to anything in the way of high jinks under the heady influence of the misty lagoon. You know what a stick-in-the-mud Benotti is.

CHARLES exits.

ROGER, barely listening, is already making his plans for ANGIE. He picks up the phone and dials her number during the following.

ROGER: I had to get you a passport, air ticket, currency, clothes – so much to do, and all in secret. It was a monumental exercise but I glowed at the prospect of tackling it. You'd be prettily contrite and pretend that you didn't deserve to come, but I'd forgive you, talk you round, and then we'd make plans. 'What a lark!', you'd cry, clapping your hands...

ANGIE's telephone rings. She sulkily answers it.

ANGIE: Yes – what do you want?

ROGER: *(His face falling.)* Oh, we haven't spoken for so long, I was just wondering how you are.

ANGIE: I'm all right.

ROGER: So I was thinking maybe it would be nice to meet up for a drink.

ANGIE: Why? I thought it was all over between us.

ROGER: Don't be silly. Look – there's something I have to speak to you about. Supposing we have lunch?

ANGIE: No, I'm not very well.

ROGER: Shall I come round to your flat, then?

ANGIE: I've already told you I don't want you here.

ROGER: Then I'll meet you at the end of your street. Half an hour. *(He hastily replaces the receiver.)*

JUDITH, laden with shopping, enters his office.

Flustered, he rises and kisses her. During the following ANGIE lethargically rises and moves outside her flat.

Judith, what a surprise!

JUDITH: I've spent all my money at the sales so now I'm looking for someone to take me to lunch.

ROGER: Darling – why didn't you say at breakfast? I already have a client.

JUDITH: Of course you do. A client. Never mind.

ROGER: In fact, I'm late already... *(He steps into the limbo area between his office and ANGIE's flat. To ANGIE.)* Great news, Angie! Four days in Venice! The two of us!

JUDITH: At any rate I'm glad I bought a new dress. Charles tells me we're going to Venice next week.

ROGER: We?

ANGIE: Won't it be awfully dank and miserable at this time of year?

ROGER: This is when Venice is at its best! All swirling mists and red sunsets, and no tourists!

JUDITH: Or aren't wives invited?

ROGER: Afraid not.

ANGIE: I don't have a passport.

ROGER: We'll get you one!

JUDITH: But they're not specifically non-invited, are they? Didn't Charles take Lucille last year?

ROGER: At his own expense, yes. *(To ANGIE.)* And you'll need clothes. I'll give you some money.

ANGIE: What's wrong with the clothes I've got? Are you ashamed of me?

ROGER: Of course not.

JUDITH: I wasn't suggesting at the agency's expense. If Charles and Lucille can afford it, I'm sure we can.

ROGER: It's not a question of it being affordable, darling, it's whether it's worthwhile, just for four days including travelling. *(To ANGIE.)* There's this wonderful island called Torcello. We'll have Sunday lunch there. *(To JUDITH.)* Besides, I have to dance attendance on Benotti.

JUDITH: We can both dance attendance on Benotti. We could take him to Sunday lunch on Torcello.

ROGER: And I do have to spend a lot of time at the Luggage Fair.

JUDITH: You won't be spending every waking minute there. If you're all that interested in luggage you can go out to Heathrow and watch the carousel go round and round.

ANGIE: Anyway, I don't have a proper suitcase!

ROGER: I'll buy you a bloody suitcase!

ANGIE: There, you see – that's how you'd be like. Making scenes and rows and holding inquests and spoiling everything.

ROGER: I won't, Angie, promise. *(To JUDITH.)* I'm sorry, darling – I'll make it up to you. Promise.

JUDITH: You really know how to make a wife feel wanted, don't you?

JUDITH angrily crosses her arms.

ROGER: Angie? Angie! Look, do you want to come to bloody Venice or not? Because if you do you're going to have to stop just standing there like some primeval fucking slug and give me some co-operation.

ANGIE turns her back on him.

Angie! Angie!

ANGIE: I'll think about it.

Both women glare at him. He is torn between them.

CURTAIN.

Act Two

SCENE 1

ANGIE's flat. It is now much less bare and altogether brighter than when we last saw it, with potted plants, table lamps and knick-knacks. A curtained wardrobe is hung with new clothes.

We discover ROGER, carrying a Canaletto print, in the limbo area. During the following he enters ANGIE's flat.

ROGER: Such as we were, Venice was the making of us. We did things we've never done before or since. Long walks, window shopping, pavement cafés, museums, even, and the sex was good. All the ups and downs, the spats, the tiffs, the arguments, the accusations, the sulks, the flare-ups, had without our appreciating it until now endowed us with an easy familiarity in bed. It was incredible to think that in all these months we'd slept with each other only once, that after Edinburgh we'd resumed an entirely vertical relationship which had continued until this Venetian re-consummation. You brought a chameleon quality to bed that I found quite extraordinary – a willingness, an ability, a talent, to adapt completely to my needs. It was as if you had me programmed on a home computer. Yet I didn't feel computerized. I felt by the time we left Venice that our love-making was exclusive, stamped 'Limited Edition'.

The telephone rings. ANGIE's answering machine goes into play. After a moment we hear Cheevers' voice on microphone. ROGER, stock-still, stares at the answering machine until the message ends.

CHEEVERS' voice: Cheevers here, Angie. Just coming up to noon, Wednesday. Give me a bell at the Gallery, would you? *Ciao.*

Pause.

ROGER: But what I couldn't get rid of, no matter how special these special feelings, was a ruminating interest in your sex life in general, Cheevers in particular. *(He hangs up the print.)*

ANGIE enters. Like JUDITH at the end of Act I she has been shopping – probably at the same store. The clothes she is wearing are new and of altogether better quality than any of her outfits we have seen earlier.

ROGER crosses and kisses her.

ROGER: Angie, you look stunning.

ANGIE: What are you doing here?

ROGER: Come to carry you off to lunch.

ANGIE: Have you been snooping?

ROGER: You did give me a key, darling.

ANGIE: Not to use *carte du jour.*

ROGER: Or even *carte blanche.*

ANGIE: Not *carte* anything. It was in case I was out when you very kindly brought round my new duvet.

ROGER: Well, today I've very kindly brought round a new print. What do you think?

ANGIE: *(Looking at it indifferently.)* Is that Venice?

ROGER: It's not the Paddington Basin.

ANGIE: Very nice. Thank you, darling.

ROGER: You don't sound too keen.

ANGIE: Possessions have never been important to me. Besides, like my lovely new clothes, they cost money. You mustn't spoil me.

ROGER: I wanted your flat to look lived in. *(He produces a bottle of champagne, already opened, and pours two glasses.)* A glass of bubbles afore we go. It's not very cold, I'm afraid – we must buy you a little fridge.

ANGIE: *(Unconvincingly.)* No, you can't!

ROGER: One more reason to hang on to your latch key. *(He moves to the answering machine.)* This thing's flashing – did you know?

ANGIE: I'll play it back later. It's probably Belle.

ROGER: No, it's Cheevers.

ANGIE: Have you been listening to my phone calls?

ROGER: *(Teasingly.)* Oh, yes – I have your telephone line tapped, didn't you know?

ANGIE: *(Relaxing again.)* I wouldn't put it past you... Don't you want to see what I've bought? *(She produces a froth of lacy underwear from her shopping.)*

ROGER: I think I'd rather see it on you.

ANGIE: I was going to buy you a present too but I ran out of money.

ROGER: You're my present.

He pours more champagne and they kiss lightly. The atmosphere is now loving and relaxed.

Angie...if I ask you something, will you promise not to ask why I want to know or what does it matter or why is it important?

ANGIE: Kiss and promise.

ROGER: I want you tell me about your friend Cheevers.

ANGIE: He's not my friend, and I don't carry his PVC about with me, darling.

ROGER: CV.

ANGIE: That either. I'll answer your questions if there's anything that's bothering you, but I've already told you as much as you need to know.

ROGER: Or as much as you want to tell me.

ANGIE: Now don't start. Take a deep breath, have some champagne, and tell me what you want to know while I get changed. *(She changes her dress during the following.)*

ROGER: All right. Why do you always call him Cheevers?

ANGIE: It's his name, darling.

ROGER: You know what I mean. Men who are known only by their surnames are usually shits or whizz-kids or possibly both. Which is he?

ANGIE: Don't be silly. He's known as that because he has the same name as his father who owns the Chelsea Auction Galleries.

ROGER: Which is where you met?

ANGIE: I never said that.

ROGER: Then where did you meet?

ANGIE: At a party. He took me home.

ROGER: To bed.

ANGIE: Perhaps. *(Defensively.)* It isn't as if I didn't know who he was, Roger. After all, I did work for his father.

ROGER: *(Drily.)* One of the family, almost.

ANGIE: So. We had a little fling, then off he went on a business course or something, and then I left the Galleries, and then he got married, and then we lost touch.

ROGER: Until?

ANGIE: I heard it hadn't worked out and he was back on the flesh market, as it's called.

ROGER: By whom?

ANGIE: Oh, the sort of set I used to go around with. You know – sort of clubby people.

ROGER: Clubby people. Clubs like the Screw, you mean? Pick-up joints?

ANGIE: If that's the quaint old-fashioned expression you want to use.

ROGER: And you came across him again in one of these places, did you?

ANGIE: Yes.

ROGER: Did you go looking for him?

ANGIE: I may have done.

ROGER: Why?

ANGIE: Boredom, I suppose.

ROGER: *(As a narrative aside.)* And so you re-started your affair. You hoped he would leave his wife but it didn't happen. He brought you her cast-offs, though, which you'd accept as a token of his serious intent. How weird.

ANGIE: It was proof of his kindness. So very few people had ever been kind to me. It showed that he cared for me.

ROGER: Not that he was a cheapskate trying to ingratiate himself into your bed?

ANGIE: He didn't have to do that.

ROGER: Of course not – the bed was always available, whenever he was of a mind to turn up at your flat for supper.

ANGIE: *(Sadly.)* Sometimes I'd make the supper and he *wouldn't* turn up.

ROGER: And then he'd come round but wouldn't stay for supper. And so you arrived at this bleak screwing arrangement, where he'd drop in late night on his way home and you'd repair to bed for a couple of hours. And your explanation was simple and heart-rending.

ANGIE: I was lonely and I didn't have any proper relationships with men. I never had had, Roger, not real ones. It was something to cling on to, however threadbare and shabby. It gave my life continuance.

ROGER: Continuity, my Lady Malaprop. Come along – let's eat.

They cross, not to the restaurant, but post-prandially to the champagne bar, swaying a little.

And let's drink. *(As a narrative aside.)* I loved you, I love you. *I* could have given you continuity, if nothing else – continuity by the bucketful...

SCENE 2

The champagne bar.

An opened bottle awaits them as they cross, continuing a discussion that has gone on all lunchtime.

ROGER: But when we first met, according to Gunby T. Gunby you were in the habit of dining frequently with Cheevers at the World's End Brasserie.

ANGIE: Not frequently – sometimes. To stop him coming round.

ROGER: Why see him at all?

ANGIE: You wouldn't understand.

ROGER: Try me.

ANGIE: I wanted his friendship. Without strings.

ROGER: You mean without sex.

ANGIE: I longed for the experience of someone – anyone – just one man – wanting to take me out with no prospect in view – at all – except the pleasure of my company. Ego trip. And the wrong choice.

ROGER: So then you chose me... You're not still seeing him, Angie, are you?

ANGIE: Yes and no.

ROGER: *(Wearily.)* Go on.

ANGIE: Don't be angry, darling.

ROGER: I'm not angry, I'm bloody astounded. When did you see him last?

ANGIE: Don't swear at me.

ROGER: When did you see him last?

ANGIE: And don't shout. If you shout I shan't tell you.

ROGER: Angela!

ANGIE: Yesterday lunchtime. Well thereabout.

ROGER: Where?

ANGIE: Here.

ROGER: *(As a narrative aside.)* I would give you up, cut my losses, retrieve my sanity – my dignity too while I was about it. Not make a scene: just thank you nicely for everything and walk away without ever turning back.

ANGIE: Don't you want to know why?

ROGER: I can answer that question myself. Because you can't keep away from the bugger.

ANGIE: Don't be ridiculous. The opposite, in fact. I came here to tell him it was all over.

ROGER: But I thought it had been all over for months and bloody months!

ANGIE: So it has, but he wouldn't take no for an answer.

ROGER: Why didn't you just tell him to piss off?

ANGIE: Not my style. So when we came back from Venice and there was a message on my answering machine, I thought I'd better see him and get it over with.

ROGER: To say what?

ANGIE: That I'd been away with someone, someone I was very much in love with, someone I was very much involved with and didn't want to lose – so would he please accept the situation and not ring me anymore.

ROGER: *(Mollified.)* Good. And what did he say to that?

ANGIE: He wished me luck.

ROGER: So he should. Then what did you say?

ANGIE: Roger... I told him I'd once been in love with him.

ROGER: *(As a narrative aside.)* I ask you to talk, Angie, but then you don't know when to stop. *(To ANGIE: dully.)* Why did you want to tell him that?

ANGIE: Not for a very nice reason, I'm afraid. To gloat, if you must know. I wanted him to realize I didn't need him anymore – that I had someone else now, someone who loved me back instead of just taking what love I had to give. Who cared about me and respected me and wanted to look after me.

ROGER: Thank you. That's the best reference I'll ever have. *(He raises his glass.)*

ANGIE: So can we put him behind us now, darling? No more inquests, investigations – no, not investigations...

ROGER: Interrogations.

ANGIE: *(Now getting quite drunk.)* Those. You'd make a good lawyer, darling, do you know that? Roger of the Bailey. I can just see you in your little wig. *(Loudly.)* Witness at the bar, do you deny that on the fourteenth –

ROGER: All right, Angie, we've got the message. Keep your voice down.

ANGIE: So you're quite sure there's nothing else you want me to tell you.

ROGER: *(As a narrative aside.)* Oh dear, you truly were asking for it, my love, weren't you? *(To ANGIE.)* Not really.

ANGIE: Oh, come on, Roger, what kind of an answer's that?

ROGER: Well, let's say not at the moment.

ANGIE: I see. You want to keep something in reserve. Something you can drag up to pull the rug from under my feet just when I think we're getting on with being happy at last.

ROGER: Now don't start, Angie. Drink your champagne.

ANGIE: There's something else you want to know from me so let's get it over with.

ROGER: There's a hundred things I want to know about you, Angie – a thousand things. It's what being in love's all about!

ANGIE: Is it? Is it? So it's never going to end. And all the time I'm with you, and all the time we were in Venice and we'd just slept together and I'd ask you what you were thinking, there it was and there it is, festering away in your petty little mind – and you call it love!

ROGER: And what do *you* call it? You don't know what love is, Angie. And as for secrets festering away in petty little minds –

ANGIE throws her glass of champagne in his face, collects her things, and walks out of the bar.

ROGER dabs the champagne from his face.

ROGER: *(In the future narrative.)* Yet however too far you went, my love, you never went too far for me. In the sixteen months we had, you exasperated, infuriated, offended, disappointed, depressed, alienated, saddened, wounded, even disgusted me, but you never bored me for a second.

ROGER crosses into:

SCENE 3

ROGER's home.

He steps out on to the patio carrying a drink. He is joined by JUDITH, also carrying a drink.

JUDITH: Have you said goodnight to Timothy?

ROGER: Yes. My God, he's growing.

JUDITH: They do, you know – especially if you don't set eyes on them from one week's end to another. You won't forget we've got Gunby coming to dinner?

ROGER: I thought you had dinner with him last week.

JUDITH: I did, in your absence, and now it's our turn. It's called socializing. And talking of which, why aren't we invited to the Pecks' on Wednesday?

ROGER: Charles and I don't live in one another's pockets. We don't necessarily go to all his dos.

JUDITH: We go to this one, Roger. It's his annual dinner party for Benito Benotti.

ROGER: Oh, that. I shouldn't worry about it, darling. *(To the absent ANGIE.)* Yes, darling, I do call Judith darling too, darling. It's an all-purpose term in marriage – sometimes even a term of abuse. *(To JUDITH.)* It's not the star event of the social calendar, you know. You're not missing out on having your name in Jennifer's Diary.

JUDITH: I'm missing out on the bloody dinner party, Roger! I want you to go to Charles and insist that he invites us.

ROGER: No, I can't do that, Judith.

JUDITH: Why not?

ROGER: *(To the absent ANGIE.)* Because I want next Wednesday evening to find me in bed with my mistress! *(He shrugs to JUDITH.)*

JUDITH: Has it crossed your mind to wonder why we're being snubbed in this way?

ROGER: Nobody is being snubbed! Charles and I are partners – remember?

JUDITH: For how long?

She abruptly exits indoors.

ROGER, picking up his briefcase, wanders down to:

SCENE 4

ROGER's office/ANGIE's flat.

The flat is at present unoccupied. In the office, ROGER moves to his desk.

ROGER: As it happens you couldn't make it on Wednesday evening and that really was a snub. You wouldn't tell me where you were going and I wondered why and where and with whom. *(He picks up the phone and punches out Angie's number.)* You told me that my jealousy of Cheevers had more than once nearly finished us, Angie. That was before it did finish us.

The telephone gives an out-of-order signal.

(Replacing the receiver.) Unobtainable. Well, we know what *that* means, don't we?

ANGIE enters the flat with some shopping and takes off her coat.

I went to see him, did that surprise you? At the Chelsea Auction Galleries. With a cock-and-bull story about an art

53

deco desk I supposedly wanted to put up for sale. What do you think of that? Fifty-one years old and I was playing hooky from my office and weaving a web of stupid little lies just to catch a glimpse of my mistress's former lover. What next?

CHARLES enters the office.

CHARLES: I know you've only had that bumf on Foster's Fibre Flakes a couple of days, Roger, but they're rather leaning on us. Any bright ideas?

ROGER: *(Distracted.)* As you say, it's only just landed on my desk.

CHARLES: Mind if I have a glance? Inspiration might just strike.

ROGER: Help yourself.

He tosses over a folder which CHARLES picks up and studies during the following. ANGIE takes a half bottle of champagne from her shopping and opens it.

(As a narrative aside.) You never believed for a second, did you, that I wanted you to have had happy times and good relationships, that had I been able to give you fond memories, even of Cheevers, instead of empty ones, they would have been yours wrapped up in ribbon... I carry a sad mental picture of something you once told me: that sometimes when we couldn't or wouldn't see one another you'd go out to the wine shop and buy a half bottle of plonk champagne which you'd drink all alone, out of a tumbler, as a reminder of the times we'd had.

ANGIE pours herself a tumbler of champagne.

CHARLES: *(Flipping through the folder.)* Not much to go on, is there?

ROGER: Not a lot.

ANGIE picks up her telephone to dial, realizes it's out of order, and after banging the receiver rest, replaces it crossly.

CHARLES: We could go down the well-worn alliterative path, I suppose. Foster's Fibre Flakes, the Family Favourite. Families Favour Foster's Fibre Flakes...

ROGER: *(In a gust of anger.)* Oh, fuck Foster's Fibre Flakes, Charles! *(To ANGIE.)* Bloody Cheevers! He was twenty-three years old, Angela! And don't deny it because I checked at Somerset House! Twenty-three! That means when you first started seeing him, and I do mean *seeing* him, he was no more than seventeen! Christ! Not so much a toy boy, more your bloody teddy bear!

CHARLES: Fuck Foster's Fibre Flakes by all means, but we've got to come up with something.

ROGER: I'm working on it! *(To ANGIE: more calmly.)* And you'd never told me.

ANGIE: I never ask people's ages, they're not relevant.

ROGER: Relevant.

ANGIE: Relevant, then. I didn't ask yours Roger – remember? *(Dismissing the subject, she picks up the phone but again has no luck. She drains her champagne glass and puts on her coat.)*

She exits.

ANGIE's flat is struck during the following.

ROGER: Seventeen! Went off on a business course, you said. Bugger off, Angie, he was still at school!

CHARLES: *(Tossing the folder back on to ROGER's desk.)* Well, rather you than me...

ROGER: And who seduced whom? As you would say, what does it matter? The young sod was everything I didn't wish him to be, exuding swagger and scorn and the arrogant confidence of a sexual spider.

CHARLES: There is something else I'd like to have a word about...

ROGER: I could see myself reflected in his hard, predatory stare – a middle-aged no-hoper in a crumpled suit, long past his sell-by date. If I'd told Cheevers I was your latest lover he would have laughed with incredulity. *(To CHARLES.)* Sorry, Charles, I thought I had something on Foster's Fibre Flakes just then.

ANGIE's flat is gone. The set changes to:

SCENE 5

ROGER's office/champagne bar.

ROGER remains at his desk, talking to CHARLES.

ANGIE enters the champagne bar and looks in her bag for change for the pay phone. During the following she dials Roger's number.

CHARLES: It'll come... *(He hesitates.)* Roger, just to help me in drawing up some kind of game plan for the work we've got to get through, could you let me know at some point whether you intend to be back at your desk this afternoon?

ROGER: I shan't even be going out. I'll have a sandwich in the office.

ROGER's telephone rings. He picks it up.

Roger Piper.

ANGIE: Can I see you for a few minutes, Roger? It's rather urgent.

ROGER: *(Guardedly.)* That's just a bit tricky at the moment. Can I ring you back?

ANGIE: I'm afraid not. I'm in Freddy's Club and they've just asked me to leave.

ROGER: You don't surprise me. What's the problem?

CHARLES: Shall I come back?

ROGER gestures that he won't be a moment.

ANGIE: They've cut my phone off.

ROGER: So I've gathered.

ROGER's other telephone rings.

CHARLES: Shall I take it?

ROGER nods. CHARLES picks up the phone.

Roger Piper's office... No, he's tied up at present but I'm sure Mrs Penn will want to speak to his partner, Charles Peck. Would you like to put her through?

ROGER looks guiltily towards the other phone, knowing he should be taking the call, but he is unable to resist ANGIE.

ANGIE: *(Over CHARLES.)* I *know* I've paid the bill but I never fill in my cheque stubs so how can I prove it?

CHARLES: *(Moving upstage with the telephone.)* Mrs Penn, how are you? How delightful to hear that soft Scottish lilt...

ROGER: *(Resignedly.)* All right – how much is it?

ANGIE: I don't know – hold on, I've got the bill somewhere in my bag... Oh dear! *(She rummages through her bag, scattering it's contents.)*

CHARLES: *(Into the phone.)* Have we not? That's very remiss of us... *(His conversation continues silently.)*

ROGER: Hallo? Look, never mind that for the moment.

ANGIE: It would only be a loan, Roger. It's just that I have to work out with Belle how much of the bill is hers, and now she's moved out I can't get in touch with her.

ROGER: Why not?

ANGIE: Because my phone's been cut off, silly.

ROGER: Angie, I have another call waiting for me.

ANGIE: Can't you come over, Roger? Just for a few minutes?

ROGER: I'm afraid not.

ANGIE: But I've ordered a bottle of champagne and I can't pay for it!

ROGER: I thought they'd asked you to leave.

ANGIE: But then they said if you were coming I could stay.

ROGER glances over at CHARLES to check that he is not being overheard, and lowers his voice.

ROGER: All right, I'll see you on one condition – that you apologize.

ANGIE: *(Genuinely puzzled.)* Apologize for what?

ROGER: For throwing drink in my face.

ANGIE: Oh, come on, darling, it was only a little drop and you know I didn't mean it.

ROGER: Whether you meant it or not, you made me look very silly and I want an apology.

ANGIE: Oh, we mustn't have Roger looking silly, must we? Very well, then – *(Mockingly.)* sorreee!

CHARLES: Just a moment, Mrs Penn. *(With his hand over the receiver.)* Roger! Where the hell's that rough copy on Penn's Shortbread Products?

ROGER: *(Distractedly.)* It's here. *(He tosses a folder over to CHARLES.)*

CHARLES: She should have had it twenty-four hours ago. *(Into the phone.)* We've located it, Mrs Penn. There's been a slip-up, I'm afraid...

ANGIE: So are you coming over or not?

CHARLES: I'll see that it's done, Mrs Penn. We'll fax it right away, don't worry. Talk to you very soon. Bye... *(He hangs up.)*

ROGER: I'll be there in a few minutes. *(He hangs up.)*

ANGIE: *(To a waiter, off.)* Could I order a bottle of Lanson Black Label please?

She exits.

The champagne bar set is lost.

ROGER: What's the old bat want now?

CHARLES: It's dealt with.

ROGER: It would've been dealt with anyway.

CHARLES: Of course it would. Fancy a spot of lunch?

ROGER: No, I'm not free.

CHARLES: I thought you were.

ROGER: Something's cropped up.

CHARLES: Roger... Is something bothering you?

ROGER: Something's bothering Judith. That was a pretty shitty stroke you pulled, Charles.

CHARLES: What?

ROGER: Your Benotti dinner party.

CHARLES: Sorry. The fact is, Roger, you're not in Benotti's best books. He feels you neglected him in Venice.

ROGER: Balls. I had breakfast with him twice and dinner once.

CHARLES: When you turned up pissed.

ROGER: For God's sake. If a man can't get pissed in Venice where can he get pissed?

CHARLES: It's not only Venice, Roger. You're getting talked about, mate. I mean in the business.

ROGER: Where's this leading, Charles?

CHARLES: I had meant to take you for a quiet lunch to talk this through, but now we've started we might as well finish.

ROGER: And you do mean finish, don't you, Charles? *(An awkward pause.)* I think you're saying you want to dissolve the partnership.

CHARLES: Yes, that's what I think I'm saying too.

ROGER: And there's no point in talking about new leaves, pulling socks up, all that?

CHARLES: I wouldn't have thought so, would you? Your personal life's your own, but it probably goes a bit beyond that, doesn't it?

ROGER: Identity crisis?

CHARLES: You said it, chum.

ROGER: *(Flippantly.)* Perhaps I'm going through the change of life.

CHARLES: That's not for me to say. You've certainly undergone some kind of personality change that I'm afraid makes us incompatible, businesswise. Sorry, Roger. Good while it lasted. We'll get the lawyers on to the paperwork tomorrow.

CHARLES exits briskly.

ROGER opens a desk drawer, takes out half a bottle of brandy and pours a large measure into a paper coffee cup. He rises and moves into the limbo area between:

SCENE 6

ROGER's home/ANGIE's flat.

JUDITH comes out on to the patio. ANGIE is sitting on her sofa. Both are nursing drinks. JUDITH is studying a piece of paper.

JUDITH: *(Reading.)* 'Leaving to develop other interests.' That's one way of putting it. What shall we tell our friends?

ROGER: Oh – say I'm working as a consultant.

JUDITH: I don't think so. That's what executives always call themselves when they're unemployable.

ROGER turns to ANGIE as she reacts to the news.

ANGIE: But how *can* he get rid of you? I thought you were supposed to be partners.

ROGER: We are partners, but partnerships are like marriages. We've decided on a legal separation.

JUDITH: What do you want to do with yourself?

ROGER: *(Looking at ANGIE.)* I want to start leading a double life full time.

JUDITH: Roger? Or don't you know?

ROGER: I don't, actually. Do you mind? You see, until today I thought I was in the advertising line.

ANGIE: But he can't throw you out just because you've got back late from lunch a few times.

JUDITH: Is there anything I can do to help?

ROGER: I don't think so, darling, thank you. I'll get something sorted out. *(He turns to ANGIE.)* There's more to it than that, Angie. Ever since you and I came together I've been neglecting my work to spend every available minute with you. Now Charles, quite rightly, has had enough.

ANGIE: I see. So you've put all the blame on me?

JUDITH: Do you think I should still go ahead with the new car?

ROGER: I don't see why not. It's your money. Besides, I may have a customer for the old one. A young auctioneer I know named Cheevers.

JUDITH: He can't be a very successful auctioneer if he's in the market for a second-hand Volkswagen.

ROGER: Actually it's for his girlfriend. *(He turns to ANGIE.)* Are you sulking?

ANGIE: No, but you only think of yourself, Roger. Don't you realize how *I've* had to neglect my work to be with *you*? You're not the only one, you know.

ROGER: What bloody work?

JUDITH: So you're going to be looking around, as they say?

ROGER: Yes. You may not see much of me.

JUDITH: Don't worry. I'm here if you need me.

JUDITH exits into the house.

ROGER at once turns to ANGIE and extends a hand. ANGIE comes forward and takes it, and they go into:

SCENE 7

A restaurant.

ROGER and ANGIE sit, looking at menus.

ANGIE: Surely all this has got to stop now, Roger? How can you afford to bring me to places like this when you're out of work?

ROGER: In this unequal life of ours, Angie, not having any work doesn't necessarily equate with not having any money.

ANGIE: *(Thoughtfully.)* Really? I still think we ought to see less of one another, not more. I really do have to find work and earn some money.

ROGER: Why wait until now to tell me?

ANGIE: Is there a right time?

ROGER: *(As a narrative aside.)* There is such a thing as picking the right moment. But do get on with it, now you've started.

ANGIE: I've got to live, like everyone else. I know you've often helped me out Roger, but somehow there's always another bill to pay.

ROGER: Forget the bills, Angie.

ANGIE: I can't take charity.

ROGER: It isn't charity – it's the very small price I'm happy to pay for seeing more of each other.

ANGIE: *(Desperately.)* But I don't *want* us to see more of each other! All this talk of coming round and coming round and coming round! Are you going to be round every day? Why don't you bring your bloody slippers with you?

ROGER: *(Hurt.)* I never meant to become part of the furniture. What's brought this on?

ANGIE: I'm sorry. You don't know what it's like being cooped up in that flat, day after day.

ROGER: You're not cooped up, what are you talking about? You can come and go as you please.

ANGIE: Except when I'm expecting you, which from now on is apparently going to be every single weekday.

ROGER: And you object to that, do you?

ANGIE: I do when you make me feel as if I'm being bricked in. You suffocate me, Roger! And every day you'll bring me flowers and champagne, won't you, like the worker bee bringing honey for the queen. Stop *bringing* me things!

ROGER: *(As a narrative aside.)* You'd rehearsed all this, of course, for delivery at the appropriate moment. But you still hadn't forgotten the business in hand.

ANGIE: And as I said, I have to start earning my living. There's so many bills.

ROGER: Let me see them.

ANGIE promptly dives into her bag and produces a sheaf of bills.

ROGER: Barclaycard...overdraft...rent book...charge card... wine shop...charge card...charge card... Some of these go back months, Angie. Why didn't you tell me you've had these hanging over you all the time I've known you?

ANGIE: I hoped they'd go away.

ROGER: *(Totting up the bills; as a narrative aside.)* And they did, didn't they, my love? What an extraordinary lunch that was. I'd arrived still licking my wounds after being heaved out of my own agency, *(He writes out a cheque.)* and I ended up writing a cheque for two thousand two hundred pounds to clear your debts. *(He hands over the cheque.)*

She leans across and gives him a kiss and a hug.

(Producing a car ignition key.) I've got something else for you.

ANGIE: What is it?

ROGER: A cure for your claustrophobia.

ANGIE: *(Incredulously.)* A car?

ROGER: *(Rising.)* Only a cast-off Volkswagen, I'm afraid. Come on.

He exits.

ANGIE: *(Following him off; excitedly.)* But Roger, it's not even my birthday!

She exits.

SCENE 8

The patio of ROGER's house.

JUDITH enters with GUNBY T. GUNBY, who carries a plateful of nibbles.

JUDITH: Roger, where are you?... He must be saying goodnight to Timothy.

GUNBY: Dutiful father.

JUDITH: Dutiful, my eye. He's usually so sloshed he thinks we're bringing up twins.

ROGER enters.

Don't look so startled, Roger, you haven't forgotten another dinner party. Gunby's just dropped in off the M4 after inspecting a clutch of motorway restaurants.

GUNBY: Actually the apple pie with shaving cream isn't half bad.

ROGER: I thought you took only the plums like the Ritz and Le Gavroche.

GUNBY: Normally I do, being of sound mind and body, but one of my inspectors has dropped off the perch.

ROGER: Ptomaine poisoning?

GUNBY: That's why I popped in – to offer Judith my hand in gastronomy.

JUDITH: It would have been fun. Lording it in all the best hotels –

GUNBY: The second-best hotels, my dear. I get the best.

JUDITH: But what with Timothy and my wonderful career, I simply couldn't think of it.

GUNBY: Turned me down flat.

JUDITH: I did suggest another candidate, though?

GUNBY: Might you be interested, Roger?

ROGER: What does it involve?

GUNBY: It's not a full-time job, so it's ideal for someone who's looking around. You'd be expected to visit three hotels a fortnight, plus a couple of restaurants within their particular area. Expenses paid, of course.

ROGER: *(As a narrative aside.)* Three hotels a fortnight. Three rooms, three beds, three nights, three golden afternoons – Christ, there are people married and living together who spend less time with one another!

GUNBY: The question is whether the money's a crucial factor.

ROGER: I don't know, Gunby – how much do you want?

Laughing, JUDITH and GUNBY go indoors.

ROGER comes down to:

SCENE 9

A hotel bedroom.

During the following ANGIE comes out of the bathroom in a kimono and sits on the bed, making up her face. ROGER enters the bedroom and puts on a dressing-gown.

ROGER: So began the mad hotel odyssey that was to be the last mad phase of our mad affair. By now it's all a jumble of champagne buckets and room service sandwiches, of king-sized beds and queen-sized beds and disappointing twin beds, of carpeted corridors and Muzak-tinkling lifts and buffet breakfasts and Do Not Disturb signs and quilted cocktail bars, and hotel bookmatches that always went into my pocket so that lighting your cigarette in Leicester with matches picked up in Nottingham I could never be absolutely sure where we were. One town is superimposed upon another. I have Cardiff with a view across Morecambe Bay, that hospital-like brick box in Swindon transplanted to the edge of the New Forest. Not all my snapshots are double exposure. A treasured one is of you walking barefoot on the sands at Lytham St Anne's with the tide far out, and perching you on a groyne to bathe your toe where a cuttlefish shell had cut it, and you looked so young and fresh and freckled and innocent with the sea breeze blowing back your hair that I wanted either to take you there and then or buy you a bucket and spade and make sand castles... *(He picks up the bedside telephone.)* I'd better ring home. *(He punches a number on the telephone. The digit tones are the first few notes of 'Send in the Clowns' by Stephen Sondheim.)*

ANGIE: It plays a tune.

ROGER: Sondheim. *(He sings.)* 'Isn't it rich? Are we a pair?' *(Into the telephone.)* Ingrid, it's Mr Piper. Is Mrs Piper there? ... I see. ... Timothy go down all right? ... Good. ... Did she leave a number at all? ... *(He notes the number down.)* Three-seven-o...yes, I've got that. ... Goodnight, Ingrid. *(He replaces the receiver.)* She's with Gunby T. Gunby.

ANGIE: Are they having an affair?

ROGER: Yes – I should think by now they very probably are.

ANGIE: Do you mind?

ROGER: I'm hardly in a position to mind, am I? *(He hums a bar of 'Send in the Clowns'.)* Angie. Would you like me to leave Judith?

ANGIE: You wouldn't, so why ask?

ROGER: *(As a narrative aside.)* It was the first time I'd ever thought about the prospect. I was surprised at how conventional my reaction was. Instead of indulging myself in daydreams of living with you I dwelt instead on the mundane practicalities of ending a marriage. It wasn't about starting a new life, it was about wondering what to tell the neighbours. Getting change-of-address cards printed. Getting my laundry done. And yes, it was about what kind of a fool I should look if I moved in with you and a week later you moved out. *(To ANGIE.)* Why wouldn't I.

ANGIE: There's Timothy, for one thing.

ROGER: I should still see him.

ANGIE: But you wouldn't like him growing up to call some other man Daddy, would you?

ROGER: Perhaps not.

ANGIE: Then why bother to ask?

ROGER: Why don't you bother to answer?

ANGIE: Because, as the politicians say, I don't answer hypocritical questions.

ROGER: Hypothetical.

ANGIE: Just for once, darling, I happen to have chosen the right word. I said hypocritical and that's what I meant. Supposing I said all right, Roger, yes, I do want you to leave Judith, what would you say then?

ROGER: That I'd think about it.

ANGIE: And what should I be doing while you thought about it?

ROGER: Looking for somewhere for us to live.

ANGIE: And how do you know I want to live with you, when you've never asked?

ROGER: I'm asking now.

ANGIE: No you're not, you're playing games.

ROGER: If I am playing games, Angie, it's only because the whole of my bloody life has become a game since I met you. Let me ask you this. Supposing I wasn't married anymore – supposing Judith left *me*, for Christsake – and I turned up on your doorstep and asked you to be the second Mrs Piper. What would you say?

ANGIE: I'm not going to answer, Roger. The plain fact is I don't see myself marrying anybody. I did once upon a time, but now I know I'm not the type.

ROGER: Then you *have* answered the question.

ANGIE: All right, I've answered it, so I might as well answer your other one as well. No, I don't want to live with you. I wouldn't know how to live with a man. I'm a homebreaker, not a homemaker.

ROGER: You mean you prefer to peer into the sweetshop window than to come into the sweetshop.

ANGIE: I've always been happy with the bags of sweets you've brought me.

ROGER: I've never given you very much.

ANGIE: More than anyone else ever has. Much, much more. *(She nestles in his arms, quietly sobbing.)*

ROGER: Tears before bedtime.

ANGIE: Hold me, Roger. I'm frightened.

ROGER: What's brought this on?

ANGIE: I've become so dependent on you.

ROGER: I like you to be dependent on me. *(As a narrative aside.)* I half did, half didn't – half wanted to keep you in a cage, half wanted you to fly away.

ANGIE: And I want to be. You're my security blanket.

ROGER: Then what frightens you, kitten? I'm not going to go away.

ANGIE: You might. I could say or do something stupid and you'd go and this time you wouldn't come back.

ROGER: If that were ever going to happen I'd be gone by now.

ANGIE: I know it's – not parasitical, what do I mean? Not wanting you to become a fixture yet at the same time terrified of losing you.

ROGER: Paradoxical. Are you?

ANGIE: My whole life revolves around you now.

The lights fade slowly during the following.

ROGER: *(Singing softly from 'Send in the Clowns'.)* 'Don't you love farce? My fault, I fear. I thought. I thought that you'd want what I want. Sorry my dear...' Our song.

ANGIE: *(Sleepily.)* It's not our song, silly. It's your telephone number.

The lights fade to blackout and quickly come back up.

The bedroom set has gone and we are now in:

SCENE 10

A restaurant.

ROGER crosses towards the restaurant.

ROGER: And was it in Norwich or Nottingham where we behaved so badly in that pretentious restaurant I was supposed to be reviewing that we were asked to leave and finished up eating fish and chips in a car park, swigging warm off-licence champagne out of the bottle like a couple of winos? ... But it was Brighton, positively Brighton, where we had that fatal last luch.

ROGER sits at the table where he is joined by ANGIE.

(To ANGIE.) Do you think we could manage another bottle?

ANGIE: Better not, darling. I have to move the car.

ROGER: But it's in the hotel car park.

ANGIE: No, I never got round to it – I left it on a double yellow line, I'm afraid.

ROGER: Then you'll get a ticket.

ANGIE: I've already got a ticket.

ROGER: To add to that great wad behind your mantelpiece clock. I hope you don't think *I'm* going to pay them.

ANGIE: I never asked you to.

ROGER: Then when are *you* going to pay them?

ANGIE: When the bank stops being so horrible to me.

ROGER: What's wrong with the bank? You paid off your overdraft.

ANGIE: Not all of it.

ROGER: But I gave you a cheque.

ANGIE: I know, and it was sweet and thoughtful of you, but I had some other debts.

ROGER: Angie, I paid them too. Bloody weeks ago.

ANGIE: Yes, but there was another credit card I forgot to tell you about.

ROGER: *(Signalling to a waiter, off; agitated.)* Bring me another bottle, please... Do I take it that Cheevers comes into this?

ANGIE: Well, I didn't give money to all and sundry. *(Pause.)* He happens to be an impulsive gambler.

ROGER: Compulsive. How much did you give him?

ANGIE: I didn't give it to him, he borrowed it.

ROGER: They always call it borrowing. How much?

ANGIE: I don't know, I never counted it up.

ROGER: No, you wouldn't have done. Silly question. *(Ironically.)* At least he brought you his wife's cast-offs in return. *(He looks at her dress.)* That's one of them, isn't it?

ANGIE: Yes. What's wrong with it?

ROGER: Nothing at all, it's very fetching. But Angie, for your birthday last week I gave you two hundred pounds to spend on a new outfit.

ANGIE: I know, darling, you're so generous, but I haven't been able to find anything yet. I thought I might look here in Brighton.

ROGER: You still have the money?

ANGIE is silent.

So you don't have the money.

ANGIE: You said it was mine to spend on what I liked.

ROGER: Did you give it to Cheevers?

ANGIE: I'm not going to tell you.

ROGER: Angela. Look at me. Your stupidity I can swallow. I never wanted to be your accountant anyway. Forget the money I gave you to pay off your debts and your overdraft – if you want to be harassed by bailiffs and bank managers, that's your lookout. The money I gave you for clothes is different. It was a present, given to you with love.

ANGIE: I said thank you, didn't I?

ROGER: Very prettily. I don't know what the hell you've done with that two hundred pounds, Angie, but I want you to get it back. I don't care how you raise it but I don't want to see you again until you've got it.

The MAITRE D'HOTEL enters with a bottle of wine.

ANGIE flourishes a cigarette, pointedly ignoring ROGER.

ANGIE: *(To the MAITRE D'HOTEL.)* Would you light my cigarette, please?

MAITRE D'HOTEL: I'm sorry, madame, we have a no-smoking policy. I know it's nice to light up after a good meal, but the chef feels it spoils it for the other diners.

ANGIE: Oh, does he? Actually, I was about to light up after a very bad meal and as for spoiling it for other diners, I would have thought the chef was doing that very well without my help. *(She rises; to ROGER.)* I'm going to look at the cathedral.

MAITRE D'HOTEL: We have no cathedral, madame.

ANGIE: Typical!

She sweeps out.

MAITRE D'HOTEL: Mr Piper, as I gather your companion didn't enjoy her meal, normally I should not dream of charging you for it, but I wouldn't want Mr Gunby to think I was trying to bribe one of his inspectors.

ROGER: Now how on earth did you know where I was from?

MAITRE D'HOTEL: *(Producing some papers.)* Your notes on the two other establishments you've been visiting – the lady dropped them on the way in. I must say I wish I'd known you were coming, Mr Piper. We have a little kitchen crisis today.

ROGER: We all have our little crises. It was a good meal. Thank you.

The MAITRE D'HOTEL bows and exits.

ROGER drains his glass and steps out of the restaurant into the limbo area.

(To the absent ANGIE.) You'd packed up and gone by the time I got back to the hotel. It was to be another two weeks before I saw you again, but I was buggered if I was going to ring you, even when Gunby T. Gunby told me ever so politely that I was fired.

GUNBY enters.

GUNBY: After all, you've been doing the job for six months now, and one hotel bed's much like another, don't you find? You must be getting fed up with it by now.

ROGER: Sometimes. Sometimes not.

GUNBY: Well, let's say one or two places have been a bit fed up with you.

ROGER: Won't you find it rather inconvenient?

GUNBY: I have a replacement.

ROGER: I mean not having me out of the way so often.

GUNBY: Do you want to go into that, Roger?

ROGER: Not particularly.

GUNBY: Is that what's been bothering you?

ROGER: Who says anything's bothering me?

GUNBY: Judith. She's worried about you.

ROGER: Does she know about Angela Caxton?

GUNBY: Not from me – I don't know what she's learned from other people. She's very loyal to you, Roger.

ROGER: Loyal not being the same as faithful.

GUNBY: What do you expect? Look, Judith looks to me for company – and as for me, I get my erotic kicks from a plate of profiteroles. If you gave up that silly little girl you'd have nothing to worry about.

ROGER: Is this Judith's doing?

GUNBY: No, I'm speaking as a friend. You don't mind, do you?

ROGER: Since you put the question, actually I do.

GUNBY: So be it.

GUNBY exits.

ROGER moves into:

SCENE 11

The patio of ROGER's house.

ROGER: And so into limbo. Mooning around the house, doing odd jobs, playing with Timothy, leading a zombified non-existence. Until at last you rang.

The telephone rings.

JUDITH enters and answers it.

JUDITH: Hallo? ... *(She replaces the receiver.)* Mr Nobody. Or Miss Nobody.

ROGER: I think I'll go to the pub.

JUDITH: Do. Have you got enough ten p pieces?

ROGER: I shan't be too late.

JUDITH: It's never too late, Roger. Timothy and I do miss you, you know.

ROGER: But I haven't been out of the house for a week.

JUDITH: I know, but you haven't been here.

ROGER: *(To the absent ANGIE.)* Perhaps it wasn't you at all. I called you from the pub – engaged, engaged, engaged. Finally, inflamed by too much gin on an empty stomach, I made the trek to Islington.

He exits.

SCENE 12

ANGIE's flat. It is empty.

ROGER enters carrying a wine shop bag containing two bottles of champagne. He lets himself into the flat. He pours himself a glass of champagne. He looks around the untidy flat and notices the answering machine, which has a light flashing.

ROGER: You never could get the hang of your answering machine. Sometimes you switched it off when you meant to switch it on, sometimes you wiped out the message before you'd hear it, and sometimes, somehow, by pressing all the wrong buttons I suppose, you managed to record your own conversation...

He presses the playback button and we hear ANGIE talking to CHEEVERS.

CHEEVER's voice: Double four-six-two...

ANGIE's voice: Guess who?

CHEEVER's voice: Angie! Listen, love, I'm in the middle of something – can I call you back?

ANGIE's voice: See that you do – we've got lots to talk about.

CHEEVER's voice: *Ciao.*

ROGER switches off the answering machine.

ROGER: There was no sense of shock or betrayal, simply cheap excitement at having found you out at last – the excitement of the chase, I suppose – tempered by the dull, dead realization that nothing could ever be the same with us again.

Giggles are heard from outside.

ANGIE and her friend BELLE enter, both of them tipsy, but BELLE less so than ANGIE.

ANGIE: Well well well, if it isn't the bad penny! At least he's bought some champagne.

BELLE shakes hands with ROGER.

BELLE: I've heard so much about you. *(To ANGIE.)* Haven't I?

ROGER: You must be Belle.

ANGIE: And he must be Roger the Lodger! He's come for his two hundred pounds, haven't you, Roger? There you are... *(She opens her bag and scatters twenty-pound notes at his feet.)* But I'm afraid there's only a hundred and sixty because we've been having our stag night.

BELLE: *My* stag night. *(To ROGER.)* I'm getting married tomorrow as ever was.

ANGIE: In Birmingham. You don't mind if I go to Birmingham, do you, Roger? Have I your permission to go to Birmingham?

ROGER: *(To BELLE.)* Why Birmingham?

BELLE: That's where the bridegroom keeps his nightclub. Don't worry, Roger, I'll see she doesn't run off with the best man this time – you do know that story?

ROGER: Yes.

ANGIE: No, he doesn't. *(She pours two glasses of champagne.)*

BELLE: *(With a laugh.)* It was all a long time ago, anyway. Why don't you come to the wedding and keep us *both* out of mischief?

ROGER: I might just do that.

ANGIE hands a glass of champagne to BELLE.

BELLE: One sip and I must dash.

ANGIE: Mustn't keep the bridegroom waiting.

BELLE: And you mustn't keep the bride waiting. *Albany Hotel* at eleven sharp. Will you see that she gets me to the church on time, Roger?

ROGER: I'll give her an alarm call. Goodbye. Good luck.

BELLE knocks back her glass in one and exits.

ANGIE, still the worse for drink, has an immediate change of mood.

ANGIE: If you must come barging in here to collect your filthy money, couldn't you have telephoned first?

ROGER: I rang for hours. You were engaged.

ANGIE: Yes, well I was talking to Belle about the wedding arrangements.

ROGER: Such as who's going to screw the best man?

ANGIE: Don't be disgusting.

ROGER: I have heard that story before, Angie. You told it to me. But as if it happened to Belle. Like the one about screwing on the Louis the sixteenth chaise-longue in the pantechnicon. That was you too, wasn't it? *(He starts to pick up the money.)*

ANGIE: You've got what you came for. I think you'd better go.

ROGER: *(Holding out the money.)* I don't want this, Angie. I just want to see it used for its intended purpose.

ANGIE: You seriously think I could go out and enjoy spending that money on clothes after all you've said.

ROGER: Please yourself. It's your money – you earned it.

ANGIE: How do you know I earned it?

ROGER: Well, didn't you?

ANGIE: I'm not going to tell you.

While they build up to the following blazing quarrel, ANGIE and ROGER continue to pour one another champagne until the supply is finished.

ROGER: Angela, I'm asking you...

She is stubbornly silent.

You didn't get it from Cheevers, by any chance?

ANGIE: Are you insane? First you ask if I gave the money to Cheevers, then when I get it back you ask if he gave it to me! You've got Cheevers on the brain!

ROGER: All right – did he procure the money for you?

She is silent.

Do you know what I mean by 'procure', Angela?

ANGIE: I'm not a child.

ROGER: You *are* a child. We know how Belle would have earned this money in your place – I'm asking how *you* earned it.

ANGIE: I'm not going to answer insulting questions.

ROGER: Then answer this one. If you didn't get it from Cheevers or through Cheevers, how did you come by it? I mean, if you earned the money temping, for instance, why can't you just come out and say so?

ANGIE: Roger – you said when you made that ridiculous scene in the restaurant that you didn't care how I got the money. You can ask till you're blue in the face but I'm not going to tell you what you said you didn't want to know.

ROGER: Is there any more champagne?

ANGIE: No. There's some brandy. *(She pours out two large brandies.)*

ROGER: When did you last speak to Cheevers, as a matter of fact?

ANGIE: Sorry – I didn't put it in my diary.

ROGER: I won't play cat and mouse with you, Angie. You had a long conversation with him only this evening.

ANGIE: Who says I did?

ROGER: Your answering machine.

ANGIE: So aren't my friends allowed to ring me up now?

ROGER: He didn't ring you – you rang him.

ANGIE: *(Defiantly.)* Well?

ROGER: You've never got over your affair with Cheevers, have you?

ANGIE: All right, I haven't – what's wrong with that?

ROGER: But you've pretended you had.

ANGIE: All right, I was pretending.

ROGER: So you're still in love with him.

ANGIE: All right, I'm still in love with him.

ROGER: Are you still seeing him?

ANGIE: That's for you to find out, since you know so much about me.

ROGER: Then I'll assume you're still seeing him.

ANGIE: Assume away.

ROGER: Look, stop fencing with me, Angie. Why did you ring Cheevers this evening?

ANGIE: Because I was lonely. Because Belle was two hours late and I had no one to talk to. Because I hadn't seen you for a fortnight, because when I do see you you're no sooner here than it's time for you to go home to your fucking wife and your fucking family and leave me on my own again. Why don't you lock me in a box when you've had enough of my company, then you could be quite sure I wasn't doing anything you didn't approve of? *(She pours herself a large drink.)*

ROGER pours himself a brandy.

You prosecute me, Roger, do you know that?

ROGER: Persecute.

ANGIE: Prosecute! I'm on trial, in the dock, and you're the judge, jury and prosecuting counsel. Well let me tell you, Mr Attorney General – in the last however many months it's been since we met –

ROGER: Sixteen.

ANGIE: Trust you to count them. In the last sixteen months I've never slept with anyone else or wanted to sleep with anyone else – which is more than can be said for you. Is that good enough?

ROGER: Come here.

ANGIE: What? Why?

ROGER: Come here.

She crosses to him. He kisses her violently. Her hands at her sides, spilling her brandy, ANGIE neither responds nor resists.

ANGIE: *(In a matter-of-fact voice.)* Are we going to bed?

ROGER: Do you want to?

ANGIE: It's the only way I know of saying goodbye.

ROGER: Brewer's droop, I'm afraid.

ANGIE: Then we may as well finish the bottle. *(She pours another large drink.)*

ROGER: *(Tossing the wad of twenty-pound notes on the bed.)* You have to be up early.

ANGIE: I know that.

ROGER: Do you think you should drive to Birmingham? Why don't you take the train?

ANGIE: Yes, I will.

ROGER: Shall I help you with the fare? Take it out of your dress money and I'll pay you back later.

ANGIE: I don't want anything from you, Roger, and there isn't going to be any later.

ROGER knocks back his drink and turns to go. ANGIE sits hunched on the bed, nursing her glass.

ROGER: Well, enjoy the wedding.

ANGIE: Roger? I don't regret anything, you know.

ROGER: Thank you for that.

ANGIE: I mean this evening, about the things I said. I meant them all. No regrets.

ROGER: Oh, I see.

He exits.

ANGIE slumps into sleep as the Lights fade to blackout.

When the lights come up, ANGIE is gone and ROGER is in the limbo area.

I was round first thing in the morning, of course. I certainly had no intention of either re-opening the inquest or resuscitating the corpse – I meant only to see that you were up, perhaps make you a cup of tea, and leave. But you'd gone.

He walks into the flat. He picks up a dog-eared railway timetable.

BELLE comes out of the bathroom wearing ANGIE's kimono.

BELLE: Good morning.

ROGER: *(Startled.)* God – I thought for a moment – what the hell are you doing here?

BELLE: I couldn't get through on the phone and I wanted to save Angie a journey. But she'd already left so I've been taking a nap.

ROGER: She must have taken an early train. But what about the wedding?

BELLE: The groom thought better of it. So I've brought back Angie's wedding present. *(She indicates an antique carriage clock.)*

ROGER: That's a very handsome clock.

BELLE: It must have cost the earth.

ROGER: It cost two hundred pounds.

BELLE: She's the most generous person I know.

ROGER: Too generous, sometimes.

BELLE: Like me.

ROGER: I'm sorry your wedding's fallen through.

BELLE: Someone told him about my scarlet past.

ROGER: Ah.

BELLE: He didn't mind my being a hooker but when he heard I'd been giving it away he went through the roof.

ROGER: The jealous type.

BELLE: It can be very destructive, jealousy.

ROGER: So I've found.

BELLE: Angie's very fond of you, you know.

ROGER: *(Ruefully.)* Very fond.

BELLE: Isn't that enough?

ROGER: No.

BELLE: She didn't care a toss for any of the others – you know that?

ROGER: Except Cheevers.

BELLE: That pimp!

ROGER: I come from a different sexual planet. I don't see how one can bear sleeping with a person one doesn't care about.

BELLE: Would you like to find out?

ROGER: Has Angie put you up to this?

BELLE: She'd thank me – if she knew.

> *BELLE extends a hand to ROGER and they fall on to the bed.*
>
> *Blackout.*

SCENE 13

A park bench. ANGIE's flat is lost.

ROGER crosses carrying a copy of the Evening Standard and sits on the bench.

ROGER: It seemed only civil to take Belle out to lunch afterwards, and then I went for a walk in the park to recover my composure. *(He opens the newspaper.)* It just wasn't your day, Angie, was it? You should have been on the front page but a big fire in Covent Garden claimed that. You were on page three, and I can just hear you joking, 'Coo! I'm a page three girl!' A jack-knifing articulated lorry on the M25 outside Waltham Abbey. Five dead including one London woman – Miss Angela Caxton of Islington, pitched through the windscreen of her white Volkswagen Polo. How many times have I told you to wear your seatbelt? *(Angrily.)* And what in God's name were you doing on the M-bloody-25? Why won't you ever look at a map? You should have been on the M-bloody-one! *(More calmly.)* The crash was around eight o'clock. You can't have had more than two and half hours' sleep. And on top of all that booze. Christ. I'd worried about you driving back from the wedding drunk. I never thought of you driving to it drunk. I felt anger and frustration. Anger at your stupidity, your lack of consideration for yourself, never mind anyone else, your final act of self-destruction. Frustration at what you'd left me with, I was trying to unlock you, Angie – why did you go off with the key?

He tosses the newspaper aside, then rises and walks into the limbo area.

I would have come to your funeral, my love – whenever and wherever it was. But I got back home that evening and collapsed, literally and melodramatically, sprawling full-length across the hall and banging my head on a marble console table. Total emotional exhaustion, that's all, but enough to keep me under sedation for a week. But you don't want to know all that. I'll find you, kitten. I'll come and see you and bring you flowers.

EPILOGUE

He now moves towards the small table with the typewriter where we discovered him in the Prologue.

ROGER: Was it love? How do I know, when I've never been along this way before? But if it wasn't, I'd like to know what the hell it was I caught from you. Sexual obsession some would say, but does that have to exclude love? Can't it be an ingredient of it? Why was every emotion heightened if it wasn't love, negative as well as positive? My anger was never angrier, my frustration more frustrating, my curiosity sharper. And I was never more alive, and never happier, and never more unhappy. *(He pecks out a few words on the typewriter.)* She thinks I'm writing a novel. I am. I'm trying to transmute you into fiction, make you as unreal in remembrance as you were in unreal life. You'll be easier to live with that way, my lovely Angie,

I'll manage it. It'll take time of course, but what the fuck!
How long's eternity?

The lights fade down to a single spot on ROGER as –

– the CURTAIN falls.

BILLY LIAR

A COMEDY

KEITH WATERHOUSE AND WILLIS HALL

This play was first presented at the Cambridge Theatre, London, on 13th September 1960, with the following cast:

FLORENCE BOOTHROYD	Ethel Griffies
GEOFFREY FISHER	George A. Cooper
ALICE FISHER	Mona Washbourne
BILLY FISHER	Albert Finney
ARTHUR CRABTREE	Trevor Bannister
BARBARA	Ann Beach
RITA	Juliet Cooke
LIZ	Jennifer Jayne

Director, Lindsay Anderson

The play is set in Stradhoughton, an industrial town in the north of England in 1960.

ACT ONE
Saturday morning

ACT TWO
Afternoon of the same day

ACT THREE
Later the same evening

No character, in this play, is intended to portray
any specific person, alive or dead.

The running time of this play,
excluding intervals, is two hours and ten minutes.

Act One

The set consists of a living-room, entrance hall and a section of the garden of GEOFFREY FISHER's house. It is a typical lower middle-class detached house in an industrial town in the north of England. To the left of the stage is the garden containing a small garden seat. The entrance to the house from the garden leads directly into the hallway with stairs going up to the bedrooms. Through the hallway is the living-room where most of the action of the play takes place. There is also a door in the living-room R, leading into the kitchen. The room is furnished with an uncut moquette three-piece suite and a dining-room suite in dark oak. The furniture is quite new, but in dreadful taste – as are also the plaster ornaments and the wall plaques with which the room is over-dressed. Above the fireplace is the usual collection of family photographs on the mantelpiece and above the mantelpiece is a large brass-studded circular mirror. The room also contains a cheap and flashy cocktail cabinet, a large television set and also a sideboard with two cupboards.

As the curtain rises we discover FLORENCE BOOTHROYD sitting on the couch. She is ALICE FISHER's mother, an old lady in her eighties, who finds it impossible to accustom herself to the modern way of life. She continually talks to herself and when she cannot be heard her lips continue to move. She is in the habit of addressing her remarks to inanimate objects. At the moment she is going through the contents of her large handbag. The handbag is open on her knee and as she takes out each object she examines it and then puts it down on the couch beside her, making a neat display. She has already taken out a few odd possessions and, at the moment, she is holding her old-age pension book. She addresses the sideboard.

FLORENCE: I don't know… They haven't stamped my book now… They haven't sent it up. It should have gone up last week but they haven't sent it up. *(She puts down the pension book and takes a white hospital appointment card from her handbag.)* That's not right, either. Doctor Blakemore? Which is Doctor Blakemore? I bet it's that black doctor. Else it's the lady doctor. I'm not seeing her. Tuesday? They know I never go on Tuesdays. I've never been on Tuesday yet. Doctor Thorpe said…

It comes to her that she is alone in the room. Putting down the handbag she rises and crosses slowly and flat-footed to the sideboard. She attempts to open the right-hand cupboard but, discovering it is locked, returns to the couch and again takes up her handbag.

He's as bad. And she encourages him. He lives in that bed. *(Noting the appointment card on the couch she picks it up.)* And where's that crepe bandage they were going to get me. *(She puts down the card.)* What's he always keep it locked up for, anyroad? There's neither sense nor reason in that. And she never tells you anything.

ALICE FISHER, GEOFFREY's wife, enters from the kitchen. She is a woman in her middle forties. Both ALICE and her husband have had working class upbringings, but GEOFFREY's success as a garage owner has moved them up into this new stratum of society. At the moment ALICE is caught up in the normal day-to-day rush of breakfast-time. She is speaking to her husband who is in the kitchen.

ALICE: Well, you do what you think fit, Geoffrey. Do what you like – it's no good me saying anything. But I know what I'd do. He still owes you for that last job you did for him.

ALICE crosses the room towards the hall, ignoring her mother who speaks to her as she passes.

FLORENCE: Who's Doctor Blakemore? Which one is that, then? Is that the one you went to?

ALICE: *(Entering the hall, calling up the stairs.)* It's time we were having you down, my lad. That bedroom clock's not fast, you know. It's half-past nine turend.

ALICE turns and enters the living room.

FLORENCE: I'll bet it's that black doctor, isn't it? I'll bet it's him.

ALICE: Who? Blakemore? Yes, I think it is.

FLORENCE: I'm not seeing him. I shan't go. I shall stop at home.

ALICE: If they say you've got to see him – you've got to see him, Mother. It's no good arguing. That's all there is to it.

GEOFFREY FISHER enters from the kitchen. He is a tall man in his early fifties. He is carrying a few invoices and, crossing and seating himself in an armchair, he begins to go through them.

FLORENCE: They caused all that bother on the buses in Birmingham. And Egypt. Mau-Mau. I make no wonder Eden's always so badly. And him upstairs. He's just as bad. I think it's time his father talked to him. I don't know why he puts up with it. I can't understand why he lets him carry on like that.

GEOFFREY: *(Looking up from the invoices he speaks to ALICE. In his speech he uses the adjective 'bloody' so frequently that it becomes completely meaningless.)* It's all right you talking, Alice, you don't understand. I've got no bloody choice. I can't turn work away.

ALICE: I've said what I've got to say. I'm not saying anything. I'm keeping out of it.

FLORENCE: They let him carry on just as he likes. I wouldn't. I'd see to him.

GEOFFREY: Where's his bloody lordship, then?

FLORENCE: I'd tell her. She lets him lead her on. She wants to go up to him with a wet dish-cloth and wring it over his face. That'll get him up.

GEOFFREY: He wants a bloody good hiding.

FLORENCE: …that'd move him…

ALICE: I've shouted him three times.

FLORENCE: …that'd shift him…

GEOFFREY: It's every morning alike.

FLORENCE: …he'd have to get up then.

GEOFFREY: You let him do just as he likes!

ALICE takes up the poker and a small shovel from the fireplace and crosses into the hall.

ALICE: *(Calling up the stairs.)* Billy! … Billy! *(She bangs the poker against the shovel.)* I shan't tell you again. If I come up there you'll know about it! I suppose you know what time it is! Your boiled egg's stone cold and I'm not cooking another.

FLORENCE: She lets him do just as he likes.

GEOFFREY: Go up to him. Go up and kick him out. He's bloody idle!

ALICE returns into the living room and places the poker and shovel back into the fireplace.

ALICE: It's all right you sitting there. You don't stand need to talk. You haven't emptied them ashes yet.

FLORENCE: She wants to go up to him. I would. *(She is now returning the objects to her handbag and pauses when she comes to the appointment card.)* It's a mystery to me about that crepe bandage. I know I had it. It's in this house somewhere.

GEOFFREY: You can't put anything down in this house. Not without somebody bloody shifting it. And who keeps taking my invoices out of that vase? Somebody bloody does.

FLORENCE: He ought to see that window's properly locked every night. He never bolts that back door properly. It wants doing. There's all sorts moving around when it gets dark.

BILLY FISHER begins to come down the bedroom stairs. He is nineteen years old and slightly built. He is wearing an old raincoat over his pyjamas. He is smoking a cigarette.

ALICE: Is that him? He's stirred himself at last, then. I'll see what his breakfast is doing.

ALICE goes out to the kitchen as BILLY reaches the foot of the stairs. BILLY takes the morning paper from behind the door and enters the living-room.

FLORENCE: She lets him do just as he likes.

BILLY: *(Reading aloud from the paper.)* Cabinet Changes Imminent.

GEOFFREY: Yes, and you'll be bloody imminent if you don't start getting up on a morning.

BILLY: Good morning, Father.

GEOFFREY: Never mind bloody good mornings. It's bloody afternoon more like. If you think your mother's got nothing better to do than go round cooking six breakfasts every morning you've got another think coming.

FLORENCE: She lets him do what he wants.

BILLY: *(Ignoring his father he turns and bows, acting out the situation to his grandmother.)* Your servant, ma'am.

GEOFFREY: And you stop that bloody game. I'm talking to you. You're bloody hopeless. And you can start getting bloody well dressed before you come down in the morning.

FLORENCE: He wants to burn that raincoat. He wants to burn it. Sling it on the fire-back. Then he'll have to get dressed whether or no.

BILLY: I gather that he who would burn the raincoat is Father and he who should get dressed of a morning is my good self. Why do you always address all your remarks to the sideboard, Grandmother?

GEOFFREY: *(Almost rising from his chair.)* Here, here, here! Who do you think you're bloody talking to? You're not out with your daft mates now. And what time did you get in last night? If it was night. This bloody morning, more like.

ALICE enters from the kitchen.

BILLY: I really couldn't say. 'bout half-past eleven, quarter to twelve. Good morning, Mother.

GEOFFREY: More like one o'clock, with your bloody half-past eleven! Well, you can bloody well start coming in of a night-time. I'm not having you gallivanting round at all hours, not at your bloody age.

BILLY: Who are you having gallivanting around, then?

GEOFFREY: And I'm not having any of your bloody lip. I'll tell you that, for a start.

ALICE: What were you doing down at Foley Bottoms at nine o'clock last night?

BILLY: Who says I was down at Foley Bottoms?

ALICE: Never mind who says, or who doesn't say. That's got nothing to do with it. You were there – somebody saw you. And it wasn't that Barbara you were with, either.

FLORENCE: He wants to make up his mind who he is going with.

GEOFFREY: He knocks about with too many lasses. He's out with a different one every night. He's like a bloody lass himself.

BILLY: Well, you want to tell whoever saw me to mind their own fizzing business.

ALICE: It is our business – and don't you be so cheeky. You're not old enough for that.

FLORENCE: If she's coming for her tea this afternoon she wants to tell her. If she doesn't I will.

BILLY: I suppose that she who's coming for her tea is Barbara and she who wants to tell her is Mother and –

ALICE: I've told you – shut up. I'm going to tell her, don't you fret yourself. You've never played fair with that girl. Carrying on. I'm surprised she bothers with you. You shouldn't mess her about like that. One and then the other. That's no way to carry on. I know where you'll finish up – you'll finish up with none of them – that's where you'll finish up.

GEOFFREY: He'll finish up on his bloody ear-hole. I'm not having him staying out half the night. Not at his age. He's not old enough. He'll wait till he's twenty-one before he starts them bloody tricks. I've told him before, he can start coming in of a night or else go and live somewhere else.

BILLY: Perhaps I will do.

ALICE: *(Ignoring him.)* I can't understand that Barbara – why she does bother with you. Are you supposed to be getting engaged to her or aren't you?

GEOFFREY: He doesn't know who he's bloody getting engaged to.

FLORENCE: He wants to make his mind up.

ALICE: *(Ignoring GEOFFREY and FLORENCE.)* Because she's not like these others, you know. That time I saw you in the arcade with her she looked respectable to me. Not like that Liz or whatever her name is. That scruffy one you reckoned to be going about with. Her in that mucky skirt. Do you ever see anything of her still?

GEOFFREY: He sees so many bloody lasses he doesn't know who he does see.

FLORENCE: He wants to make his mind up – once and for all. He wants to make his mind up who he is going with.

BILLY: I haven't seen Liz for three months.

ALICE: Well, who were you with then? Down at Foley Bottoms? Last night?

BILLY: Rita.

GEOFFREY: Who the bloody hell's Rita?

FLORENCE: She wants to see that he makes his mind up.

ALICE: I shall tell Barbara this afternoon – I shall tell her, make no mistake about that.

GEOFFREY: He's never satisfied with what he has got – that's his bloody trouble. He never has been. It's ever since he left school It's ever since he took that job – clerking. Clerking for that undertaker – what kind of a bloody job's that?

BILLY: Perhaps I might not be doing it much longer.

GEOFFREY: You what?

ALICE: What do you mean?

BILLY: I've been offered a job in London.

GEOFFREY: *(Turning away in disgust.)* Don't talk bloody wet.

ALICE: How do you mean? A job in London? What job in London?

BILLY: *(Taking a crumpled envelope from his raincoat pocket.)* What I say, I've been offered a job in London. Script-writing.

GEOFFREY: Bloody script-writing.

ALICE: What script-writing?

GEOFFREY: Script-writing! He can't write his bloody name so you can read it. Who'd set him on?

BILLY: *(Proudly.)* Danny Boon.

ALICE: Danny who?

BILLY: *(Going into a slow, exasperated explanation.)* I told you before. Boon. Danny Boon. I told you. He was on at the Empire the week before last. When he was there I told you. I went to see him. I went to his dressing room. I took him some of my scripts. Well, he's read them. He's read them and he likes them. And he's sent me this letter. He's offered me a job in London. Script-writing. Danny Boon. The comedian. He's been on television.

FLORENCE: *(Addressing the television.)* It's always boxing; boxing and horse shows.

ALICE: *(Ignoring her.)* Danny Boon? I don't remember ever seeing him.

GEOFFREY: No, and neither does anybody else. It's another of his tales. Danny Boon! He's mad him up.

ALICE: What kind of job?

BILLY: I've told you. Script-writing.

GEOFFREY: It's like all these other tales he comes home with. He can' t say two words to anybody without it's a bloody lie. And what's he been telling that woman in the fish shop about me having my leg off? Do I look as though I've had my leg off?

BILLY: It wasn't you. It was Barbara's uncle. She gets everything wrong – that woman in the fish shop.

ALICE: You'll have to stop all this making things up, Billy. There's no sense in it at your age. We never know where we are with you. I mean, you're too old for things like that now.

BILLY: *(Displaying the letter.)* Look – all right then. I've got the letter – here. He wants me to go down to see him. In London. To fix things up. I'm going to ring up this morning and give them my notice.

ALICE: You can't do things like that, Billy. You can't just go dashing off to London on spec.

GEOFFREY: *(Disparagingly.)* He's not going to no bloody London. It's them that'll be ringing him up, more like. You'll get the sack – I'll tell you what you'll get. What time are you supposed to be going in there this morning, anyroad?

BILLY: I'm not. It's my Saturday off this week.

GEOFFREY: You said that last bloody week. That's three bloody weeks in a row.

BILLY: I got mixed up.

GEOFFREY: I've no patience with you. *(He places the invoices in his pocket and rises from his chair.)* Anyway, I've got some work to do if you haven't.

ALICE: Are you going in towards town, Geoffrey?

GEOFFREY: I'm going in that direction.

ALICE: You can drop me off. I'm going down as far as the shops.

GEOFFREY: I can if you're not going to be all bloody day getting ready. I'm late now.

ALICE: *(Crossing towards the hall.)* I'm ready now. I've only to slip my coat on.

ALICE goes out into the hall and puts on a coat which is hanging on the rack. GEOFFREY turns to BILLY.

GEOFFREY: And you can get you mucky self washed – and get bloody dressed. And keep your bloody hands off my razor else you'll know about it.

FLORENCE: *(Raising her voice.)* Is she going past Driver's? 'Cause there's that pork pie to pick up for this afternoon's tea.

ALICE: *(Entering the living room.)* I'm ready. I'll call in for that pie. *(To BILLY.)* Your breakfast's on the kitchen table. It'll be clap cold by now.

GEOFFREY: *(Crossing towards the door; turning for a final sally at BILLY.)* And you can wash them pots up when you've finished. Don't leave it all for your mother.

ALICE: I shan't be above an hour, Mother.

ALICE and GEOFFREY go out through the hall and into the garden. BILLY goes into the kitchen.

FLORENCE: I shouldn't be left on my own. She's not said anything now about the insurance man. I don't know what to give him if he comes.

ALICE and GEOFFREY exit.

BILLY enters from the kitchen. He is carrying a cup and a teapot.

BILLY: I can't eat that egg. It's stone cold.

FLORENCE: There's too much waste in this house. It's all goodness just thrown down the sink. We had it to eat. When I was his age we couldn't leave nothing. If we didn't eat it then it was put out the next meal. When we had eggs, that was. We were lucky to get them. You had to make do with what there was. Bread and dripping.

BILLY: *(Sitting down, pouring himself a cup of tea.)* Do you want a cup of tea?

FLORENCE: And if you weren't down at six o'clock of a morning you didn't get that.

BILLY drinks and grimaces.

BILLY: They don't drink tea in London at this time of a morning. It's all coffee. That's what I'll be doing this time next week.

FLORENCE: Sundays was just the same. No lying-in then.

BILLY and his grandmother are now in their own separate dream-worlds.

BILLY: Sitting in a coffee-bar. Espresso. With a girl. Art student. Duffel-coat and dirty toe-nails. I discovered her the night before. Contemplating suicide.

FLORENCE: If you had a job in them days you had to stick to it. You couldn't get another.

BILLY: *(Addressing his imaginary companion.)* Nothing is as bad as it seems, my dear. Less than a week ago my father felt the same as you. Suicidal. He came round after the operation and looked down where his legs should have been. Nothing.

FLORENCE: We couldn't go traipsing off to London or anywhere else. If we got as far as Scarborough we were lucky.

BILLY: Just an empty space in the bed. Well, he'll never be World Champion now. A broken man on two tin legs.

BILLY slowly levers himself out of his chair and limps slowly and painfully around the room leaning heavily against the furniture.

FLORENCE: *(Addressing BILLY in the third person.)* He's not right in the head.

BILLY realizes he is being watched and comes out of his fantasy.

I wouldn't care, but it makes me poorly watching him.

BILLY: *(Rubbing his leg and by way of explanation.)* Cramp.

FLORENCE: He wants to get his-self dressed.

ARTHUR CRABTREE enters the garden and approaches the front door. He is about the same age as BILLY. He is wearing flannels, a sports coat and a loud checked shirt. He pushes the doorbell which rings out in two tones in the hall.

As BILLY crosses to answer the bell.

He shouldn't be going to the door dressed like that.

BILLY opens the door and, together with ARTHUR, goes into a routine – their usual way of greeting each other. ARTHUR holds up an imaginary lantern and peers into an imaginary darkness.

ARTHUR: *(In a thick north-country accent.)* There's trouble up at the mill.

BILLY: *(Also in a thick north-country accent.)* What's afoot, Ned Leather? Is Willy Arkwright smashing up my looms again?

ARTHUR: It's the men! They'll not stand for that lad of yours down from Oxford and Cambridge.

BILLY: They'll stand for him and lump it. There's allus been an Oldroyd at Oldroyd's mill and there allus will be.

ARTHUR: Nay, Josiah! He's upsetting them with his fancy college ways and they'll have none of it. They're on the march! They're coming up the drive!

BILLY: Into the house, Ned, and bar the door! We've got to remember our Sal's condition.

They enter together and march into the living room where they both dissolve into laughter.

FLORENCE: Carrying on and making a commotion. It's worse than Bedlam. Carrying on and all that noise. They want to make less noise, the pair of them.

ARTHUR: Good morning, Mrs Boothroyd.

FLORENCE: He wants to make less noise and get his-self dressed.

BILLY: Do you want a cup of tea, Arthur? I'm just having my breakfast.

ARTHUR: You rotten idle crow! Some of us have done a day's work already, you lazy get.

BILLY: Why aren't you at work now?

ARTHUR: Why aren't you at rotten work, that's why I'm not at work. Come to see where you are. They're going bonkers at the office. You never turned in last Saturday either.

BILLY: Isn't it my Saturday off this week?

ARTHUR: You know rotten well it isn't.

FLORENCE: *(Getting up from the couch.)* They're all idle. They're all the same. They make me badly.

FLORENCE crosses the room and disappears up the stairs into the bedroom.

BILLY: I could say I forgot and thought it was.

ARTHUR: You can hellers like. You said that last week.

BILLY: Tell them my grandad's had his leg off.

ARTHUR: You haven't got a rotten grandad. Anyroad, I can't tell them anything. I'm not supposed to have seen you. I've come up in my break. I'm supposed to be having my coffee. I'm not telling them anything. I'm having enough bother as it is with our old lady. What with you and your lousy stories. Telling everybody she was in the family way. She's heard about it. She says she's going to come up here and see your father.

BILLY: Cripes, she can't do that! It was only last night I told him she'd just had a miscarriage. She's not supposed to be up yet.

ARTHUR: What the hell did you tell him that for?

BILLY: I hadn't any choice. My mother was going to send a present round for the baby.

ARTHUR: The trouble with you, cocker, is you're just a rotten pathological liar. Anyway, you've done it this time. You've dropped yourself right in with not coming in this morning.

BILLY: I can get out of that. I'll think of some excuse.

ARTHUR: There's more to it than than, matey. Shadrack's been going through your postage book.

BILLY: When?

ARTHUR: This morning, when do you think? There's nearly three rotten quid short. All there is in the book is one stinking lousy rotten threepenny stamp and he says he gave you two pound ten stamp money on Wednesday.

BILLY: Fizzing hell! Has he been through the petty cash as well?

ARTHUR: Not when I left. No. Why, have you been fiddling that as well?

BILLY: No, no... I haven't filled the book up, though.

ARTHUR: And he was going on about some calendars – I don't know what he meant.

BILLY: *(Crossing to the sideboard.)* I DO. *(He takes a small key from his raincoat pocket and opens the right-hand cupboard. As he does so a pile of large envelopes fall out on to the carpet followed by a few odds and ends.)* There you are, Tosh, two hundred and sixty of the bastards.

ARTHUR: What?

BILLY: Maring calendars.

ARTHUR: *(Crossing and picking up an envelope from the floor.)* What do you want with two rotten hundred and sixty calendars? *(Reading the address on the front of the envelope.)* 'The Mother Superior, The Convent of the Sacred Heart!' *(He tears open the envelope and takes out a large wall calendar illustrated with a colourful painting of a kitten and a dog. Reading the inscription.)* 'Shadrack and Duxbury, Funeral Furnishers.' These are the firm's! 'Taste, Tact and Economy.' You skiving nit! You should have posted these last Christmas.

BILLY: Yes.

ARTHUR: Well, what are they doing in your sideboard cupboard?

BILLY: I never had enough stamps in the postage book.

ARTHUR: You think that postage money's part of your bloody wages, don't you? *(He bends down and sorts through the pile of papers on the floor.)* Why do you keep them in there?

BILLY: It's where I keep all my private things.

ARTHUR: *(Picking up a small package.)* Private things! A naffing crepe bandage! *(He throws down the package and picks up a piece of blue notepaper.)* What's this then?

BILLY: *(Making a grab for the letter.)* Gerroff, man! Give us that here! That's personal!

ARTHUR: *(Evading BILLY's hand.)* What the hell are you writing to Godfrey Winn for?

BILLY: It's not for me. It's my mother.

ARTHUR: *(Reading the letter.)* 'Dear Sir, Just a few lines to let you know how much I enjoy *Housewives' Choice* every day, I always listen no matter what I am doing, could you play "Just a Song at Twilight" for me.' That's a turn-up for the top ten! She isn't half with it, your old lady! *(Reading.)* 'I don't suppose you get time to play everyone that writes to you, but this is my favourite song. You see my husband often used to sing it when we were a bit younger than we are now. I will quite understand if you cannot play. Yours respectfully Mrs A. Fisher.' So why didn't you post this then?

BILLY: I couldn't be bothered. *(He makes a further attempt to grab the letter.)* Give us it here!

ARTHUR: *(Holding him off.)* 'P.S. My son also writes songs, but I suppose there is not much chance for him as he has not had the training. We are just ordinary folk.'

BILLY: *(Snatching the letter and tossing it into the cupboard.)* I'm not ordinary folk even if she is. *(He crams the envelopes containing the calendars back into the cupboard.)* I keep trying to get rid of them. It was bad enough getting them out of the office.

ARTHUR: How long have they been here?

BILLY: Not long. I used to keep them in that coffin in the basement at work. You can't get rid of the fizzing things! It's like a bloody nightmare. They won't burn. I've tried tearing them up and pushing them down the lavatory – all they do is float.

ARTHUR: Makes no difference what you do with them. Duxbury's on to you. He knows about them.

BILLY: *(Stuffing the last of the calendars into the cupboard and locking the door.)* Oh well…so what. He knows what he can do with his calendars. I don't give a monkey's. I'm leaving. I've got another job.

ARTHUR: Leaving?

BILLY: I'm going to ring him up this morning and give him my notice.

ARTHUR: Yes, and we've heard that one before.

BILLY: No, straight up. I'm going to London.

ARTHUR: What as – road-sweeper?

BILLY: *(Grandiloquently.)* Ay road sweepah on the road – to fame! *(He returns to his normal voice.)* I've got that job with Danny Boon.

ARTHUR: You haven't!

BILLY: Yes – script-writer. Start next week.

ARTHUR: You jammy burk! Have you though, honest?

BILLY: Yeh – course I have. It's all fixed up. He sent me a letter. Asking me to work for him.

ARTHUR: What's he paying you?

BILLY: A cowing sight more than I get from Shadrack and flaming Duxbury's.

ARTHUR: What? Counting the postage?

BILLY: What's it to you? This is it for me, boy! Success! 'Saturday Night Spectacular!' 'Sunday Night at the Palladium!' Script by!

ARTHUR: Ta-ra-ra-raaa!

BILLY: Billy Fisher! Directed by!

ARTHUR: Ta-ra-ra-raaa!

BILLY: William Fisher! Produced by!

ARTHUR: Ta-ra-ra-raaa!

BILLY: William S. Fisher!

ARTHUR: Ta-ra-ra-raaa!

BILLY: A W.S. Fisher Presentation! 'Mr Fisher, on behalf of the British Television Industry, serving the needs of twenty million viewers, it gives me great pleasure to present you with this award, this evening, in recognition of the fact that you have been voted Television Script-writer of the Year – for the seventh year running.'

ARTHUR: *(Picking up a vase from the sideboard he places it in BILLY's hands.)* Big-head.

BILLY: *(Returning the vase to the sideboard.)* Rot off. You wait and see.

ARTHUR: *(Taking a small bottle of tablets from his trouser pocket.)* So you won't be needing these now, then, will you?

BILLY: What's them?

ARTHUR: Passion pills. What I said I'd get for you.

BILLY: *(Taking the bottle incredulously.)* Let's have a look, mate. *(He opens the bottle and is about to swallow one of the tablets.)* What do they taste like?

ARTHUR: Here, go steady on, man! They'll give you the screaming ad-dabs.

BILLY: *(Returning the tablet to the bottle.)* How did you get hold of them?

ARTHUR: From a mate of mine who got demobbed. He brought them back from Singapore.

BILLY: I'll bet they're bloody aspirins.

ARTHUR: Do you want to bet? You want to ask this bloke, tosher.

BILLY: How many do you give them?

ARTHUR: Just one. Two two-and-nines at the Regal, a bag of chips and one of these and you're away. Who's it for anyway?

BILLY: Barbara… Bloody hell!

ARTHUR: What's up?

BILLY: She's supposed to be coming round this morning.

ARTHUR: I thought it was this afternoon? For her tea?

BILLY: *(Placing the bottle of tablets on the sideboard.)* No, I've got to see her first. Our old man'll go bald if he sees her before I've had a word with her. She thinks he's in the Merchant Navy.

ARTHUR: You what?

BILLY: *(Crossing hurriedly towards the hall.)* On petrol tankers. *(He indicates the tea-things.)* Shift them into the kitchen for me. Shan't be a tick.

BILLY runs up the stairs in the hall and into his bedroom.

ARTHUR picks up the teapot and goes into the kitchen. He re-enters and crosses to the sideboard where he picks up the bottle of tablets.

BILLY appears at the top of the stairs with his clothes in his hands.

BILLY moves down the stairs and enters the living room. ARTHUR replaces the tablets on the sideboard.

ARTHUR: What time's she supposed to be coming?

BILLY: *(Dressing hastily.)* Quarter of an hour since. Where's them passion pills?

ARTHUR: On the sideboard. You're not going to slip her one this morning are you?

BILLY: Why not? I'm pressed for time, man. I'm going out with Rita tonight.

ARTHUR: Well, what about our grandmother?

BILLY: Oh, she's spark out till dinner-time.

ARTHUR: I've lost track of your rotten sex life. Which one are you supposed to be engaged to, anyway?

BILLY: That's what they call an academic question.

ARTHUR: Well, you can't be engaged to both of them at once, for God's sake.

BILLY: Do you want to bet?

ARTHUR: Crikey! Well, which one of them's got the naffing engagement ring?

BILLY: Well, that's the trouble. That's partly the reason why Barbara's coming round this morning – if she did but know it. She's got it. I've got to get it off her. For Rita.

ARTHUR: What for?

BILLY: Ah, well… You see, she had it first – Rita. Only I got it from her to give it to Barbara. Now she wants it back. I told her it was at the jeweller's – getting the stone fixed. There'll be hell to pay if she doesn't get it.

ARTHUR: The sooner you get to London the better.

BILLY: *(Tucking his shirt in his trousers and slipping on his jacket.)* Are you sure them passion pills'll work on Barbara? She's dead from the neck down.

ARTHUR: You haven't tried.

BILLY: Tried! Who hasn't tried! If you want to try you're welcome. All she does is sit and eat stinking oranges.

ARTHUR: What I can't work out is why you got engaged to her in the first place. What's wrong with Liz?

BILLY: Don't talk to me about Liz. I've not seen her for months. She's tooled off to Bradford or somewhere.

ARTHUR: Well, she's tooled back again then. I saw her this morning.

BILLY: What? Liz?

ARTHUR: Yeh – scruffy Lizzie. I bumped into her in Sheepgate. Mucky as ever. It's about time somebody bought her a new skirt.

BARBARA approaches the house. She is about nineteen years old, a large well-built girl in a tweed suit and flat-heeled shoes. She is carrying a large handbag.

BILLY: Did she say anything about me?

ARTHUR: I didn't stop. Just said 'Hallo'. I wouldn't be seen stood standing to that scruffy-looking bird.

BILLY crosses and, taking the bottle from the sideboard, he places it in his breast pocket. ARTHUR crosses towards the door.

ARTHUR: I'll have to get going, anyway. I'll get shot when I get back to work. I've been gone nearly half an hour now.

BILLY: *(Crossing towards the door.)* Hang on a couple of minutes, man. Don't make it look too obvious! If she sees you going out and leaving her with me she'll be out of that door like a whippet.

ARTHUR: I'm late now!

BILLY: You can chat her up for a minute.

He crosses into the hall and opens the door to admit BARBARA.

Hallo, darling!

BARBARA: *(Who uses endearments coldly and flatly.)* Hallo, pet.

BILLY: *(Leading the way.)* Come through into the lounge.

BARBARA: *(Following BILLY into the living room.)* Hallo, Arthur.

ARTHUR winks at her. BARBARA looks round the room.

What a nice room! *(She crosses to examine the cocktail cabinet.)* What a beautiful cocktail cabinet!

BILLY: I made it.

ARTHUR reacts to this statement.

BARBARA: How clever of you, sweet. I didn't know you could do woodwork.

BILLY: Oh yes, I made all the furniture. *(A pause and then, wildly.)* And the garage.

BARBARA looks around the room doubtfully.

ARTHUR: *(Coughing.)* It's time I was making a move, mate.

BARBARA: You're not going because of me, Arthur?

ARTHUR: No, I'm supposed to be at work. *(To BILLY.)* So long, tosh!

BILLY: So long.

BARBARA: Bye! ... Isn't your sister in, Billy?

ARTHUR: *(Stopping short on his way to the door and turning.)* What bloody sister?

BILLY, unnoticed by BARBARA, gesticulates to ARTHUR to leave.

ARTHUR does so – hastily.

BILLY: Barbara, I'm glad you asked me that question. About my sister.

BARBARA: What is it?

BILLY: Sit down, darling.

BARBARA sits on the couch.

Darling, are you still coming to tea this afternoon?

BARBARA: Of course.

BILLY: Because there are some things I want to tell you.

BARBARA: What things, Billy?

BILLY: You know what you said the other night – about loving me? Even if I were a criminal.

BARBARA: Well?

BILLY: You said you'd still love me even if I'd murdered your mother.

BARBARA: *(Suspiciously.)* Well?

BILLY: I wonder if you'll still love me when you hear what I've got to say. you see – well, you know that I've got a fairly vivid imagination, don't you?

BARBARA: Well, you have to have if you're going to be a script-writer, don't you?

BILLY: Well, being a script-writer, I'm perhaps – at times – a bit inclined to let my imagination run away with me. As you know.

BARBARA is even more aloof than usual.

You see, the thing is, if we're going to have our life together – and that cottage – and little Billy and little Barbara and the lily pond and all that... Well, there's some things we've got to get cleared up.

BARBARA: What things?

BILLY: Some of the things I'm afraid I've been telling you.

BARBARA: Do you mean you've been telling me lies?

BILLY: Well, not lies exactly... But I suppose I've been, well, exaggerating some things. Being a script-writer... For instance, there's that business about my father. Him being a sea captain. On a petrol tanker.

BARBARA: You mean he's not on a petrol tanker?

BILLY: He's not in the navy.

BARBARA: Well, what is he?

BILLY: He's in the removal business.

BARBARA: And what about him being a prisoner-of-war? And that tunnel? And the medal? Don't say that was all lies?

BILLY: Yes.

BARBARA turns away abruptly.

Are you cross?

BARBARA: No – not cross. Just disappointed. It sounds as though you were ashamed of your father.

BILLY: I'm not ashamed. I'm not – I'm not!

BARBARA: Otherwise why say he was a prisoner-of-war? What was he?

BILLY: A conscientious ob... *(He checks himself.)* He wasn't anything. He wasn't fit. He has trouble with his knee.

BARBARA: The knee he's supposed to have been shot in, I suppose.

BILLY: Yes. Another thing, we haven't got a budgie, or a cat. And I didn't make the furniture... Not all of it, anyway.

BARBARA: How many other lies have you been telling me?

BILLY: My sister.

BARBARA: Don't tell me you haven't got a sister.

BILLY: I did have. But she's dead. If you're still coming for your tea this afternoon they never talk about her.

BARBARA remains silent, her head still turned away.

You remind me of her... If you're not coming, I'll understand... I'm just not good enough for you, Barbara... If you want to give me the engagement ring back – I'll understand.

BARBARA: *(Turning towards him.)* Don't be cross with yourself, Billy. I forgive you.

BILLY: *(Moving to kiss her.)* Darling...

BARBARA: *(Moving away.)* But promise me one thing.

BILLY: That I'll never lie to you again?

BARBARA nods.

I'll never lie to you again. Never, I promise... Darling, there is one thing. I have got a grannie.

BARBARA: I believe you.

BILLY: Only she's not blind. She's not very well, though. She's upstairs. Sleeping. She might have to have her leg off.

BARBARA: *(Kissing him.)* Poor darling.

BILLY: *(Moving quickly towards the cocktail cabinet.)* Would you like a drink?

BARBARA: Not now, pet.

BILLY: *(Opening the cabinet.)* Port. To celebrate.

BARBARA: All right. Well, just a tiny one.

BILLY: I'm turning over a new leaf.

Unnoticed to BARBARA he pours the drinks and taking a tablet from the 'passion pill' bottle, places it in her glass. He crosses with the glasses and sits beside her on the couch.

That's yours, darling.

BARBARA: *(Sitting on the edge of the couch she sips the port.)* Let's talk about something nice.

BILLY: Let's talk about our cottage.

BARBARA: Oh, I've seen the most marvellous material to make curtains for the living room. Honestly, you'll love it. It's a sort of turquoise with lovely little squiggles like wine-glasses.

BILLY: Will it go with the yellow carpet?

BARBARA: No, but it will go with the grey rugs.

BILLY: *(Taking her in his arms.)* I love you, darling.

BARBARA: *(Moving away.)* I love you.

BILLY: Do you? Really and truly?

BARBARA: Of course I do.

BILLY: Are you looking forward to getting married?

BARBARA takes an orange from her handbag and peels it and eats it during the following dialogue.

BARBARA: I think about it every minute of the day.

BILLY: Darling… *(He again attempts unsuccessfully to kiss her.)* Don't ever fall in love with anybody else.

BARBARA: Let's talk about our cottage.

BILLY: *(Simulating a dreamy voice.)* What about our cottage?

BARBARA: About the garden. Tell me about the garden.

BILLY: We'll have a lovely garden. We'll have roses in it and daffodils and a lovely lawn with a swing for little Billy and little Barbara to play on. And we'll have our meals down by the lily pond in summer.

BARBARA: Do you think a lily pond is safe? What if the kiddies wandered too near and fell in?

BILLY: We'll build a wall round it. No – no, we won't. We won't have a pond at all. We'll have an old well. An old brick well where we draw the water. We'll make it our wishing well. Do you know what I'll wish?

BARBARA: *(Shaking her head.)* No.

BILLY: Tell me what you'll wish first.

BARBARA: Oh, I'll wish that we'll always be happy. And always love each other. What will you wish?

BILLY: Better not tell you.

BARBARA: Why not, pet?

BILLY: You might be cross.

BARBARA: Why would I be cross?

BILLY: Oh, I don't know… You might think me too…well, forward. *(He glances at her face but can see no reaction.)* Barbara…? Do you think it's wrong for people to have – you know, feelings?

BARBARA: Not if they're genuinely in love with each other.

BILLY: Like we are.

BARBARA: *(Uncertainly.)* Yes.

BILLY: Would you think it wrong of me to have – feelings?

BARBARA: *(Briskly and firmly.)* I think we ought to be married first.

BILLY: *(Placing his head on BARBARA's knee.)* Darling…

BARBARA: Are you feeling all right?

BILLY: Of course, darling. Why?

BARBARA: Look where your hand is.

BILLY: Darling, don't you want me to touch you?

BARBARA: *(Shrugging.)* It seems…indecent, somehow.

BILLY: Are you feeling all right?

BARBARA: Yes, of course.

BILLY: How do you feel?

BARBARA: Contented.

BILLY: You don't feel…you know – restless?

BARBARA: No.

BILLY: Finish your drink.

BARBARA: In a minute. *(She opens her handbag and offers it towards him.)* Have an orange.

BILLY, snatching the bag from her, throws it down and oranges spill out across the floor.

BILLY: You and your bloody oranges!

BARBARA: *(Remonstratively.)* Billy! … Darling!

BILLY: *(Placing his head on her shoulder.)* I'm sorry, darling. I've had a terrible morning.

BARBARA: Why? What's happened?

BILLY: Oh, nothing. The usual. Family and things. Just that I've got a headache.

BARBARA: I'm sorry, pet. You know, you ought to see a doctor.

BILLY: I've seen doctors – specialists – I've seen them all. All they could give me was a huge crepe bandage.

BARBARA, unimpressed, licks her fingers.

You know, my darling, I think you have feelings, too. Deep down.

BARBARA: *(Examining her hands distastefully.)* Oooh, sticky paws!

BILLY: Wipe them on the cushion. *(He rises as a thought strikes him.)* You can go upstairs if you want. Use our bathroom.

BARBARA: Thank you.

BARBARA, picking up her handbag, crosses into the hall and goes upstairs.

BILLY, picks up her glass and crosses to the cocktail cabinet, where he pours out two more drinks. Taking the 'passion pills' from his pocket, he adds two pills to BARBARA's glass and then, on impulse, he adds the entire contents of the bottle into her glass. He is standing admiring the glass and its contents as the telephone rings in the hall. He places the glass on the table and crosses into the hall where he picks up the phone.

BILLY: The Fisher residence? Can I help you? *(His manner changes.)* Oh, hullo, Mr Duxbury. No, well, I'm sorry but I've had an accident. I was just leaving for work and I spilt this hot water down my arm. I had to get it bandaged. … Oh, well, I think there's a very simple explanation for that, Mr Duxbury. You see, there's a lot of those figures that haven't been carried forward. … I use my own individual system. … No. No, not me, Mr Duxbury. Well, I'm sure you'll find that there's a very simple explanation. … What? Monday morning? Yes, of course I'll be there. Prompt. Thank you, Mr Duxbury. Thank you for ringing. Goodbye, then. *(He puts down the telephone for a moment and is lost in depression. He brightens as, in his imagination, he addresses his employer.)* Well, look Duxbury – we're not going to argue over trivialities. As soon as I've finalized my arrangements with Mr Boon I'll get in touch with you. *(He picks up the telephone.)* Hello, Duxbury? … I'm afraid the answer is 'no'. I fully agree that a partnership sounds very attractive – but frankly my interests lie in other directions. I'm quite willing to invest in your business, but I just have not the time to take over the administrative side… Oh, I agree that you have a sound proposition there. … Granted! I take your point, Mr Duxbury. What's that little saying of yours 'You've got to come down to earth.' It's not a question of coming down to earth, old man. Some of us belong in the stars. The best of luck, Mr Duxbury, and keep writing…

He breaks off as

BARBARA approaches down the stairs.

For her benefit, he goes into another fantasy as she passes him and enters the living room.

Well, Doctor, if the leg's got to come off – it's got to come off... *(He replaces the telephone and looks speculatively at the living room door.)* It's not a question of coming down to earth, Mr Duxbury. *(He pauses.)* Some of us, Mr Duxbury, belong in the stars.

BILLY, who has now regained his self-confidence, enters the living room and crosses towards BARBARA with her glass of port.

CURTAIN.

Act Two

Afternoon of the same day.

It is late afternoon and just after tea-time in the Fisher household. ALICE is moving in and out of the kitchen clearing the tea-things from the living room table. The best tea-service has been brought out for BARBARA's benefit, although FLORENCE has insisted upon having her usual pint-pot. A strange silence has fallen upon the living room caused partly by BARBARA's disclosure that she has recently become engaged to BILLY – and partly by FLORENCE's insistence on taking her time over her tea. FLORENCE, in fact, is the only one remaining at the table. GEOFFREY has moved away to a chair and BARBARA is seated on the couch. BILLY is in the hall engaged in a phone conversation and has closed the door to the living room.

BILLY: ...Rita, will you listen for a minute! ... No, listen to what I'm telling you! The ring's still at the jeweller's! Of course it's all right... Well, what's the sense in coming round here now! It isn't here – I've just told you, it's at the jeweller's... Rita! *(He puts down the phone.)* Oh blimey! ... *(He takes up the phone and dials a number.)*

BARBARA: *(In an attempt to break the silence.)* Of course, we haven't fixed the date or anything. *(There is a pause.)* We won't be thinking of getting married for quite a while yet.

GEOFFREY: *(A slight pause.)* Well, what you going to live on? The pair of you? He'll never have a bloody penny.

FLORENCE: And there was none of this hire purchase in them days. What you couldn't pay for you didn't have. I don't agree with it. He didn't either. It's only muck and rubbish when it's there.

ALICE returns from the kitchen and fills a tray with used tea-things. She picks up FLORENCE's pint-pot.

I haven't finished with that yet.

ALICE replaces the pot.

BILLY puts down the phone in exasperation. He picks it up and dials another number. ALICE returns into the kitchen with the tray.

BARBARA: We had thought of a cottage in Devon.

GEOFFREY: Bloody Devon! He'll never get past the end of our street.

FLORENCE: She needn't have opened that tin of salmon – it's not been touched hardly.

BARBARA: I don't believe in long engagements – but I don't mind waiting.

GEOFFREY: You'll wait till bloody Domesday if you wait for that sackless article. He's not had a shave yet.

ALICE: *(Putting her head round the kitchen door.)* Come on, Mother! It's only you we're waiting for.

FLORENCE: *(Mumbling to herself.)* She knows I haven't got to be rushed. I don't know what she does it for...

An awkward silence falls upon the living room. BILLY speaks into the telephone.

BILLY: Arthur? ... Look, you've got to do something for me. Stop Rita coming round here. ... Well, go round to their house! She's after the ring and Barbara's still got it. ... No, did she heckerslike! I told you they were aspirins. Don't stand there yattering, get your skates on!

He slams down the receiver.

FLORENCE: *(Who has been mumbling quietly to herself throughout the above now raises her voice to address the sideboard.)* It's every tea-time alike. Rush, rush, rush. They've got no consideration. She knows I'm not well.

BARBARA: *(Politely.)* Billy was saying you'd not been well.

GEOFFREY: Take no notice of what she says – he'll have you as bloody daft as his-self.

BILLY opens the door and enters the living room.

You'll stand talking on that phone till you look like a bloody telephone.

Who was it, then?

BILLY: Only Arthur.

GEOFFREY: What's he bloody want?

BILLY: Oh – nothing.

GEOFFREY: He takes his time asking for it.

ALICE: *(Entering from the kitchen.)* How's his mother?

BILLY: *(Crossing to the fireplace.)* All right – considering.

BARBARA: Arthur's mother? Has she been ill?

GEOFFREY: That's the bloody tale he's come home with.

BILLY: *(Shuffling awkwardly in front of the fire.)* She's been off colour, but she's all right.

GEOFFREY: By, if I don't knock some sense into you! Stand up straight and get your hands out of your pockets! You want to get married, you do!

FLORENCE: She wants to sew them up. With a needle and cotton. She should sew them up.

GEOFFREY: You'll have to brighten your ideas up, then!

FLORENCE: A needle and a bit of black cotton. That'd stop him. Then he couldn't put them in his pockets.

ALICE: Mother, haven't you finished that tea yet! Why don't you finish it by the fire. I've got to get cleared up.

FLORENCE: *(Rising and crossing slowly to sit by the fire.)* I can't be up and down – up and down – every five minutes. She knows it doesn't do me any good. And that fire's too hot. He banks it up till it's like a furnace in here. I can't be putting up with it.

ALICE: *(Clearing the remains off the table.)* Well, it's all very well, Mother, I like to get things done. Then it's finished with.

BARBARA: Can I be giving you a hand, Mrs Fisher?

ALICE: It's all right, Barbara. I don't know why our Billy doesn't wash up once in a while.

GEOFFREY: He can't wash his bloody self, never mind the pots.

BARBARA: *(Rising and crossing towards the kitchen.)* I don't mind.

BARBARA and ALICE exit into the kitchen.

BILLY crosses to sit on the couch and GEOFFREY rises. There is an embarrassed silence. There is a first attempt at contact between BILLY and his father.

GEOFFREY: She doesn't have much to say for herself... Where do you say she works, then?

BILLY: Turnbull and Mason's.

GEOFFREY: Who?

BILLY: Solicitors. Up Sheepgate.

GEOFFREY: Oh aye?

BILLY: Shorthand-typist.

GEOFFREY: She likes her food, doesn't she? She'll take some keeping. By bloody hell! She had her share of that pork pie, didn't she?

BILLY: She lives up Cragside. On that new estate.

GEOFFREY: She'll need to live up Cragside the way she eats. She can shift them tinned oranges when she starts, can't she? Mind you, she needs it. She's a big lass, isn't she? Big-boned.

BILLY: Yes.

GEOFFREY: *(After a pause.)* You're reckoning on getting married then?

BILLY: Thinking about it.

GEOFFREY: You've got your bloody self engaged, anyroad.

BILLY: Yes.

GEOFFREY: So she was saying. You never told us.

BILLY: No. I was meaning to.

GEOFFREY: That was a bit of a daft trick to do, wasn't it?

BILLY: Oh, I don't know.

GEOFFREY: I mean, at your age like. You're only young yet. You're not old enough to start thinking about getting married.

BILLY: There's no hurry.

GEOFFREY: No. But you'll have to put your mind to it sometime.

BILLY: Yes.

GEOFFREY: I mean, you can't go carrying-on the way you've been carrying-on – now, you know. Messing about with different lasses.

BILLY: No – I know. I realize that.

GEOFFREY: You've not only yourself to consider. I don't see why you couldn't have waited a bit. I don't see why you couldn't have told us – your mother and me.

BILLY: I've said – I was meaning to.

GEOFFREY: She's not – you haven't got her into trouble – I mean, there's nothing like that about it, is there?

BILLY: No. … No – 'course not.

BILLY looks across at his father and we feel for a moment, that they are about to make some point of contact.

GEOFFREY: Well, that's something, anyroad. I suppose she's all right. Just with you not saying anything, that's all.

BILLY: Yes.

GEOFFREY: Only you'll have to start thinking about getting married. Saving up and that.

BILLY: There's plenty of time yet.

FLORENCE: Well, she didn't touch none of that salmon, I know that. Nobody did. She puts too much out. There's some folk would be glad of that. I tell her…

BILLY shows some impatience.

GEOFFREY: 'Course, I don't believe in interfering. You've made your mind up. I don't want you to come to me and say that I stopped you doing it.

BILLY: Well, Dad, it's not that simple. I've not really decided what we'll be doing yet.

GEOFFREY: You couldn't do no worse than us when we started. Me and your mother. We'd nothing – I hadn't two ha' pennies to scratch my backside with. We had to manage.

BILLY: I'm not bothered about managing, Dad. It's just that I hadn't made my mind up.

GEOFFREY: *(Almost reverting back to his normal antagonism.)* Well, you want to get your bloody mind made up, lad. Right sharp. Before she does it for you.

BILLY: You see…

FLORENCE: *(Interrupting.)* I told her, you don't get married till you're twenty-one.

BILLY: Just a minute, Grandma…

FLORENCE: *(Ignoring him.)* You can do as you like then, I said. Only, I said, don't come running back to me when you can't manage. I said you'll have it to put up with…

BILLY: *(Completely exasperated.)* For Christ's sake belt up!

GEOFFREY: *(Losing his temper completely.)* You what! *(He moves across and grabs BILLY by his shirt.)* You what did you say? What was that? What did you say?

BILLY: *(Frightened but unrepentant.)* I merely remarked…

GEOFFREY: *(Shouting.)* Talk bloody properly when you talk to me! You were talking different a minute ago, weren't you? What did you just say to your grandma? What did you just say?

ALICE enters from the kitchen.

ALICE: Hey, what's all this row? *(She indicates the kitchen.)* Don't you know we've got somebody here?

GEOFFREY: I can't help who's here! She might as well know what he is! Because I'll tell her! *(Shaking him.)* He's ignorant! That's what you are, isn't it? Ignorant! Ignorant! Ignorant! Isn't it?

ALICE: Well, don't pull him round. That shirt's clean on.

GEOFFREY: *(Releasing his hold on BILLY.)* I'll clean shirt him before I've finished!

ALICE: Well, what's he done?

GEOFFREY: I'll clean shirt him round his bloody ear-hole. With his bloody fountain pens and his bloody suede shoes. Well, he doesn't go out tonight. I know where he gets it from. He stops in tonight and tomorrow night as well.

BILLY: Look…

GEOFFREY: Don't 'look' me! With you look this and look that! And you can get all that bloody books and rubbish or whatever it is cleared out of that sideboard cupboard as well! Before I chuck 'em out – and you with 'em!

BILLY: What's up? They're not hurting you are they?

BARBARA enters and stands in the kitchen doorway uncertainly.

GEOFFREY: No, and they're not bloody hurting you either!

ALICE: *(Quietly.)* Well, I don't know what you've done now.

GEOFFREY: Answering back at his grandmother. If that's what they learned him at grammar school I'm glad I'm bloody uneducated! Anyroad, I've finished with him! He knows where there's a suitcase. If he wants to go to London he can bloody well go.

ALICE: *(Sharply.)* Oh, but he's not.

GEOFFREY: I've finished with him. He can go.

ALICE: Oh, but he's not.

GEOFFREY: He's going! He can get his bloody things together! He's going out!

ALICE: Oh, but he's not. Oh, but he's not. Oh, but he is not!

BILLY: *(Trying to get a word in.)* Look, can I settle this…

GEOFFREY: *(Interrupting.)* It's ever since he started work. Complaining about this and that and the other. If it isn't his boiled eggs it's something else. You have to get special bloody wheatflakes for him because there's a bloody plastic bloody submarine in the packet. Splashing about in the kitchen at his age. He wants pulling away. Well, I've had enough – he can go.

ALICE: Oh, but he's not. Now, you just listen to me, Geoffrey. He's not old enough to go to London or anywhere else.

GEOFFREY: He's old enough to get himself engaged. He thinks he is. He's old enough and bloody daft enough.

ALICE: Well, you said yourself. He doesn't think. He gets ideas in his head.

GEOFFREY: He can go. I've finished with him.

ALICE: Oh, but he is not. Not while I'm here.

BARBARA: *(Who has been staring at FLORENCE.)* Mrs Fisher...

GEOFFREY: *(Ignoring her.)* He wants to get into the bloody army, that's what he wants to do.

ALICE: *(Spiritedly.)* Yes, and you want to get into the bloody army as well.

BARBARA: Mrs Fisher. I don't think Billy's grandma's very well.

ALICE, GEOFFREY and BILLY turn and look at FLORENCE who is sitting slumped in her chair.

ALICE: *(Rushing across to her mother.)* Now look what you've done!

GEOFFREY: *(To BILLY.)* I hope you're bloody satisfied now. She's had another do.

ALICE: It's no use blaming him, Geoffrey. You're both as bad as each other. Well, don't just stand there – get me the smelling salts.

BARBARA: *(Coming forward.)* Can I be doing anything, Mrs Fisher?

ALICE: No...no, it's all right. She's getting old, that's all. He'll see to it.

GEOFFREY: *(Crossing to the sideboard, searching through the drawers.)* It's happening too bloody often is this. We can't be having this game every fortnight – neither sense nor reason in it.

ALICE: Well, she can't help it, Geoffrey. It's not her fault.

GEOFFREY: She'll have to see that bloody doctor. If I've to take time off and take her myself – she'll have to see him.

ALICE: She won't see him.

GEOFFREY: It's getting past a joke is this. It's not his fault he's bloody black. *(Rifling through a second drawer.)* I wish you'd keep them salts in the same place. Never here when you want them.

ALICE: *(Patting her mother's wrists.)* Hurry up, Geoffrey!

FLORENCE: *(Who has been slowly coming round during the above begins to mumble.)* I told her about that fire. Banking it up. I get too hot and then I go off. They don't think. Rushing me with my tea.

ALICE: It's all right, Mother. You'll be all right.

GEOFFREY locates the bottle of smelling salts.

GEOFFREY: *(Crossing and handing them to ALICE.)* Does she want these bloody salts or not?

ALICE: *(Taking the bottle from GEOFFREY.)* She'd better have them. *(She opens the bottle and holds it under FLORENCE's nose.)*

FLORENCE: Feathers.

GEOFFREY: She's off. She's bloody rambling.

FLORENCE: She wants to burn some feathers. Never mind salts. I can't be doing with salts. They make me bilious.

ALICE: It's all right, Mother. *(To GEOFFREY.)* We'd better get her upstairs. She's too hot in here anyway.

GEOFFREY: She'll be too bloody cold if she doesn't see that doctor. It's not fair on us. It's us that has it to put up with.

BARBARA: Shall I fetch you a glass of water?

ALICE: No – she doesn't have water. She'll be all right in a minute.

GEOFFREY: It's happening too regular is this. It's every week alike. And it's always on bloody Saturdays. We can't even sit down to us tea in peace.

ALICE: Don't go on at her – you'll only make her worse. Just help me get her off to bed.

GEOFFREY: *(Putting his arm round FLORENCE and raising her to her feet; gruffly compassionate.)* Come on then, Mother. Let's be having you. She's a bloody ton weight. She puts some weight on for somebody who never eats nothing. *(To FLORENCE.)* You're putting weight on.

ALICE: Don't stand there, Billy. Help your father.

GEOFFREY: *(Piloting FLORENCE towards the door.)* By bloody hell – don't ask him to do nothing. He'll drop her down the bedroom stairs.

ALICE: *(Crossing to help him.)* You never give him a chance.

ALICE and GEOFFREY support FLORENCE and move off through the hall and up the stairs.

FLORENCE: They ought to put a bed down here… Them stairs is too steep…

GEOFFREY: Now steady… Steady on, lass… Plenty of time.

FLORENCE continues to mumble to herself as they go upstairs. We cannot hear what she is saying but one sentence comes out plainly as they disappear into the bedroom.

FLORENCE: They could have got the bungalow.

In the living room there is an embarassed silence between BILLY and BARBARA. BILLY absent-mindedly picks up FLORENCE's handbag and looks inside it. He goes through the contents idly and takes out an obsolete ration book.

BILLY: Do you know, she still keeps her old ration book?

BARBARA: I noticed she didn't look very well. Even at tea-time. I noticed but I didn't like to say anything.

BILLY: *(After a pause.)* You wouldn't think she'd been all over the world, would you? Paris – Cairo – Vienna.

BARBARA: *(Incredulously.)* Who? Your grandma?

BILLY: My grandad was in the Diplomatic Corps. Before he had his leg off. He could speak seven languages, you know. They went all over.

BARBARA: *(Completely disbelieving him she decides to ignore this statement.)* Do you think your mother's going to like me, pet?

BILLY: He was in the French Foreign Legion for nine years.

BARBARA: I think we should get on with each other. It's better when you do – **really.** When families stick together. Why didn't you tell them we'd got engaged?

BILLY: I was going to. Did you show them the ring?

BARBARA: *(Examining the ring.)* Of course. I show it to everybody. It's lovely. I won't be completely happy until I've got the other one to go with it.

BILLY: Darling… *(Taking her hand.)* You will always love me, won't you?

BARBARA: You know I will.

BILLY: *(His fingers on the engagement ring.)* I still say this ring's too big. Why won't you let me get it altered?

BARBARA: *(Pulling her hand away.)* I don't think it's too big. Anyway, I want everybody to see it first.

BILLY: Well, don't blame me if you lose it. My mother was saying it was nearly coming off while you were washing up. It'll only take a couple of days. And then it'll be there for ever. *(Romantically.)* For ever and ever…

BARBARA: Sweet…

BILLY: So go on, then. Give me it. You can have it back on Wednesday.

BARBARA: No, I'll never take it off. Never – never.

BILLY: Give me the cowing ring!

BARBARA: Billy!

BILLY: *(Moving away from her in disgust.)* Oh, please yourself then. Don't say I didn't warn you.

RITA approaches the house through the garden. She is a small girl with blonde hair – seventeen years old but she dresses to look much older. She is common and hard and works in a snack bar.

BARBARA: Now you're cross. Don't be, pet. I'll take care of it. And I'll never lose it.

RITA rings the bell.

BILLY: Just a minute. *(He crosses into the hall and opens the front door.)* Rita!

RITA: *(Moving forward menacingly.)* Right, I suppose you…

BILLY: *(Interrupting her.)* Just a minute!

He slams the door on RITA and moves across the hall to speak to BARBARA.

Just a minute! *(He closes the living room door.)*

ALICE appears at the top of the staircase.

ALICE: Who is it, Billy?

BILLY: Just a minute!

BILLY opens the front door and enters the garden, closing the door behind him.

ALICE goes back into her bedroom.

BARBARA takes an orange from her handbag and is peeling it as the lights fade down on the living room and the lights come up on the garden set.

Hallo, Rita.

RITA: *(Her conversation consists mainly of clichés and expressions picked up on amorous evenings spent with friendly American airmen.)* Ooh! Look what's crawled out of the cheese!

BILLY: Hallo, Rita – sorry I can't ask you in.

RITA: Get back in the knife-box, big-head.

BILLY: We're flooded. The pipes have burst.

RITA: Are you kidding? Here, pull the other one – it's got bells on it.

BILLY: What's the matter, darling? Is anything wrong?

RITA: Hark at Lord Muck. Don't come the innocent with me. You know what's wrong. I thought you were going to your uncle's on Wednesday night.

BILLY: I did go to my uncle's. My Uncle Herbert's.

RITA: Well, you didn't then – because somebody saw you. Sitting in the Gaumont. With your arm round a lass eating oranges.

BILLY: They didn't see me. I was at my Uncle Ernest's playing Monopoly.

RITA: *(Imitating him.)* At my Uncle Ernest's playing Monopoly. You rotten liar! You're just muck. You're rotten that's what you are. And where's my engagement ring?

BILLY: I'm glad you asked me that question. Because I called into the shop this morning and the man said it might be another week.

RITA: *(Again imitating him.)* The man said it might be another week. You're worse than muck. You're rotten.

BILLY: No, because they can't do it up here. They've got to send it to Bradford. They've got three people off ill.

RITA: *(Again imitating him.)* Three people off ill. Yes, I suppose they're all having their legs off. To hear you talk everybody's having their leg off. And another thing, I thought I was coming round for my tea this afternoon. To meet your rotten mother.

BILLY: Yes, darling, but something happened. My grandma was taken ill. Last Thursday. They've got her in bed.

RITA: Well, I am going to see your rotten mother – I'll tell you that. My name's not 'Silly', you know. Either you get me that rotten ring back or I'm going to see your rotten mother.

BILLY: *(Attempting to quieten her.)* Sssh, darling!

RITA: *(Raising her voice.)* And your rotten father! And your rotten grandmother!

In a wild attempt to quieten RITA, BILLY takes her in his arms and kisses her. She responds with an automatic animal passion. They break away.

You are rotten to me, Billy. I'm not kidding, you know. I still want that ring back. *(Her voice rises again.)* And my dad wants to know where it is as well. We're supposed to be engaged, you know.

BILLY: You once said you didn't want to marry me.

RITA: Don't come that tale with me. I said I didn't want to live in a rotten cottage in Devon – that's all.

BILLY: We'll live wherever you like, darling. Nothing matters as long as we're together.

RITA: Well, can you get it back tonight, then?

BILLY: Of course I can, darling. If that's what you want. *(He kisses her again.)* Darling, darling, darling.

RITA: *(Pushing BILLY away as his hand creeps round her back.)* Hey, Bolton Wanderer! Keep your mucky hands to yourself!

BILLY: Tell me you're not cross with me, darling.

RITA: *(Imitating him.)* Tell me you're not cross… Put another record on, we've heard that one. And get that ring back.

BILLY: I will. I promise, darling. I'll go down to the shop. I'll give it to you tonight – at the dance.

RITA: You'd better do – or else there'll be bother. I wouldn't like to be in your shoes if my father comes round. And he will, you know. And he won't stand arguing in the garden.

BILLY kisses her again.

Go on, then. Go in and get your coat on – and get off for that ring.

BILLY: See you tonight, darling.

RITA: Never mind see you tonight, shops'll be shut in half an hour. You'll get off now. Go on, then, get your coat. You can walk me down as far as the bus-stop. Go on, Dateless, don't stand there catching flies.

BILLY: I can't go yet.

RITA: Why not? What's stopping you?

BILLY: I'm waiting to go to the lavatory. My mam's on.

RITA: I'l be walking on. You catch me up.

RITA walks off slowly, down the garden and goes.

BILLY enters the house. As he crosses through the hall the lights fade down in the garden and come up in the living room. BARBARA is just finishing eating the orange.

BILLY: Hey, listen! I've just had my fortune told by a gipsy.

BARBARA: I've eaten a whole orange while I've been waiting.

BILLY: She says there's a curse on me.

BARBARA: Your mother's not come down yet. Neither has your father.

BILLY: I'm going to experience sorrow and misfortune but after a long journey things will start to go right. Hey, she had a baby on her back like a Red Indian.

BARBARA: Do you think she'll be all right – our grandmother?

BILLY crosses and sits in the armchair.

BILLY: Who? Oh, my grandma! Yes, she'll be all right. It's just that she's got this rare disease – they're trying a new drug out on her.

BARBARA: She looked as though she was having some kind of fit at first. I noticed when you were having that row with your father.

BILLY: They've only tried it out three times – this drug. Once on President Eisenhower, then the Duke of Windsor and then my grandma.

BARBARA: Honestly! No wonder your father gets cross with you.

BILLY: How do you mean?

BARBARA: Well, all these stories you keep on telling – no wonder he keeps losing his temper.

BILLY: Oh, you don't take any notice of him.

BARBARA: Billy?

BILLY: What?

BARBARA: What was your father saying? About you going to London?

BILLY: Did he? When? I never heard him.

BARBARA: When he was talking about answering back at your grandmother. When he got hold of your shirt. He said, 'If you want to go to London you can "B" well go.' He swore.

BILLY: I know. He's been summonsed twice for using bad language.

BARBARA: Yes, but what did he mean?

BILLY: What? About going to London?

BARBARA: Yes.

BILLY: Ah, well – there's a very interesting story behind that.

BARBARA: No, Billy, this is important – to us. You've got to think about me now.

BILLY: *(Rising and crossing towards her.)* It's for you I'm doing it, my darling.

BARBARA: What do you mean?

BILLY: *(Sitting down beside her and taking her hand, he goes off into a fantasy.)* Isn't it obvious? How can we go on living like this?

BARBARA: *(Automatically freeing her hand, she takes an orange from her handbag.)* What do you mean, pet? Like what?

BILLY: In this – this atmosphere. Do you honestly think that we could ever be happy – I mean really happy – here?

BARBARA: Where?

BILLY: In this house. There's the shadow of my father across this house. He's a bitter man, Barbara.

BARBARA: *(Settling down and beginning to peel the orange.)* Why? What for? What about?

BILLY: He's jealous. Every time he looks at me he sees his own hopes and the failure of his own ambitions.

BARBARA: Your father?

BILLY: He had his dreams once. He can't bear it – seeing me on the brink of success. He was going to be a writer too.

BARBARA: Billy if this is going to be another of your stories…

BILLY: You don't have to believe me. The evidence is here – in this house.

BARBARA: Evidence? How do you mean – evidence?

BILLY: *(Pointing to the sideboard.)* It's all in there.

BARBARA: What is?

BILLY: Go and look for yourself. In that cupboard.

BARBARA rises and crosses to the sideboard. She tugs at the handle on BILLY's cupboard.

BARBARA: It's locked.

BILLY: *(Menacingly.)* Yes.

BARBARA: Where's the key?

BILLY: God knows. I was four years old when that was locked, Barbara. It's never been opened since.

BARBARA: *(Crossing towards BILLY.)* Well, what's supposed to be in it?

BILLY: Hopes! Dreams! Ambitions! The life work of a disillusioned man. Barbara, there must be forty or fifty unpublished novels in that cupboard. All on the same bitter theme.

BARBARA: *(In half-belief.)* Well, we can't all be geniuses.

BILLY: Perhaps not. But he crucified himself in the attempt. Sitting night after night at that table. Chewing at his pen. And when the words wouldn't come he'd take it out on us.

BARBARA: But what about going to London? What about our cottage in Devon?

ALICE emerges from the bedroom and comes down the stairs.

BILLY: Well, it's all down south, Barbara. We could live in the New Forest. We could have a cottage there – a woodman's cottage – in a clearing.

BARBARA: I think I'd be frightened. Living in a forest.

BILLY: *(Putting his arm round her.)* Not with me to look after you, you wouldn't.

BILLY rises awkwardly as ALICE enters the room. ALICE is faintly preoccupied. She crosses towards the kitchen and speaks almost to herself.

ALICE: Well, she seems to be resting.

ALICE goes into the kitchen. There is a slight feeling of embarassment between BILLY and BARBARA and then BARBARA speaks to break the silence.

BARBARA: Are we going out dancing tonight?

BILLY: If you like… *(He claps his hand to his forehead in an over-dramatic gesture.)* Oh, no! Just remembered!

BARBARA: *(Suspiciously.)* What?

BILLY: I promised to go round to my Uncle Herbert's tonight. To play Monopoly. It's his birthday.

BARBARA: Funny you never told me before. You're always having to go round to your Uncle Herbert's. Anyway, I thought it was your Uncles Ernest who played Monopoly?

BILLY: Ah, well... I'm glad you asked me that question. You see, my Uncle Herbert...

BARBARA: *(Interrupting.)* Oh, don't bother. You and your relatives. If I didn't know you better I'd think you had another girl.

BILLY: Darling! What a thing to say!

BARBARA: You know that Liz is back in town, don't you?

BILLY: Liz who?

BARBARA: You know who. That dirty girl. I'm surprised you weren't ashamed to be seen with her.

BILLY: Oh, her... I haven't seen her for donkey's years.

ALICE enters from the kitchen. She is carrying a tumbler containing a white liquid which she is stirring with a spoon.

ALICE: Her breathing's all right – she's still awake, though. I think she'd be better if we could get her off to sleep.

BARBARA: She was looking tired this afternoon.

ALICE: *(Gently reprimanding.)* Well, I blame you as much as anybody. You set your father off and then it sets her off. I've told you time and time again.

BILLY: *(Half ashamed.)* She's all right now, is she, then?

ALICE: Is she ever all right?

BARBARA: Are you quite sure there's nothing I can do? Could she eat an orange?

ALICE: I'm going to get the doctor in to her – be on the safe side. Whether she wants him or not. Your father's sitting with her. *(She hands him the tumbler.)* Can you take this up without spilling it?

BILLY: *(Taking the tumbler reluctantly.)* Who? Me?

ALICE: Either that or ring the doctor up for me. *(Rather impatiently.)* But do something, lad, don't just stand there.

ALICE turns away from him and walks briskly into the hall where she picks up the phone. BILLY stands indecisively for a moment and then crosses through into the hall and up the stairs as ALICE dials the number. She waits for a reply and glances up at BILLY who has, for no reason at all, developed a limp.

(Calling up to him.) Now, what are you playing at!

BILLY stops limping and quickens his pace and goes into the bedroom.

(Turning back to the phone.) Hallo, is that the surgery? ... Well, it's Mrs Fisher, forty-two Park Drive. ... Yes, that's right. Only it's my mother again. Mrs Boothroyd. Do you think the doctor could call round? ... Oh, dear. Only we've got her in bed again... I've given her her tablets – and the mixture. ... Well, will you ask him to come round as soon as he can? ... Yes, yes, I will, I will – thank you very much. Goodbye. *(She replaces the phone and crosses into the living room.)* You don't like to bother them on a Saturday but what else can you do?

BARBARA: Is the doctor coming, Mrs Fisher?

ALICE: He's coming sometime – when he's ready. It'll be nine o'clock again, I suppose. He's already out on his calls.

BARBARA: I shouldn't worry. He'll be round as soon as he can.

ALICE: *(Sitting.)* You can't help worrying sometimes. If I don't worry nobody else will. It's just getting me down, is this. It's just one thing after another.

BARBARA: *(Returning to her seat on the couch and taking up the orange.)* Would you like a piece of orange, Mrs Fisher?

ALICE looks up and, for the first time, realizes that BARBARA is trying to help.

ALICE: No. No, thank you. Not just at this minute, love. Thank you.

BARBARA: Would it be better if I went? *(Half rising.)* I mean if I'm in the way.

ALICE: No, don't be silly. You sit yourself down. I'm only sorry it's happened while you were here.

BARBARA: *(Returning to her seat.)* You can't arrange illnesses, can you?

ALICE: You can't. I only wish you could. Only she has these turns and all you can do is put her to bed. Bus she always seems to pick the most awkward times. Still, you can't blame her. It's not her fault. You might think it is to hear him talk. You'd think she does it on purpose, to listen to him.

BARBARA: She might be better before the doctor comes.

ALICE: It wears me out, I know that. And if it isn't her it's our Billy. I don't know what we're going to do with him.

BARBARA: I think he wants to help – but he doesn't like to offer.

ALICE: He didn't used to be like this. He's got to grow up sometime. I don't know, it might be better if he did go to London. It might put some sense into him if he had to look after himself.

BARBARA: Well, that's what I don't understand, Mrs Fisher. Is he going to London?

ALICE: Well, he reckons he is. Hasn't he said anything to you?

BARBARA: Well, not really. I only heard what his father said. I tried to ask him.

ALICE: What did he say to you?

BARBARA: Nothing, really. *(She indicates the sideboard.)* He just started talking about that cupboard.

ALICE: Oh, don't talk to me about that cupboard. I don't know what he keeps in there. I'm frightened to ask, to tell you the honest truth.

BARBARA: He said it had been locked since he was four years old.

ALICE: I don't know why he says these things. I mean, what good does it do to him? It's not as if he gets anything out of it.

BARBARA: I'm sure I don't know. He told me Mr Fisher was a captain on a petrol ship.

ALICE: Don't let his father hear you say that – else there'll be trouble. He'll murder him one of these days. If he knew all I know he'd have murdered him long ago. I could do it myself sometimes. And he says things we can find out about, that's what I don't understand. He told me that young lad who works in the fruit shop had gassed himself – and he knows I go in there every Tuesday.

BARBARA: I know. He says all kinds of things.

ALICE: I don't know where he'll end up – it's not our fault, I do know that. We've done our best for him. His father says it's since he started work – but I know different. It's ever since he went to that grammar school. He wanted to go, so we let him – he'd not been there five minutes before he wanted to leave. And we had it all to pay for, you know – he never appreciated it. School uniform, he loses his cap first week. Cricketing trousers, he never wore them. We bought him a satchel and he let a lad run away with it. Then there was his books to pay for – well, he never reads them. It's just been a waste of time and money. You'd think he'd been dragged up. He's not cleaned his shoes for six months.

BARBARA: I tell him about his shoes. He takes no notice. And his hair – he won't have a haircut, will he?

ALICE: Well, he doesn't take after me – or his father. And it's us that's got to clean up after him. He got them suede shoes so he wouldn't have to bother cleaning them – but you can't just not touch them. He trod in some dog-dirt on Tuesday and – do you know? – he walked it round this house for three days. I had to get a knife and scrape it off myself in the finish. *(Distastefully, recalling the incident.)* Pooh! You could smell it all over the house.

BARBARA: My mother won't have a dog. And she hates cats.

ALICE: You can't keep on telling him – it just goes in one ear and out the other. He wants watching all the time, that's his trouble. You see, if he'd gone into the business with his father, like we wanted him to, we could have kept an eye on him more. But he won't listen. He went after all kinds of daft jobs. That lady in the Juvenile Employment Bureau, she lost patience with him. He wouldn't have this and he wouldn't have that. And she offered him some lovely jobs to begin with. He could have gone as a junior trainee at the Co-op Bank if he'd wanted to. She offered him that.

BARBARA: I know somebody who works there, she likes it. They've got their own social club.

ALICE: She just stopped bothering. She couldn't get any sense out of him. She asked him what he did want in the end and he told her he wanted to be either a merchant seaman or a concert pianist. Grammar school! You'd think he'd been to the Silly School. He shows me up.

BARBARA: How did he come to work for Shadrack and Duxbury's?

ALICE: Don't ask me. He'd been left school a fortnight and he was still no nearer a job – he wanted to work in the museum by this time. We were sick and tired of having him lounging about the house. His father comes home one morning at twelve o'clock and finds him playing with some Plasticine. He went mad. He told him straight out. He says, you get out of this house and get yourself a job, my lad, he says. And, he says, don't you dare come back without one – or I'll knock your blooming head right off your shoulders – only he didn't say blooming.

BARBARA: No, I can imagine.

ALICE: So, of course, our Billy goes out and waltzes back two hours later and says he's working for an undertaker – start on Monday. He's been there ever since.

BARBARA: I don't think he likes it, though, does he?

ALICE: Like it or lump it, he's got to work for his living. Never mind going to London. He's got no mind of his own, that's his trouble. He listens to these pals he's got. What they do he's got to do. I'm only glad he's found himself a sensible lass, for once.

BILLY emerges from the bedroom and comes down the stairs.

BARBARA: I think it was that girl he used to go about with before he met me, Mrs Fisher. That funny girl. That Liz. She used to put a lot of ideas into his head.

BILLY pauses at the foot of the stairs and listens to their conversation.

ALICE: Oh, that one. I've seen him with her. She looked as though a good bath wouldn't do her any harm. I don't know what kind of a family she comes from. I'm only glad she's gone.

BARBARA: She's come back again, didn't you know? She goes off all over, all the time. By herself. I don't think she's got any family. Do you know what I don't like about her, Mrs Fisher? She smokes and she keeps her cigarette in her mouth when she's talking. I could never do that. It looks common.

ALICE: You could always tell when he'd been out with her. The ideas he used to come home with. He comes home one night and says he wants to go off on holiday with her. To the Norfolk Broads, if you like. I told him – straight. I said, that's not the way we do things in this house. I said, if you want to go on holiday you can come to Morecambe with us – and if you don't you can stop at home.

BARBARA: I don't believe in mixed holidays – not before you're married.

ALICE: I'm sure you don't, love. You wouldn't be sitting here if you did, I can tell you.

BARBARA: He was saying you wouldn't mind if I went to Blackpool with him for a week – but I wouldn't. I don't believe in anything like that.

ALICE: He was saying that!

BILLY: *(Entering hastily and changing the subject.)* Hey, listen!

ALICE and BARBARA turn to BILLY who is trying to think of something to say next.

(He tries to joke in desperation.) Fifteen men under one umbrella and not one of them got wet. *(He evokes no reaction.)* It wasn't raining.

ALICE: *(To BARBARA.)* Well, you can't say you don't know what you're letting yourself in for. *(To BILLY.)* Stop acting so daft with people poorly. We've got enough on our plates without you.

BARBARA: How's your grandma, Billy? Is she any better?

ALICE: Has she gone off to sleep yet?

BILLY: She looks all right to me.

ALICE: Is your father all right with her? Would he like me to go up? Does he want anything?

BILLY: I don't know.

ALICE: No, and I don't suppose you care. *(Losing her temper.)* Have you had a wash since you got up this morning?

BILLY: Course I have.

ALICE: Yes, a cat-lick. I bet you didn't take your shirt off, did you? You'll have to smarten your ideas up, you know, if you want to go scriptwriting. They don't have them on the BBC with mucky necks. You'll start washing your own shirts in the future, I can't get them clean.

BILLY: *(Acutely embarrassed but, for BARBARA's benefit, he pretends to be amused and winds an imaginary gramophone handle.)* Crikey Moses, she's off!

BARBARA: Well, you can't say you've had a shave this morning, Billy because you haven't.

BILLY: I'm growing a beard, if you want to know.

ALICE: Oh no, you're not. We're having no beards in this house.

BARBARA: I don't think I'd like you with a beard, Billy.

ALICE: He's not having a beard.

BILLY: I'm having a bloody beard.

ALICE: Hey, hey, hey! Language! Don't you start coming out with that talk! Else you'll get a shock coming, big as you are! We get enough of that from your father.

BILLY: Well, I'm still having a beard. I can grown one in six weeks.

BARBARA: I don't think you should, Billy. Not if your mother doesn't want you.

ALICE: He's got no say in the matter. If I say he doesn't grow a beard, he doesn't grow one.

BILLY: What's up with you? It's my stinking face!

ALICE: I'll not tell you again about that language! You can start to alter yourself, that's what you can do, my lad. We're not going on like this for much longer. Either brighten your ideas up or do as your father says – and get off to London or where you like. Because we're not going on like this, day in and day out! It's not fair on nobody!

BILLY: Oh, shut up!

ALICE: And you can start watching what you say to people, as well. What did you say to me about that lad in the fruit shop? Gassing himself? And what have you been telling Barbara about that cupboard?

BILLY: What cupboard?

ALICE: You know very well what cupboard!

BILLY: I don't know what cupboard. How do you mean – cupboard?

BARBARA: Your sideboard cupboard.

BILLY: What about it?

BARBARA: That evidence you were talking about. In the cupboard. When you were four years old. All these unpublished novels. Where you father was chewing his pen up.

BILLY: Oh that! Oh, you should have said. No, you're getting mixed up. I was talking about his invoices that he writes out. He keeps them in that vase – I didn't say anything about any cupboard.

BARBARA: *(Shocked.)* Billy Fisher! I don't know how you can stand there! He'll be struck down dead one of these days.

BILLY: *(With a pretence at innocence.)* What's up?

ALICE: He can stand there as if butter wouldn't melt in his mouth.

BILLY: I don't know what you're all on about.

BARBARA: Oh yes, you do. Don't try and make it out as if it's me, Billy.

BILLY: It is you. Look – Barbara – you were sitting over there, weren't you? On that couch. Because you were eating an orange. And I was standing over there. Right? It is right, isn't it? You were sitting there and I was standing there.

BARBARA: Yes, but then you said your father…

ALICE: Never mind what he said, love, I know what he is.

RITA enters the garden and stands, for a moment, hesitantly outside the front door.

BILLY: Yes, you'll believe her, won't you?

ALICE: I'd believe anybody before you, Billy I'm very sorry, but there it is. I'd believe Hitler before I'd believe you.

BILLY: Why don't you come straight out and call me a liar, then!

ALICE: Well, you are one. I don't care who knows it.

BILLY: Well, that's a nice thing for a mother to say, isn't it?

ALICE: Yes, and you're a nice son for a mother to have, aren't you? You don't think what you're doing to me, do you? You never consider anybody except yourself.

BILLY: I suppose you do, don't you?

ALICE: Yes, I do. I worry about you, I know that.

BILLY: Well, what about me? Don't you think I worry? I worry about the H-bomb. You didn't know I nearly went on the Aldermaston march last Easter, did you? I don't want another war, you know. And what about all them refugees? You never stop to consider them, do you? Or South Africa.

At which point RITA makes up her mind, and, without knocking, marches into the house and into the living room.

Do you know, Barbara, if you were black and we lived in South Africa I'd be in gaol by now. Doing fifteen years. *(At which point he breaks off as RITA makes her entrance.)* Hallo, Rita.

RITA: *(To BILLY, indicating ALICE.)* It takes some time to come out of the lavatory, doesn't it? What's she been doing? Writing her will out?

ALICE: *(Outraged.)* Do you usually come into people's houses without knocking?

RITA: I do when people have got my private property. *(To BILLY.)* Come on – give.

BILLY: Rita, I don't think you've ever met my mother, have you?

RITA: No, but she'll know me again, won't she? Come on, you and your stinking rotten jewellers. I'm not daft, you know.

ALICE: *(Shocked.)* We're not having this! Where does she think she is?

BILLY: *(Attempting to guide RITA towards the door, he takes her elbow.)* I'll just take Rita as far as the bus stop, Mother.

RITA: *(Shrugging him away.)* Take your mucky hands off me, you rotten toffee-nosed get. You didn't think I'd come in, did you?

ALICE: No, but I think you'll go out, young lady. And if you've anything to say to my son you'd better just remember where you are.

BILLY: Well, I'm very glad you have come, Rita, because I feel I owe you a word of explanation.

RITA: Oooh, I feel I owe you a word of explanation. Get back in the cheese, with the other maggots.

ALICE: I'm not putting up with this – I shall bring his father down.

RITA: You can bring his rotten father down. I hope you do. And his rotten grandma.

BARBARA: Billy's grandma, for your information, happens to be ill in bed.

RITA: *(Turning to BARBARA for the first time.)* Oooh, look what the cat's brought in. Get Madam Fancy-knickers. I suppose this is your rotten sister. I thought she was supposed to be in a rotten iron lung.

BARBARA: For your information, I happen to be Billy's fiancée.

RITA: *(Imitating BARBARA.)* Oooh, for your information. Well, for your information, he happens to be engaged to me. In front of a witness.

BILLY: How do you mean? What's witnesses got to do with it?

BARBARA: Billy, will you kindly tell me who this girl is?

RITA: *(Imitating her.)* Oooh, Billy, will you kindly tell me? Aw, go take a long walk on a short pier, you squint-eyed sow, you're nothing else.

ALICE: Barbara, would you kindly go upstairs and ask Mr Fisher to come down for a minute?

RITA: You can fetch him down. Fetch all the rotten lot down. You can fetch the cowing iron lung down as well, for all I care.

ALICE: I've never been spoken to like this in all my days.

BARBARA: Shall I go up, Mrs Fisher?

RITA: *(Imitating her.)* Oooh, shall I go up, Mrs Fisher? If you can get up the stairs with them bow legs, you can.

ALICE: It's all right, Barbara. I'll deal with this young madam. I've met her type before.

BILLY: I think I can explain all this.

BARBARA: Yes, I think you've got some explaining to do, Billy.

RITA: He can explain until he's blue in the rotten face. It makes no difference to me.

ALICE: If I knew your mother, young lady, wouldn't I have something to say to her.

RITA: You can keep out of this. It's between me and him. *(To BILLY.)* Where's my ring? Has she got it?

BARBARA'S right hand instinctively goes to her left.

She has, hasn't she? You've given it to her, haven't you?

BILLY: Ah, well – yes, but you see… Only there's been a bit of a mix-up. You see, I thought Barbara had broken the engagement off.

BARBARA: Billy!

RITA: Yeh, well you've got another drink coming if you think I'm as daft as she is. You gave that ring to me. And don't think you can go crawling out of it, 'cause you can't. You seem to forget I've got a witness, you know. I've got two. 'Cause Shirley Mitchem saw you giving me it, as well – so you needn't think she didn't. I can go down to the Town Hall, you know.

ALICE: Now, don't you come running in here with them tales, my girl. You know as well as I do he's under-age.

RITA: Ask him if he was under-age down at Foley Bottoms last night. 'Cause I'm not carrying the can back for nobody. He wasn't under-age then. He was over-age more like.

ALICE: Get out! Get out of my house!

BARBARA: Have you been untrue to me, Billy? I've got to know.

RITA: *(Imitating her.)* Oooh, have you been untrue to me, Billy! Get out of your pushchair, babyface. *(To BILLY.)* You're just rotten, aren't you? You are – you're rotten, all through. I've met some people in my time, but of all the lying, scheming…anyway, you gave that ring to me.

BILLY: Yes, but, look, Rita…

RITA: *(Interrupting.)* Don't talk to me, you rotten get. Well, she can have you – if she knows what to do with you, which I very much doubt. You rotten lying get. Garr – you think you're somebody, don't you? But you're nobody. You miserable lying rotten stinking get.

BILLY: Does this mean you're breaking off our engagement?

RITA: You don't get out of it like that. I want that ring.

BARBARA: *(Finding the right word at last.)* Billy, have you been – having relations with this girl?

RITA: *(Swinging round on BARBARA.)* What do you think he's been doing? Knitting me a pullover? You know what you can do, don't you? You can give me that ring. Because it's mine.

ALICE: If you don't stop it this minute! *(To BILLY.)* As for you, I hope you know what you've done, because I don't.

RITA: Are you going to give me that ring?

BARBARA: I shall give the ring back to Billy – if and when I break off the engagement.

BILLY: *(Moving towards her.)* Barbara.

RITA: Yes, you can go to her. She can have you. And she knows what she can do, the squint-eyed, bow-legged, spotty, snotty-nosed streak of nothing.

BARBARA: And you know what you can do as well. You can wash your mouth out with soap and water.

RITA: *(Imitating.)* Oooh, you can wash your mouth out with soap and water. You could do with some soap in your ears, you've got carrots growing out of them. Well, you can give me that ring. Before I come over there and get it.

ALICE: You can get out of this house. I won't tell you again.

RITA: Save your breath for blowing out candles. I want my ring. *(Crossing towards BARBARA.)* Yes, and I'm going to get it.

ALICE: Get out of my house! Get out! Get out!

GEOFFREY FISHER emerges from the bedroom and comes slowly down the stairs.

RITA: *(Moving right up to BARBARA.)* Are you going to give me that ring, or aren't you?

GEOFFREY: *(Halfway down the stairs.)* Mother! ... Mother!

RITA: Because you'll be in *Emergency Ward Ten* if I don't get it – right sharpish.

BARBARA: Don't you threaten me.

RITA: I won't threaten you – I'll flatten you! Give me that cowing ring back!

(She makes a grab for BARBARA's hand.)

BARBARA: *(Pushing her away.)* I won't... I won't...

ALICE: Will you stop it, the pair of you!

GEOFFREY enters the room and stands in the doorway. He appears not to comprehend what is happening.

GEOFFREY: Mother!

GEOFFREY's word silences ALICE, BILLY and BARBARA who turn and look at him.

RITA: *(Unconcerned.)* Give me the ring!

GEOFFREY: You'd better come upstairs. Come now. I think she's dead.

CURTAIN.

Act Three

Later the same evening.

*It is about half-past nine and quite dark in the garden outside the Fishers'
house. When the action of the play takes place in the garden, however,
a street lamp comes up from the road beyond the garden and off stage.
There is also a small light in the porch of the house. As the curtain rises
GEOFFREY FISHER is going through the contents of BILLY's cupboard
which are, at the moment, spread across the floor of the living room by the
sideboard. ALICE FISHER is sitting in a chair by the fire. She is obviously
distraught by the death of her mother. GEOFFREY rummages through the
envelopes and papers and then rises, shaking his head.*

GEOFFREY: Well, I can't bloody find it. It's not in here,
anyway. He hasn't got it. It's about the only bloody thing
he hasn't got.

ALICE: She might not have had one, Geoffrey – you know
what she was like.

GEOFFREY: *(Although he hasn't changed his vocabulary there is a
more tender note than usual in his voice.)* Don't talk so bloody
wet, lass. Everybody's got a birth certificate.

ALICE: Well, you don't know, Geoffrey, they might not have
had them in those days. She was getting on.

GEOFFREY: Everybody's got a bloody birth certificate.
They've had them since the year dot. If he's got it squat
somewhere I'll bloody mark him for life.

ALICE: You can't blame our Billy for everything, Geoffrey.
What would he want with it?

GEOFFREY: *(Indicating the papers on the floor.)* What's he want
with this bloody lot? There's neither sense nor bloody
reason in him. And where is he, anyway? Where's he taken
himself off to?

ALICE: I don't know, Geoffrey. I've given up caring.

GEOFFREY: You'd think he could stay in one bloody night
of the year. He ought to be in tonight. He ought to be

in looking after his mother. He's got no sense of bloody responsibility, that's his trouble.

ALICE: Well, she liked her cup of tea. We'll have that pint-pot to put away now. She's used that pint-pot for as long as I can remember.

GEOFFREY: She liked her bloody tea, there's no getting away from it. *(He half-jokes in an attempt to lift ALICE out of her depression.)* If I had a shilling for every pot of tea she's supped I'd be a rich man today. Well, there's one good thing to be said for it, when does the dustbin man come around? 'Cause he can take all them tins of condensed milk out of her bedroom.

ALICE: We can't throw them away. Somebody might be glad of them. We could send them round to the Old People's Home, or something.

GEOFFREY: Get away with you, you'd poison the bloody lot of them. That stuff doesn't keep for ever you know. They'll be green mouldy.

ALICE: I thought it was supposed to keep – condensed milk.

GEOFFREY: It won't keep twenty bloody years, I'm sure. She's had that pile of tins stacked up there since nineteen thirty-nine. And there's not one of them been opened – not one.

ALICE: Well, they went scarce, Geoffrey, when the war started, you know. That's why she started saving them.

GEOFFREY: Went scarce? Too bloody true they went scarce, she had them all. She hoarded them – she was like a squirrel with them. If Lord Woolton had heard about her in nineteen forty-one she'd have got fifteen years. By bloody hell, she would. *(He reminisces gently.)* Hey! I say! Do you remember how I used to pull her leg about it? How I used to tell her the food office was ringing up for her? You couldn't get her near that bloody telephone. She used to let it ring when we were out – she must have lost me pounds.

ALICE: *(Not cheered by GEOFFREY's attempt at humour.)* Well, I only hope you manage as well when you're as old as she was. She's not had an easy life – I wish I could have made it easier for her. She had all us to bring up, you know. And that took some doing.

GEOFFREY: No – she didn't do too bad, to say. What was she? Eighty – what?

ALICE: She'd have been eighty-three in August. Either eighty-three or eighty-two. She didn't seem to know herself.

GEOFFREY: Well, I shan't grumble if I last as long – she had a fair old crack of the whip.

ALICE: She didn't suffer, that's something to be grateful for. Some of them hang on for months and months. What did you say she was talking about? Before she went?

GEOFFREY: Don't ask me. I couldn't hear for that bloody shambles that was going on down here. I've never heard anything like it in all my born days.

ALICE: Well, you can blame our Billy for that, because I do. I've not finished with that Rita-whatever-her-name-is. I shall find out where she lives. I shall go round and I shall find out.

GEOFFREY: I know her. She works in that milk-bar in Sheepgate. I know her and I know her bloody father as well. You know him. Him that's always racing that whippet on the moor. Him with them tattoos all up his arms. Supposed to work in the market, when he does work. They live in them terrace-houses. Down Mill Lane.

ALICE: Well, I shall go round. I shall go round and see her mother.

GEOFFREY: You'll go bloody nowhere. You keep away. We've got enough to cope with without getting mixed up with that lot.

ALICE: I only wish she could have been spared it. If you can't die in peace, what can you do?

GEOFFREY: You don't want to go fretting yourself about that. She heard nothing about it. She was miles away.

ALICE: And what do you say she said? Did she know you?

GEOFFREY: Well, she did at first. She was all right after you went down. And she was all right when our Billy came up with her medicine. She took that all right and kept it down. She was just ramblin' on – like she does. She was chuntering on about a tin of salmon going to waste. Then something about getting her pension book changed at the post office next week. She never knew, you see. It was just this last five minutes when she started to slaver. I was holding her up in bed and she just slumped forward. I thought she was having a bloody fit. But no – she just gave a little jerk with her head – like that. Then she started to slaver. She was just like a baby, Alice. Just like a baby, slavering and gasping for breath. She wet my handkerchief through, I know that. Then she sits straight up – by herself – and says, 'Where's my Jack?' I had to think who she was talking about. Then I remember she must have meant your father. Only she always used to call him John, didn't she?

ALICE: *(Half to herself.)* She hardly ever called him Jack.

GEOFFREY: Then she said, 'I love you, Jack'. Oh, and before she said, 'What are you thinking about?' – she must have been talking to your father, she couldn't have been talking to anyone else. But you had to listen close to, to hear what she was saying. She could hardly speak. By the time she went she couldn't speak at all. She was just slavering.

There is a pause.

ALICE: You should have called me.

GEOFFREY: *(Suddenly compassionate.)* She wouldn't have known you. And you wouldn't have liked to have seen her like that. You couldn't have done anything for her – nobody could.

ALICE: You should have called me, Geoffrey.

GEOFFREY: I didn't think it would have done you any good to see her, that's all. *(Reverting to his normal tones.)* And, listen! If he thinks he's going to the funeral in them bloody suede shoes, he's got another think coming. There'll be all them

Masonics coming – I'm not having him showing me up. He'll get some bloody black ones or stop at home.

ALICE: He's got some black ones but he won't wear them.

GEOFFREY: Well, make him. And think on and see that he gets a bloody good wash on Tuesday morning. When did he have a bath last?

ALICE: Well, there'll be no baths on Tuesday, 'cause I'm not lighting any fires – I shall be too busy. And I still know nothing about the funeral. I wish I'd have seen Mr Duxbury.

GEOFFREY: You only just missed him. If you'd have gone to your Emily's five minutes later you would have seen him. Anyway, they're doing everything. Shadrack and Duxbury's. He says they'll fix the tea for us – the lot.

ALICE: And you still haven't told me what Mr Duxbury said about our Billy – about him getting into bother at work.

GEOFFREY: Don't talk to me about our Billy. I'm going to start putting him in the coal cellar when people come. Duxbury comes to the door – I take him straight upstairs. He starts measuring her up so I left him to it. Come down here and walk into the living room and there's bloody Dopey sat in here. He's let the fire go out. Kettle boiling its bloody heady off. He's sitting with his shoes and socks off and all muck between his toes watching bloody Noddy on television. *(Losing his temper.)* His grandmother bloody dead upstairs and all he can do is watch Noddy.

ALICE: I can't understand him. He doesn't seem to have any feeling for anybody.

GEOFFREY: I told him. I said to him, 'What are you bloody doing? Do you know Mr Duxbury's upstairs?' He was out of that chair and through that door like a shot. I watched him out of our bedroom window – putting his shoes and socks on in the street. I'll bloody swing for him before I've finished, I will.

ALICE: Well, what did Mr Duxbury say about him?

GEOFFREY: He wasn't going to say anything. Not today. Until I asked him if our Billy had rung up and asked for his cards, like he said he was. Then the lot came out. *(He indicates the calendars.)* There's all these calendars he's supposed to have posted, for one. Then there's his petty cash – that doesn't add up. Then there's his postage book. Two pound ten postage money he's had. And he's supposed to have pinched a brass plate off a coffin. What does he want to do a bloody trick like that for?

ALICE: You didn't say anything about postage money before – you just said petty cash.

GEOFFREY: I don't know. Don't ask me. The whole bloody lot's wrong from start to finish. He can't keep his hands off nothing.

ALICE: But what did he say about not taking him to court?

GEOFFREY: How many more bloody times? He says if he stays on – and does his work right, and pays this money back – and stops giving back-chat every five minutes – he'll hear no more about it.

ALICE: But what about him going to London?

GEOFFREY: How the bloody hell can he go to London? He'll go to Dartmoor if he's not careful. He's to stop on there until he's paid this money back – and I know I'm not paying it, if he goes down on his bended knees I'm not paying it.

ALICE: It's a mystery to me why he wanted to take that money in the first place. He never buys anything – and if he does go short he knows he's only to come to me.

GEOFFREY: You've been too soft with him, that's been the bloody trouble, all along. Anyway, you know what he's spent it on, don't you? That bloody engagement ring. That's where the money's gone. Well, he can get that back to the shop for a start. And he can get engaged when he's twenty-one and not before. And he brings no more bloody lasses round here. And he comes in at nine o'clock in future – never mind half-past eleven. There's going to be some changes in this house.

ALICE: Yes, and you've said that before and it's made no difference. He used to get on her nerves.

GEOFFREY: Well, she's not got him to put up with any more. He used to lead her a dog's life. I've seen him – mocking her. And where is he? He's got no bloody right to be out.

ALICE: I don't know where he's got to.

GEOFFREY: He'll know where he's got to when he rolls in here. He'll go straight out again – through the bloody window.

ALICE: We don't want any more rows tonight, Geoffrey. My nerves won't stand it. You've had one row today and you saw what happened. She was all right till you started on our Billy.

GEOFFREY: Don't start blaming me for it. For God's sake. I told her often enough to go to see that doctor.

ALICE: You know very well why she wouldn't go.

GEOFFREY: It was your bloody job to see that she did. I'm not on tap twenty-four hours a bloody day. I've got work to do.

They are building up to an argument.

ALICE: And I've got my work to do as well. I did my best. I tried to make her go. You know why it was. It was because he was black.

GEOFFREY: I don't care if he was sky-blue bloody pink with yellow dots on. You should have gone with her.

ALICE: *(Almost in tears.)* It was only this afternoon she was sitting in that chair with a pot of tea. You can say what you like, she was all right till you started on to our Billy.

GEOFFREY: She was never all right. She hadn't been all right for bloody months.

ALICE: It's tomorrow morning I'm thinking about. When I should be taking her up her pot of tea and a Marie Louise biscuit.

GEOFFREY: Will you shut up about bloody pots of tea! You won't fetch her back with pots of bloody tea. She'll get no pots of tea where she's gone.

ALICE: Well, I like to think she will! *(She rises and crosses towards the kitchen.)*

GEOFFREY: Where are you going now?

ALICE: I'm going to make myself one.

GEOFFREY: Sit you down. I'll see to it.

ALICE: No. No. I'm better when I'm doing something. I'd rather be occupied.

ALICE goes into the kitchen.

GEOFFREY: *(Crossing to join her.)* I'll give you a hand, anyway.

GEOFFREY goes into the kitchen as the lights fade down in the living room. The lights come up in the garden – both from the porch and the street lamp. We discover BILLY sitting on the garden seat, rather cold and his hands dug deep in his pockets. He lights a cigarette, then rises and crosses to the front door where he listens for a moment through the letter box. Hearing nothing he returns towards the garden seat and sits disconsolately.

BILLY hums to himself and then turns on the seat and takes up a garden can. He toys with the cane for a moment, attempting to balance it on his fingers. His humming grows louder and he stands and conducts an imaginary orchestra using the cane as a baton. He is humming a military march and he suddenly breaks off as the garden cane becomes, in his imagination, a rifle. He shoulders the cane and marches briskly up and down the garden path.

BILLY: *(Marching.)* Lef', ri', lef', ri', lef'-ri'-ler'! Halt! *(He halts.)* Order arms! *(He brings the cane down to the 'Order' position. He pauses for a moment and the garden cane becomes, in his imagination, an officer's baton which he tucks under his arm and then he marches smartly off to an imaginary saluting base a few paces away. He has become, in his imagination, a major-general.)* Dearly beloved Officers and Gentlemen of the Desert Shock Troops. We are assembled at the grave-side here this evening to pay our respects to a great lady. There are many of us here tonight who would not be alive now but for her tender mercies although in her later years she was limbless from the waist down. She struggled valiantly to combat ignorance and disease. Although she will be remembered by the world as the inventor of penicillin and radium we, of this proud regiment, will remember her as our friend – the Lady of the Lamp. I call upon you all to join with me in observing two minutes' silence. *(He removes an imaginary hat which he places under his arm. He lowers his head respectfully and stands in silence. Imitating a bugle he hums the 'Last Post'.)*

He is still standing, his head lowered, as ARTHUR and LIZ enter the garden.

Although LIZ is about the same age as BARBARA and RITA she has more maturity and self-possession. Although she is dressed casually and is, in fact, wearing the black skirt we have heard so much about, she is not as scruffy as we have been led to believe. She is also wearing a white blouse and a green suede jacket. She is not particularly pretty but is obviously a girl of strong personality. LIZ is the only girl for whom BILLY has any real feelings. LIZ and ARTHUR stand for a moment looking at BILLY, who has not noticed them.

ARTHUR: What's up with him, then?

BILLY: *(Startled and embarrassed.)* I didn't hear you coming…
(He sees LIZ for the first time and is even more embarrassed.) Liz.

LIZ: Hallo, Billy.

ARTHUR: What are you on, then? He's saying his prayers.

BILLY: *(Scratching the ground with the cane with an assumed casualness.)* No, I was just standing. Just thinking to myself. *(To LIZ.)* Arthur told me you were back.

ARTHUR: You looked like one of them stinking gnomes we've got in our garden. With a maring fishing rod.

BILLY tosses the garden cane into the garden.

What are you standing out here for? Won't they let you in?

BILLY: *(Irritated.)* Can't I stand in my own rotten garden now? *(To LIZ.)* When did you get back?

LIZ: Last week.

ARTHUR: *(Before she can continue.)* Hey, is it right your grandma's snuffed it?

BILLY: You what? Yes. This afternoon. Funeral's on Tuesday.

ARTHUR: Fizzing hell! I was only talking to her this morning.

BILLY: *(To LIZ.)* Why didn't you ring up?

ARTHUR: *(Before she can reply.)* You don't half drop me in it! I thought you'd made it up. I told our old lady you'd made it up! She'll go stinking bald.

BILLY: *(To LIZ.)* You've got the number. You could have rung me up.

LIZ: I was going to, Billy.

ARTHUR: *(Again before she can continue.)* Do you know what I was going to do? If I'd had enough money. I was going to send a wreath round. With a little card saying in capital letters: 'You Stinking Louse-bound Crowing Liar'. I was sure you'd made it up.

BILLY: *(Annoyed.)* What are you talking about? What would I want to make up a thing like that for?

ARTHUR: Oh, get George Washington. *(In a mimicking falsetto.)* Please sir, I cannot tell a lie. I chopped up Grandma.

BILLY: *(Turning to ARTHUR.)* Look, why don't you just jack it in – eh?

ARTHUR: All right, all right. Keep your shirt on. Don't go biting my head off.

BILLY: Well, you want to grow up.

ARTHUR: You what! Listen who's talking. You're a right one to talk. Grow up? Blimey! *(He turns to LIZ.)* Do you know what he once did? He saves up these plastic boats you get out of cornflake packets. He does! He saves them all. He keeps them in his desk. Well, do you know what he once did? He filled up a baby's coffin with water – down in the basement – and started playing naval battles. He thinks I don't know.

BILLY: Aw, shut up. Anyway, I don't sit in the lavatory all morning. Reading mucky books.

ARTHUR: No, and I don't go around playing at Winston Churchills when I think nobody's looking.

BILLY: Aw, belt up, man!

ARTHUR: *(Tapping BILLY on the chest.)* You just want to stop telling people to belt up. You want to go careful, man. Or else somebody's going to belt you.

BILLY: Yeh – you and whose army?

ARTHUR: I'm not talking about me. I'm talking about somebody else.

BILLY: Who?

ARTHUR: Somebody's brother.

BILLY: Whose naffing brother? What are you talking about?

ARTHUR: Rita's naffing brother. Who do you think? That's what I came up to tell you – thanks very much for asking. It's the last favour I'll do you, I know that. I've just seen him down at the dance hall. Screaming blue murder. I wouldn't like to be in your shoes, man, when he gets you.

BILLY: *(Uneasily.)* I'm not frightened of him.

ARTHUR: You what! He'll bloody slaughter you. He will, you know, he's not kidding.

BILLY: So what.

ARTHUR: So what, he says. I knew you should never have given her that ring in the first place. I told you, didn't I? Well, she still want it back, you know. You've had your chips.

BILLY: Aaahh – who cares.

ARTHUR: You'll bloody care when you're in the infirmary getting stitched up. Well, you've had it coming, matey let's face it. You and your rotten lying. Well, I know what I'd do if I was you – and I didn't want to get crippled. I'd get off to that job in London, dead smartish – that's if there is a job in London.

BILLY: What do you mean – if there is a job in London?

ARTHUR: I mean, if it isn't another of your stinking lies!

BILLY: I'll go – don't you worry.

ARTHUR: I'm not worrying, Tosh. I've got more to do with my time. But I'll tell you this much, you can stop going round giving out the patter about our old lady. Because if I hear – once more – about her being in the family way, I'll be round here myself. Never mind Rita's brother.

BILLY: Aw – dry up.

ARTHUR: *(Going off.)* Well, I've told you, man. *(He turns to BILLY.)* And don't think I'm covering up for you any more – 'cause I'm not.

BILLY: *(Softly.)* Aw – get knotted.

ARTHUR goes.

(Turning to LIZ.) He talks too much.

There is a slight pause as they stand and look at each other.

Hallo, Liz.

LIZ: Hallo, Billy.

BILLY: When did you get back?

LIZ: Last week.

BILLY: Why didn't you ring me up?

LIZ: I was going to.

BILLY: Thank you very much.

LIZ: No – really. I was going to. I thought I'd see you at the dance tonight. I went to the dance. I thought you'd be there.

BILLY: I couldn't go.

LIZ: No. No – I know. I heard about your grandma. I'm sorry.

BILLY: Yes. *(Changing the subject.)* I haven't seen you for months.

LIZ: Five weeks. You didn't waste much time, did you?

BILLY: Why? What do you mean?

LIZ: Getting engaged. To everybody.

BILLY: Oh – that.

LIZ: You're mad.

BILLY: *(Shrugging his shoulders.)* Where have you been?

LIZ: Oh – here and there.

BILLY: Why didn't you write?

LIZ: I did – once. I tore it up.

BILLY: You're always tearing it up.

LIZ: *(Changing the subject.)* How's everything with you? How's the script writing? How's the book coming along?

BILLY: *(Enthusiastically.)* Oh, I've finished it. It's going to be published next Christmas.

She gives him a long, steady look.

I haven't started writing it yet.

LIZ: You are mad.

BILLY: Yes.

LIZ sits on the garden seat.

Liz?

LIZ: Mmmm?

BILLY: *(Sitting beside her.)* Do you find life complicated?

LIZ: Mmmm. So-so.

BILLY: I wish it was something you could tear up and start again. Life, I mean. You know – it's like starting a new page in an exercise book.

LIZ: Well, it's been done. Turning over a new leaf.

BILLY: I turn over a new leaf every day – but the blots show through.

LIZ: What's all this about London?

BILLY: I've been offered a job down there.

LIZ: Honestly?

BILLY: Honestly. A sort of job.

LIZ: Good. I'm glad. Perhaps it's your new leaf.

BILLY: *(Proud of the phrase.)* I turn over a new leaf every day – but the blots show through the page.

LIZ: Well, perhaps a new leaf isn't good enough. Perhaps you need to turn over a new volume.

BILLY: Yes.

LIZ: Are you going to take that job?

BILLY: I think so.

LIZ: You only think so.

BILLY: I don't know.

LIZ: You know, my lad, the trouble with you is that you're – what's the word? – introspective. You're like a child at the edge of a paddling pool. You want very much to go in, but you think so much about whether the water's cold, and whether you'll drown, and what your mother will say if you get your feet wet...

BILLY: *(Interrupting.)* All I'm doing is wondering whether to dive or swim.

LIZ: Perhaps you need a coach.

BILLY: Do you know why I'm so fascinated by London?

LIZ: No. Why?

BILLY: A man can lose himself in London. London is a big place. It has big streets – and big people.

LIZ: *(Giving him another look.)* Mad.

BILLY: Perhaps I need to turn over a new paddling pool.

There is a pause as they look at each other.

LIZ: Who do you love?

BILLY: *(Adopting his thick north country accent.)* Thee, lass.

LIZ: Yes, it sounds like it, doesn't it?

BILLY: I do, lass.

LIZ: Say it properly, then.

BILLY: I do, Liz, I do.

LIZ: What about Barbara?

BILLY: Well, what about her?

LIZ: Well, *what* about her?

BILLY: All over.

LIZ: You've said that before.

BILLY: I know. This time it is all over.

LIZ: And what about the other one? Rita-whatever-her-name-is?

BILLY: That's all over, too.

There is a pause, BILLY takes out a packet of cigarettes, lights two and gives one to LIZ.

LIZ: I want to marry you, you know, Billy.

BILLY: I know, Liz – I know. We will – one day.

LIZ: Not one day. Now.

BILLY: Do you?

LIZ: Next week will do. Before you go to London. Or when you get there. Whichever you prefer.

BILLY: I think I get engaged a bit too often.

LIZ: I don't want to get engaged. I want to get married.

BILLY: Is that why you keep sloping off every few weeks? Because you want to get married?

LIZ: I want to get married.

BILLY: All right. All right.

LIZ: How do you mean – all right? I've just proposed to you and you say 'all right'. Aren't you supposed to say 'this is so sudden' or yes or something?

BILLY: I don't know.

She puts her arms round him and kisses him. He responds. They break away.

LIZ: Billy?

BILLY: Yes?

LIZ: You know what you wanted me to do? That night? When we walked through the park? And I said 'another night'?

BILLY: I remember.

LIZ: Well, it's another night tonight, isn't it?

BILLY: *(Afraid, but excited.)* Are you sure?

LIZ: Yes.

BILLY: Where could we go?

LIZ: I've got a room. There's no one there.

BILLY: What do you think we ought to do about – you know, babies.

LIZ: Have them. Lots and lots of them.

BILLY: No, I mean tonight.

LIZ: It's all right. *(After a pause.)* Billy?

BILLY: Yes?

LIZ: Ask you something?

BILLY: What?

LIZ: Do you know what *virgo intacta* means?

BILLY: Yes.

LIZ: Well, I'm not.

BILLY: No. I somehow didn't think you were.

LIZ: Want me to tell you about it?

BILLY: No. *(He kisses her.)* All right, yes. Tell me about it.

LIZ: No – not now.

BILLY: Tell me about it.

LIZ: You think that's why I'm always going away, don't you?

BILLY: I don't know.

LIZ: Ask me where I've been for the past five weeks.

BILLY: What difference does it make?

LIZ: None – I suppose. It's just that every so often I want to go away. It's not you, Billy. I want to be here with you. It's the town. It's the people we know. I don't like knowing everybody – or becoming a part of things. Do you see what I mean?

BILLY: Yes…yes.

LIZ: What I'd like is to be invisible. You know, to be able to move around without people knowing, and not having to worry about them. Not having to explain all the time.

BILLY: Liz…Liz! Listen! Listen! Liz, do you know what I do? When I want to feel invisible. I've never told anybody. I have a sort of – well, it's an imaginary country. Where I go. It has its own people…

LIZ: *(Interrupting.)* Do you do that? I knew you would. Why are we so alike, Billy? I can read your thoughts. A town like this. Only somewhere over by the sea. And we used to spend the whole day on the beach. That's what I used to think about.

BILLY: This is more than a town – it's a whole country. *(He is getting excited.)* I'm supposed to be the Prime Minister. You're supposed to be the Foreign Secretary – or something.

LIZ: *(With mock obedience.)* Yes, sir.

BILLY: I think about it for hours. Sometimes I think, if we were married, with a house of our own, we could just sit and imagine ourselves there.

LIZ: Yes, we could.

BILLY: I want a room, in the house, with a green baize door. It will be a big room, and when we go into it, through the door, that's it, that's our country. No one else would be allowed in. No one else will have keys. They won't know where the room is. Only we'll know. And we'll make models of the principal cities. You know, out of cardboard. And we could use toy soldiers. Painted. For the people. We could draw maps. It would be a place to go on a rainy afternoon. We could go there. No one would find us. I thought we could have a big sloping shelf running all the way down one wall, you know, like a big desk. And we'd have a lot of blank paper on it and design our own newspapers. We could even make uniforms, if we wanted to. It would be our country... *(He falters away.)*

LIZ: Let's have a model train that the kids won't be allowed to use.

BILLY: Liz...? Will you marry me?

LIZ: Yes.

He kisses her.

Billy?

BILLY: Yes?

LIZ: Are you really going to London or just pretending?

BILLY: I'm thinking about it.

LIZ: Only thinking?

BILLY: Well, going. Soon, anyway.

LIZ: When's soon?

BILLY: Well, soon.

LIZ: That's a bit vague. Soon. Why not now?

BILLY: It's difficult.

LIZ: No, it's easy. You just get on a train and four hours later there you are – in London.

BILLY: It's easy for you, you've had the practice.

LIZ: I'll come with you.

BILLY: That'd be marvellous – if we could.

LIZ: *(Rising.)* But we can, Billy! We can! What is there to stop us?

BILLY: *(Thinking seriously about it for the first time.)* Well, there's... I don't know...you've got to make all sorts of arrangements, haven't you?

LIZ: You buy a ticket, that's all. You buy a ticket and get on a train. That's all there is to it.

BILLY: I've never thought about it like that.

LIZ: Billy, we can! We can go! We can go tonight!

BILLY: But, Liz.

LIZ: There's a midnight train. We can catch that. It gets in at King's Cross Station. Breakfast at Lyons Corner House. Then we get a tube – we get a tube from Piccadilly Circus to Earl's Court. I've got friends there, Billy. They'll put us up. They'd give us a room.

BILLY: *(Almost convinced; rising.)* Tonight, Liz?

LIZ: Yes, tonight! Twelve-five from New Street Station. We'll be in London tomorrow. We can go to Hyde Park in the afternoon. We'll go to the pictures tomorrow night – the Odeon, Marble Arch. What time is it now?

BILLY: *(Glancing at his watch.)* Just after ten.

LIZ: I'm going, Billy. Are you coming?

BILLY: *(His mind made up.)* Yes, Liz. I'm coming.

LIZ: Are you sure?

BILLY: I'm coming with you.

LIZ: *(Briskly.)* Right, then. I'm going home. Now. And I'm going to pack my things. I'll meet you at the station. In that refreshment room. In an hour's time. Eleven o'clock. I'll get the tickets. Two singles to London. You won't let me down, Billy?

BILLY: I'm coming.

LIZ: What will you tell your father and mother?

BILLY: They know already – more or less.

LIZ: You won't let them talk you out of it?

BILLY: I'm coming.

The lights begin to come up in the living room.

GEOFFREY enters from the kitchen, takes up a newspaper, sits down and begins to read.

The lights fade slightly in the garden. LIZ kisses BILLY.

LIZ: Eleven o'clock.

BILLY: Eleven.

LIZ goes off down the garden.

BILLY watches her go and then turns and enters the house. GEOFFREY rises at the sound of the door. BILLY enters the living room. He registers shock as he sees that his cupboard has been opened.

GEOFFREY: What time of bloody night do you call this?

BILLY: It's only ten.

GEOFFREY: I don't care what bloody time it is. Who said you could go out? And where've you been?

BILLY: I've only been out. Why? Did you want some chips bringing in?

GEOFFREY: I'll chip you. I'll chip you round your bloody ear-hole if I start on you. Have you been out dancing?

BILLY: No, 'course I haven't.

GEOFFREY: If you've been out dancing with your grandma lying dead I'll bloody murder you, I will.

BILLY: *(Feigning innocence.)* What's up?

GEOFFREY: What's up – you know what's up. What have you done with that letter of your mother's?

BILLY glances in fear at the envelopes on the floor.

Do you hear me? I'm talking to you!

BILLY: What letter?

GEOFFREY: What, what, what! Don't keep saying bloody 'what'. You know what letter. That what she gave you to post to 'Housewives' Choice'.

BILLY: I told her once. I posted it.

GEOFFREY: *(Taking the letter from his pocket.)* You posted bloody nothing. You've had it in that cupboard. It was given to you to post. You bloody idle little swine.

BILLY: I did post it. That's just the rough copy.

GEOFFREY: What are you talking about? Rough copy? It's your mother's letter. How could you have posted it?

BILLY: Look – the letter my mother wrote was full of mistakes, that's all. I just thought it would stand a better chance if I wrote it out again – properly. That's all.

ALICE enters from the kitchen.

GEOFFREY: Well, who told you to write it out again? And who told you to open it? You keep your thieving hands off other people's things! And where did you get all them bloody calendars from, as well?

BILLY: What calendars?

GEOFFREY: *(Fingering his belt.)* By bloody hell! I'll give you 'what' if you don't stop 'what, what,' my lad! You know what! Don't think I haven't been talking to Mr Duxbury – because I have. I've heard it all. You make me a laughing-stock. You can't keep your hands off nothing. And where's that monkey wrench out of my garage? I suppose you know nothing about that?

BILLY: No, 'course I don't. What do I want with a monkey wrench?

GEOFFREY: What do you want with two hundred bloody calendars! And what have you been doing with their name-plates as well? You're not right in the bloody head.

BILLY: *(Losing his temper.)* I'm not right! I'm not right! I didn't want to work for Shadrack and flaming Duxbury's! You made me take the rotten job! Now you can answer for it.

GEOFFREY: Don't bloody shout at me, you gormless young get – or I'll knock your eyes out.

BILLY: God give me strength.

GEOFFREY: Give you strength, he wants to give you some sense! You're like a bloody Mary-Ann! Well, I hope your mother gets more sense out of you.

ALICE: Well, you've got yourself into a fine mess, lad, haven't you?

BILLY: Have I?

ALICE: I'm only thankful she knows nothing about it. *(She glances up at the ceiling.)* Why didn't you post that letter of mine?

BILLY: I did post it. I was telling Dad. I just wrote it out again, that's all. There was some mistakes in it.

ALICE: Yes, well we can't all be Shakespeares, can we? And what's all this about you taking money from work?

BILLY: What money?

GEOFFREY: *(Warningly.)* I've told you.

BILLY: What? I haven't taken any money.

GEOFFREY: There's two pound ten short in your postage book. Never mind petty cash.

BILLY: Oh, that...I...

ALICE: What did you do with it, Billy?

GEOFFREY: He's spent it. That's what he's bloody done with it.

ALICE: Well, it's just beyond me. You didn't have to take money, Billy. You could have come to me.

GEOFFREY: You've had things too bloody easy. That's been your trouble. You can't carry on at work like you do at home, you know.

BILLY: Well, I told you I didn't want to work there when I first started, didn't I?

GEOFFREY: You didn't want to work for nobody, if you ask me anything. You thought you'd live on me, didn't you?

BILLY: No, I didn't. I could have kept myself.

ALICE: Kept yourself – how?

BILLY: Writing scripts.

GEOFFREY: Writing bloody scripts, you want to get a day's work done, never mind writing scripts. Who do you think's going to run this bloody business when I'm gone?

BILLY: You said you didn't want me in the business.

GEOFFREY: Only because you were so bloody idle! Somebody's got to carry on with it! Who's going to keep your mother?

BILLY: *(With an attempt at humour.)* Why, you're not retiring, are you?

GEOFFREY: Don't try and be funny with me, lad! Or you'll laugh on the other side of your face!

ALICE: And what did you tell me about Arthur's mother? She wasn't having a baby, you know very well she wasn't.

BILLY: It was only a joke.

GEOFFREY: A joke – it sounds like a bloody joke!

ALICE: And why did you tell her I'd broken my leg?

BILLY: I didn't know you knew Arthur's mother.

ALICE: Yes, you don't know who I know and who I don't know, do you? If you want to know, she rang me up. And what did you do with that cardigan she gave you for me, last Christmas?

BILLY: *(Vaguely.)* I think I gave it to the refugees.

ALICE: Well, you've got a new cardigan to find by tomorrow morning. Because she's coming round to see me.

BILLY: *(Emphatically.)* I won't be here tomorrow morning.

GEOFFREY: You won't be here to bloody night if you talk to your mother in that tone of voice!

BILLY: I'm not going to be here tonight. I'm leaving.

ALICE: What are you talking about?

BILLY: *(Decisively.)* I'm getting the midnight train. Tonight. I'm taking that job in London.

ALICE: If you're in any more trouble, Billy, it's not something you can leave behind you. You put it in your suitcase and take it with you.

GEOFFREY: Well, he's not taking that suitcase of mine upstairs. *(Turning to BILLY.)* Anyway, you're not going to London or nowhere else – so you can get that idea out of your head, for a kick-off.

BILLY: I mean it, Dad. I'm going.

GEOFFREY: And I bloody mean it, as well. *(Raising his voice.)* You stop here till that money's paid back. You can thank your lucky stars Mr Duxbury's not landed you in court. You want to be grateful.

BILLY: Grateful! Grateful! Grateful for this, grateful for that! That's all I've ever heard! Grateful you let me go to the grammar school! We've been hearing that one since the first day I went there. What am I supposed to do? Say 'thank you very much' three times a day for my marvellous education?

GEOFFREY: Well, it's a chance we never had!

BILLY: Yes, and don't we bloody well know it! I even had to be grateful for winning my own scholarship! And what did you say when I came running home to tell you I'd won it? Don't think I've forgotten! I was eleven years old! I came belting out of those school gates and I ran all the way! And what did you say? That you'd have to pay for the uniform and I'd have to be grateful! And now I'm supposed to be grateful to Shadrack and stinking Duxbury! Why? What for? For letting me sit at one of their rotten desks all day?

ALICE: *(Gently reasoning.)* Well, you took the job, Billy.

GEOFFREY: Yes, and he's stopping there till that money's paid back.

BILLY: I'm not arguing about it. I'm going! *(He crosses towards the door.)*

GEOFFREY: Go, then! I've finished with you!

BILLY enters the hall and moves up the stairs. During the following he goes into the bedroom.

(Crossing to the door, calling after BILLY.) They'll take you to court, you know! I won't stop them! I'm not paying it back! And don't think you're taking my suitcase!

GEOFFREY crosses back in to the living room and stands silent. ALICE sits in the chair by the fire.

ALICE: Oh, dear me... Oh, dear me.

BILLY enters from the bedroom and charges down the stairs and into the living room.

He is carrying a small battered suitcase. He crosses to the sideboard and, opening a drawer, begins to pack the case with shirts, socks, ties and pullover. GEOFFREY watches him in silence.

(Concerned.) What time train do you reckon you're catching?

BILLY: Midnight.

ALICE: Well, what time does it get in?

BILLY: Tomorrow morning.

ALICE: And where are you going to live when you get there?

GEOFFREY: He'll finish up in the Salvation Army Hostel.

ALICE: *(As BILLY packs a pair of socks.)* All them socks need darning, you know.

BILLY makes no reply.

Well, you'll want more than one suit... And what about your grandma's funeral on Tuesday?

BILLY has now placed all his clothing in the case. He stoops and begins to pack the calendars.

GEOFFREY: *(In disbelief.)* What the thump are you packing them bloody calendars for?

BILLY: I thought I'd post them.

ALICE: Well, you'll be expected at the funeral, you know.

GEOFFREY: *(Disparagingly.)* He's not going anywhere.

BILLY: *(Slamming the case shut, rising.)* I'm going.

He picks up the case and crosses to the door.

GEOFFREY: *(Half relenting.)* Don't act so bloody daft.

BILLY pauses for a moment, his hand on the door, caught up in the embarrassment of leaving.

BILLY: Well, I'll write to you then. Soon as I've got fixed up. *(Acutely embarrassed.)* I'm sorry about my grandma.

He goes out.

ALICE: Oh, dear me… Oh, dear me.

GEOFFREY: They can summons him. I've finished.

ALICE: You'll have to pay it, Geoffrey. Will he be all right on his own?

GEOFFREY: He won't bloody go – he'll be back in five minutes.

ALICE: We know nothing about where he's going and what he's supposed to be doing. Who's that fellow he says he's going to work for? That comedian?

GEOFFREY: I don't bloody know.

ALICE: It was in that letter he had in his pocket in that old raincoat.

GEOFFREY crosses and takes the envelope from the raincoat which is hanging in the hall. He returns into the living room reading the letter to himself as he walks. He then reads the letter aloud to ALICE.

GEOFFREY: 'Dear Mr Fisher, Many thanks for script and gags, I can use some of the gags and pay accordingly. As for my staff job, well I regret to tell you, you might be interested in this. *(He pauses.)* Why not call in for a chat next time you are in London? Best of luck and keep writing. Danny Boon.'

ALICE: *(After pause.)* Run down to the station and fetch him back.

GEOFFREY: He's off his bloody rocker.

ALICE: You'll have to go stop him, Geoffrey.

GEOFFREY: Nay, he's big enough to look after himself now. He can stand on his own two feet for a change. I've finished. I've done my whack for him.

ALICE: I wonder if he's got any money?

GEOFFREY: That's his look-out. It doesn't belong to him if he has. You can depend on that.

ALICE: Oh, dear me… Oh, dear me.

GEOFFREY: There's no need for him to starve. He can get a job if he sets his mind to it. And gets up in a morning.

ALICE: Well, what's he going to do?

GEOFFREY: He can go clerking – same as here. There's a lot of offices in London. Well, there's one thing certain. I know what I'm going to bloody do: I'm off to bed. I've enough on my plate without worrying my head over that one. He can go to hell, he can.

ALICE: Do you want a cup of Ovaltine, or anything?

GEOFFREY: No. You want to get off to bed as well, lass.

ALICE: *(Rising.)* I always used to take her one up at this time. I'll have to get used to it – not having to.

GEOFFREY: Aye, well…

ALICE: Is the back door locked, Geoffrey?

GEOFFREY: I've seen to it.

They cross into the hall. GEOFFREY switches off the light in the living room and automatically drops the catch on the Yale lock. GEOFFREY follows ALICE up the stairs. As they go up the porch light fades up.

RITA and ARTHUR enter the garden.

(With assumed cheerfulness.) Well, he'll come home at holiday times. And happen some weekends.

GEOFFREY switches out the hall light from the top of the stairs and follows ALICE into the bedroom.

ARTHUR: *(With relief, seeing the hall light go out.)* They've gone to bed.

RITA: Have a look through the rotten letter-box.

ARTHUR: You can see! They've gone to bed. You don't think they're sitting there with no lights on, do you?

RITA: Well, he's not getting out of it – 'cause I shall come round in the morning. Our kid'll come round as well. Our kid'll duff him up. He'll get that ring back.

ARTHUR: You and your kid and that louse-bound ring! Come on, let's get down to Foley Bottom. Get some snogging hours in.

RITA: He needn't think he's got away with it – 'cause he hasn't. He'll be a stretcher case tomorrow morning! You wait! You rotten yellow-bellied-squint-eyed get! You're nothing else! You closet!

We hear the sound of a window being flung open and ALICE shouting.

ALICE: Get away! Don't you know we've got somebody dead in this house!

We hear the window slammed shut.

RITA: *(Screaming.)* You want to be all rotten dead! You want gassing!

ARTHUR: Shut up, Rita! She knows my mother.

RITA: I don't care.

ARTHUR: They're not worth bothering about. Come on – let's get down to Foley Bottoms. We're just wasting time stuck here.

RITA: *(Allowing ARTHUR to place his arm around her and pilot her out of the garden.)* Well, we'll be round here first thing tomorrow morning. *(As they go.)* We get up before they do.

ARTHUR and RITA go off.

There is a pause and then BILLY enters and walks slowly and dejectedly to the front door. He puts down his case and, taking a key from his pocket, opens the door and enters. He crosses into the living room and, closing the door behind him, switches on the light. He stands indecisively for a moment and then crosses and switches on the radio. He crosses to his suitcase and opens it as the sound of a dance-band comes from the radio. He stands for a moment, and, as the music continues, he compulsively lifts his hand and begins to conduct. He glances towards the ceiling, wondering if he is making too much noise, then crosses and switches off the radio. He returns to the suitcase which he carries over to the sideboard. He opens his cupboard and is neatly stacking the calendars back into the cupboard.

CURTAIN.

JEFFREY BERNARD IS UNWELL

BASED ON THE LIFE AND WRITING OF JEFFREY BERNARD

Presented by Michael Redington at the Apollo Theatre, London, on 18th October, 1989, with the following cast of characters:

JEFFREY BERNARD, Peter O'Toole

POETS		
HACKS		
WIVES		
GIRLFRIENDS		
THESPIANS		
PUBLICANS		
SINNERS		
POLICEMEN		
WAITERS		
FRIENDS		
NEIGHBOURS		
JOCKEYS		
TRAINERS		
BORES		
ARTISTS		
DOCTORS		
NURSES		
CUSTOMS AND EXCISE OFFICIALS		
MAGISTRATE		
DRUNKS		
TARTS	all played by	Timothy Ackroyd
		Sarah Berger
		Annabel Leventon
		Royce Mills

Director, Ned Sherrin
Settings, John Gunter
Costumes, Stephen Brimson-Lewis

The play is set in the Coach and Horses, Soho, London.

Time
The present, with excursions into the past.

Production Note

The frequent entrances and exits of various characters are not usually indicated in the stage directions. The characters may enter and exit from any point except the street door, which remains ostentatiously locked throughout.

For the sake of pace, many of the 'one-liners' in the London production were delivered from a serving hatch with a sliding door over the bar. Others were delivered as simple crossover lines as characters crossed to one of six exit points.

Act One

The set is the Coach and Horses pub in Soho. Getting on towards dawn.

As the Curtain rises, the stage is set in darkness.

The poet, ELIZABETH SMART, appears in a spot.

SMART: My dear Jeff,
    I can't say enough
    how much I admire
    the way you have
    conducted your entire
    life, and the way you have
    used your marvellous Muse.
    And how right she was to
    choose you. Because
    She's a Rare Bird who would
    have retired or died
    if you hadn't known how
    to amuse
    her, and her you
    That's one non-bogus
    marriage made
    on Parnassus
    and *true.*

    She knew
    exactly what and who
    she was letting herself
    in for: the real You.
    Drink, betting shops and pubs
    are the sort of thing that rubs
    her up the right way;
    she'll always stay
    and make you more beautiful

and witty
every day.

This is a loose love
Ode, owed
to one of my friends
who is in my special
collection of people
who make amends
for endless excruciating
boring hours
so often lived
when foolishly pursuing
stimulation,
and none occurs.
Sterne, Benchley, Leacock
Carroll, and Nash, and Lear
are not more dear
to me than bedrock
Bernard…

Her voice fades as we lose the spot.

Pause. Then a groan, a stirring, and the sound of a head hitting a piece of furniture in the darkness.

JEFF: Shit!

Another pause as he searches his pockets for matches. Finding a box, he up-tips it in the dark.

Fuck.

But finally he finds one of the spilled matches on the floor, strikes it, and finds that he is lying under a pub table. As the match goes out we hear him blundering about until he switches on a single wall light. He is in shirtsleeves and has been using his jacket for a pillow. He picks up the jacket, brushes it down, and puts it on. Lighting a cigarette, he crosses unsteadily to the street door and tries to open it. Then he looks up at the pub clock.

Five in the morning. Mark you, that's the pub time. It's only ten to really…

He rattles the door ineffectively then, switching on another light, goes behind the bar and is about to pour himself a large vodka when he pauses.

(Crying feebly.) Help…! *(Pouring the vodka.)* And answer came there none, as they say in the saloon bars. So nobody can say I didn't try to get out… Still, there are worse places to find yourself locked in for the night than a pub, I suppose. I know a bloke who woke up at dawn in the back stalls of a cinema in Dover. All he could remember was a poster for *High Noon* in the foyer and the fact that he'd got married at twelve o'clock the previous day in the Marylebone Road Registry Office. He's divorced now. He can't even bring his ex-wife's name to mind but he does remain a very great fan of Gary Cooper…

He sits on a bar stool, nursing his drink, and broods for a while.

At least the Coach and Horses has a roof. One night, when I was working on the *Sporting Life*, I woke up in a field outside Pontefract and I still have no idea how I got there. Come to that, I've no idea how I got here. I must have come in for the one, then gone down to the bog and crashed out till well after closing time, then I suppose I came back up here for the other one and quietly dozed off. It does happen. Another time when I was on the *Sporting Life* I remember opening eyes to find myself in bed with Barry Brogan a great jockey, true, but not my idea of a desirable bed companion. Then, on yet another occasion, I wasn't on the *Sporting Life* any longer.

The entrances and exits of the various characters who populate JEFF's life are not indicated. They appear as required and then fade back into the shadows.

EDITOR: Dear Mr Bernard, It will come as no surprise to you that following your unpardonable exhibition at the point-to-point dinner, which you attended as a representative of the *Sporting Life* on Friday evening, it is no longer possible for you to continue in our employ…

JEFF: Oh, God. I was supposed to be making a speech sometimes I'd never done before. I was nervous, I went down to the *Sporting Life* office at crack of dawn to work on it. Smithfield market was open, so I thought if I had a couple of drinks to get me going I'd probably write rather a good one.

EDITOR: … This was not, you will agree, the first time your behaviour has compromised us, and to protect myself and all connected with the *Sporting Life* from further embarrassment, I have no alternative but to terminate your engagement forthwith…

JEFF: I drank steadily from six in the morning to seven in the evening, at which time I arrived at the hotel where I was proposing to speak and immediately passed out. Two waiters had to carry me upstairs and put me to bed.

EDITOR: … I am sorry this has become necessary, but you will agree you were given every chance. I would be obliged if you would return to me your metal Press badge at your earliest convenience. Yours faithfully, Editor, *Sporting Life.*

JEFF: From the Jeffrey Bernard collection of letters from the editor. Some people are in the habit of writing angry letters to the Press. I get it the other way round. The Press in the habit of writing letters to me.

KINGTON: Dear Jeffrey, Are you going to do the fucking article or aren't you? Yours, Miles Kington, Literary Editor, *Punch.*

JEFF: One day I was asked to write my autobiography and I put a letter in the *Spectator* asking if anyone could tell me what I was doing between nineteen sixty and nineteen seventy-four.

MOLLOY: Dear Mr Bernard, I read with interest your letter asking for information as to your behaviour and whereabouts between the years nineteen sixty to nineteen seventy-four. On a certain evening in September nineteen sixty-nine, you rang my mother to inform her that you were going to murder her only son. If you would like further information, I can put you in touch with many people who have enjoyed similar bizarre experiences in your company. Your sincerely, Michael J. Molloy, Editor, *Daily Mirror.*

JEFF goes behind the bar and pours himself another stiff vodka.

JEFF: I could die here. It's a good thing I can hold this stuff tolerably well. I mean, if I were a yob or a Hurrah Henry, by the time the pub opens again I could be one of those cases found by the coroner to have choked on their own vomit. Disgusting phrase. When did you hear of anyone coking on someone else's vomit? I'm putting these on the slate, by the way. I don't believe in freeloading.

Carrying his drink, he comes round from behind the bar and prowls around the pub.

Dear Sir, May I add a few words to your excellent obituary of Jeffrey Bernard who has regrettably died from choking. I knew him intimately for over fifty years and I feel that many of his remarkable qualities were left unsung in your otherwise comprehensive review of his messy life. He was born in nineteen thirty-two probably by mistake covered from head to foot in eczema. One of the first things he did was to wet the bed and continued to do so until he was fifteen. A weak, thin-skinned and over-sensitive boy, he had few friends at school. He usually chose to sit at the very back of the classroom so that he could play with himself unobserved. His early obsession with sex prevented him from obtaining any worthwhile academic honours. By the time he left school he had become a chain smoker and compulsive writer of fan letters to Veronica Lake.

In nineteen forty-six he paid his first visit to Soho and from that point he was never to look forward. It was here in the cafes and pubs of Dean Street and Old Compton Street that he was to develop his remarkable sloth, envy and self-pity. It was about this time we began to realize that Jeffrey was not cut out for a career as a naval officer as his mother had hoped.

He drifted from job to job and, between jobs, he spent months at a time accepting small sums of money from homosexuals and friends. He began to develop a greed for unearned money and the growing conviction that he was cut out for better things. After a short, undistinguished spell in the army, from which he was given a medical discharge with his pay-book marked 'Mental stability nil', he returned to Soho, got married for the first time out of four, and split up with his wife a few weeks later.

It was during this period that he first became involved with horse-racing and gambling, and the feelings of infantile omnipotence, that this activity prompted were to last him for the rest of his life. These feelings were particularly noticeable in his dealings with women and some even said that his life was a never-ending cliché of a search for his mother. His drinking began to escalate to such an extent that he was unable to hold down the most ordinary of jobs and he was consequently advised to take up journalism. Even in this field he was never offered a staff appointment, and he gradually drifted into writing a series of personal and, at times, embarrassing columns about his own wretched experiences.

After a spell in the alcohol and drug-addiction unit at St Bernard's Hospital (no relation), Hanwell, he developed the fantasy that starting tomorrow, it would all be different. My last memory of Bernard is of seeing him staring at his typewriter and fighting yet another battle against his chronic amnesia. He leaves two unwritten books and a circle of detached acquaintances.

His perambulations have taken him back to the bar where there is a telephone. He is about to pick it up when his extemporized self-obituary reminds him.

Did you know, by the way, there's a bloke in America who sells talking tombstones? Before someone pegs out, as it might be a wife, they record a message on tape, then, when a husband comes to put a jar of dandelions on her grave on Sunday, he presses a button and lo, it's the same old story again.

WIFE: So there you are. I'm amazed you managed to tear yourself away from the pub. Your dinner's in the oven. You're drunk again aren't you? You make me sick. Honestly, I thought you'd change and settle down. Don't you ever think of the future? Christ, this headache's killing me. And stop staring at the women in the next grave. You needn't bother to come next Sunday. I'll be all right. Don't worry about me – you never did before so why start now? Always thinking of yourself. Me, me, me. Good-bloody-bye and where do you think you're taking those flowers? You make me sick!

JEFF picks up the receiver.

JEFF: I'll try giving old Norman a bell. The landlord – maybe he'll come and bail me out. Old Norman. He likes being called old Norman, that's why I do it, sycophant that I am. He slings down a vodka, snarls 'There you are, get your own fucking ice, haven't you got anything smaller?' and we all say good old Norman. Fancies himself as 'a big character'. Most landlords do, have you noticed? And if they're not bits of characters themselves, they know plenty of people who are…

Forgetting his phone call for the time being, he puts the receiver down.

One time when I was working as a barman, the publican was one of those dreadful men who call you 'squire' and think of themselves as 'your genial host'. On my first day, he came up to me where I was polishing the Smirnoff bottle and said –

LANDLORD: You see that bloke going out? Now *he's* a bit of a character.

JEFF: *(Yawning.)* Oh yes? Well, Guvnor, you mustn't keep me from my work.

LANDLORD: Yes, Would you believe that man must lose at least six umbrellas a year?

JEFF: Well, well. *(Resuming his narrative.)* I mean, I know the
shortage of eccentrics is acute these days, but you'd think
a pub landlord of all people could come up with someone
slightly more interesting than an umbrella loser. Even I can
do better than that. For instance, an antique dealer I know
who was once voted Rat of the Week by the old *Sunday
Pictorial*, a doctor who's had a cold for five years, and an
ex-embassy press attaché who now writes the flagellation
column for a seedy magazine, and that's just off the top of
my head.

*He picks up the telephone again, is about to dial, then remembers
something else.*

Dennis Shaw. Does that name mean anything? Now
there was a character. The face that closed a thousand
cinemas. He used to play villains and Gestapo men in
those wonderfully-awful British B pictures. Twenty stone
and encrusted in warts – imagine a toad wearing a dinner
jacket and that was Dennis Shaw, or Den-Den as he called
himself. One night that dear, sweet man John Le Mesurier
– now there was another character – one night, John Le
Mes was walking along Piccadilly when he saw Dennis
Shaw being bundled into a Black Maria for drunk and
disorderly. John Le Mes gave him one of his affable smiles
and said –

JOHN LE MES: Hello, Dennis. Working?

JEFF: He must have been drunker and even more disorderly
than usual because the police didn't like taking him in very
much, as I found once when I tried to get him arrested for
being boring. He'd gate crashed my table in a restaurant
and thoroughly spoiled my dinner by just sitting there
being Dennis Shaw, then he got into my cab and wouldn't
get out so I made the driver take us to Tottenham Court
Road police station. Where upon, he bounded in to the
nick, reappearing a moment later with four policemen and
booming –

SHAW: Gentlemen, I'd like you to meet Jeffrey Bernard, the
biggest idiot in Soho.

JEFF: He then sat down on the pavement and refused to budge. But all the desk sergeant said was –

SERGEANT: We'd rather not arrest Mr Shaw, sir, if you don't mind. He's a bit difficult in the cells, you see.

JEFF: One night I was out on the piss with Den-Den – a rather difficult enterprise, considering he was barred from every pub within a six-mile radius of Charing Cross – and we finished up in the *Stork Club* where we went through the card. Dinner, the full works, a bottle of champagne for me and a bottle of Gordon's gin for Den-Den. Now I'd been playing all evening and in any case the bugger owed me for enough dinners to feed the five thousand sop when the bill came I refrained from picking it up. So did Den-Den. After a while the waiters started stacking chairs on the tables and after another while the cleaners arrived and started vacuuming the floor, but still we sat there finishing Den-Den's gin with the bill untouched and unread on the table. Finally, the head waiter came over and even in the cold, grey light of dawn you could see his face turn white as he saw who it was.

By now JEFF and SHAW are sitting at a table.

WAITER: Good-morning, Mr Shaw.

SHAW: So you remember me.

WAITER: I do indeed, Mr Shaw.

SHAW: Tell this gentleman where we last met.

WAITER: At the *Pigalle*, Mr Shaw, when I was head waiter there.

SHAW: Under what circumstances did we become acquainted?

WAITER: You refused to pay your bill, Mr Shaw.

SHAW: Tell this gentleman what your response was to that.

WAITER: I called the police, Mr Shaw.

SHAW: *(Thumping the table.)* Call the bastards again!

JEFF: *(Rising.)* He was a collector's item, was Den-Den. And never lost an umbrella in his life. He found quite a few, though.

He crosses to the telephone again. Lighting a cigarette, he finally dials.

(After a while.) He's got to be home, so he must be out for the count. I wonder if I put a call through the engineers whether they could somehow make it ring louder...

Cradling the phone on his shoulder, he idly picks up a discarded copy of 'The Times' from a bar stool.

(After reading for a moment.) I think this has been left here for my benefit. One of those crappy features on the subject of alcoholism...

Putting the paper down again, he jiggles the telephone receiver impatiently against the ear.

What the opposite of insomnia is, Norman has got it. An enviable talent. The only time I get a good sleep is face down in the blueberry pie over lunch at the *Groucho Club*...

Giving up on his phone call he replaces the receiver and picks up 'The Times' again.

'Have you a drinking problem?' – the usual list of odd questions, and if you answer yes, it shows there's 'serious cause for alarm'. The trouble is the more I look at these questions the less alarmed I feel. In fact, I've just this minute come to the conclusion that I don't drink enough...

He moves behind the bar where he pours himself another stiff one.

I wish someone'd pay *me* to write a quiz on boozing. I'd be laughing all the way to the *Groucho*... I wonder if they'd pay me to supply the answers?

'The Times' Questioner is a very starchy disapproving-looking lady.

QUESTIONER: Do you have time off from work because of drinking, or has your work performance suffered because of alcohol?

JEFF: The situation is very much the reverse. Work frequently interferes with my drinking. Besides, drinking *is* my work.

I was once paid five hundred pounds for an article on this very subject.

QUESTIONER: Do your family –

JEFF: Just a minute, I haven't finished. I'll have you know I once fired my agent for being pissed all the time. I told her. 'One of us has to be sober, and it isn't going to be me.'

QUESTIONER: Have there been family quarrels because of your drinking?

JEFF: I believe there was a tremendous row in nineteen thirty-four as to whether I should be fed Nestles or Cow & Gate.

QUESTIONER: And are you becoming difficult, irritable and testy after drinking?

JEFF: You must be joking. I'm impossible. After crossing time last Tuesday I bit a Greek greengrocer in Goodge Street who asked me not to feel his cucumbers.

QUESTIONER: Do you find your memory is getting worse?

JEFF: Could you repeat the question?

QUESTIONER: Have you ever had loss of memory after a heavy drinking session?

JEFF: Quite honestly I can't remember ever having had a heavy drinking session.

QUESTIONER: Do you order yourself a double when the rest of the party is drinking singles, or do you order yourself a quick extra drink while collecting an order from the bar?

JEFF: None of my 'party' drinks singles. They do have some style, you know. As to ordering a quick drink, I can tell you there's no such thing in this fucking place. It takes longer to get a drink in here than it takes to get a refund out of the Inland revenue.

QUESTIONER: Has your sexual drive and ability suffered because of your drinking?

JEFF: Mind your own fucking business.

QUESTIONER: And finally do you – ?

JEFF: Sorry – no more questions. It'll soon be opening time in Billingsgate.

QUESTIONER: You make me sick!

JEFF speaks confidentially as the QUESTIONER departs.

JEFF: In fact, I didn't want to say this in front of *The Times*, but owing to some tablets I've been taking in conjunction with a small port, to which I am not accustomed – that's what drunk chartered accountants always claim when hauled up at Bow Street – I find myself on the verge of suffering from impotence, or incompetence as women call it. Though suffering's the wrong word – impotence has its drawbacks: like you stand no chance of being held down and raped by three nubile girls, which is what once happened to a bloke on Malibu Beach and the next night you couldn't see the sea for the entire male population of Southern California. But it's not in the least uncommon, you know. There are fifty-five thousand impotent men in the Avon and Somerset area alone – that's what I read in the *Daily Telegraph*. I wonder how they know. Were they shopped to the medical authorities by fifty-five thousand disgruntled women? And why is the West Country so heavily afflicted? Could it be the cider? No – apparently the causes of impotence are given as stemming from diabetes, alcohol, pelvic injuries, drugs and psychological problems. *(Lighting a cigarette.)* If smoking sixty of these things a day counts as a drug then I'm holding a full house for the first time since I played poker in the army. But I personally welcome impotence and wish it would hurry up and come, so to speak. I raise my glass to it, though not much else. What a release – for the first time since the age of fourteen, when I formed an ambition to a sex object instead of a good seam bowler, I will no longer be led about by my prick. When I ponder the fact that my life lies in ruins solely because I have always followed the direction in which my various erections were pointing, I wish to God I'd been born a girl. Which reminds me. In the steam bath one day I found

Solly, a seventy-year-old taxi driver, staring at his private member and moaning –

SOLLY: We were born together. We grew together. We went courting together. We got married together. We had children together. Why, oh why, oh why did you have to die before me?

JEFF: Another of the delights of impotence is that I should set fire to the bed a bit less often. You see, I am somewhat in the habit of being asked for cigarettes by ladies while lying in my bed. Not after the event – that's always been the man's prerogative but before it. Usually what's happened is that I've jumped the gun by getting into the bed in belief I was being followed. But what these ladies do is light up a cigarette and then give you a hundred specious reasons for having to go home.

1ST GIRL: My husband may be phoning from Paris.

2ND GIRL: My cat can't bear to be left alone.

3RD GIRL: But we've only known each other for a day…

4TH GIRL: Half a day…

5TH GIRL: Half an hour…

6TH GIRL: The baby-sitter will go mad if I'm late.

7TH GIRL: But people simply don't *do* it in broad daylight, do they?

JEFF: One more advantage, by the way. Not having to wrestle with one-liners like those any more means not having to put up with one-liners like these any more, after they've moved in.

1ST GIRL: And where do you think you're going?

2ND GIRL: You've been drinking.

3RD GIRL: Can we go home now, please?

4TH GIRL: Your dinner's in the oven.

5TH GIRL: You make me sick.

JEFF: But to get back to the bedside manner…

8ᵀᴴ GIRL: I like you, Jeff, I like you a lot. But not in that way.

JEFF: So. I resign myself to the situation, take a Valium,
fall asleep with the last fag in my mouth and wake up
to find the bedspread in flames. I started keeping a fire
extinguisher by my bed but I never really knew whether to
aim it at the mattress, the lady – if she was still there or my
private parts.

Once more he crosses to the telephone, picks it up and dials.

(After listening for a while.) Maybe he's taken a Valium too.
Perhaps I should call the fire brigade... Come on, Norman,
some of us have got homes to go to, as you landlords so
often remind us... *(Recollecting with a frown.)* Though now
that I come to think about it, some of us haven't.

*He replaces the telephone and, during the following, brings out a
suitcase and a couple of carrier bags, stuffed with possessions, from
behind the bar where they have been stored.*

Woman again. Why haven't they got labels on their heads
saying 'Danger Government health warning: women can
seriously damage your brains, genitals, current account,
confidence, razor blades and good standing among
friends'? Sometimes they walk out on you, sometimes they
throw you out, all depending on whose bed you were in
when you set it on fire. This was a throwing-out job. At
least I was allowed access to my worldly goods. Love
locked out is one thing, but when it's love plus your books
and Mozart tapes, all your spare clothes and shoes plus
your framed photograph of yourself with Lester Piggott, it
can be well-nigh unbearable while it lasts.

*Rummaging among his belongings he locates the Lester Piggott picture
and puts it on a table.*

No-one would ever call Lester a laugh a minute but don't
let anybody tell you he has no sense of humour. He even
sends up his own legendary meanness. There's a story
about the time years and years ago when he'd ridden
another winner and the stable lad was kept waiting for the
customary tip.

LAD: Excuse me Lester, but do you think you could drop me a pound for that winner I did you?

PIGGOTT: *(Cocking a hand to his ear.)* What?

LAD: That winner I did you. You were going to drop me a pound.

PIGGOTT: Can't hear you. That's my bad ear.

LAD: *(Close up to the other ear.)* What about a couple of quid for that winner I did for you?

PIGGOTT: Still can't hear. Try the one pound ear again.

Rummaging again, after a reflective moment, JEFF unearths a bundle of letters and riffles through them.

JEFF: Some letters tied with barbed wire. I don't know why I bother keeping them. Or why they bother writing them. They're all identical.

MISTRESS: Dear Jeffrey, It was madness from the start. You must have known as well as I did that it could never work. Why on earth did we ever start it? Your moods crushed me. I put out a hand, but never took it. Well. You did take. My God, that's all you ever did – take, take, take. You say you like women, but I really think you hate them. Not once did you ever listen to me when I wanted to talk about me. You were just waiting for me to stop talking and get my clothes off. Then, in that Chinese restaurant in Gerrard Street, you finally did it. You insulted everything I hold sacred. The family unit. Carshalton Beeches. Cosmopolitan, and money. No, I'm sorry, it's all over. I hope you find true happiness, as I have.

JEFF: No doubt with a film-maker aged about thirty who drives a Ferrari coupe with on bronze arm leaning nonchalantly over the offside door, and who lives in a riverside penthouse with a Burmese cat, several gold medallions, a bottle of after shave, an extremely expensive hi-fi set and no self-doubt whatsoever.

MISTRESS: PS. You make me sick.

JEFF: She could have been the fifth Mrs Bernard if I'd played my cards wrong. Trouble was, she had the most extraordinary ideas about what's called 'settling down'. This is a very curious phrase used only by women. I've seen feathered birds settling down and I've seen dust settling down and I've seen bookmakers settling *up* even, but what do all these women mean by settling down? I suspect they mean that life is no laughing matter. You could have fooled me. But what puzzles me is what on earth did my four wives think they were getting when they married me? I mean, you can see a train when it's coming. But they thought I'd change and settle down.

He unearths framed photographs of himself with various ladies and displays them on one of the pub tables.

As a matter of fact, I think I *have* settled down insofar as I'm pretty set in my ways. I have come to terms with the fact that my dinner is in the oven and always will be. I have also learned to accept the fact that –

BORE: You only get out of life what you put into it.

JEFF: The sagacious prick who gave me that piece of information would have had his teeth knocked out if I hadn't been in an alcoholic and diabetic coma at the time, but he meant well. And bless my soul, don't the ladies mean well when they ask you to change and settle down? Never trust people who mean well. Hitler probably meant well and Cromwell certainly hoped we'd change and settle down.

Anyway, I was tremendously flattered when this girl said to me –

MISTRESS: When I first saw you in the pub I thought to myself, what's this handsome man doing surrounded by rogues?

JEFF: Apart from her suspect eyesight, she's answered her own question, if you see what I mean. Surrounded by rogues. Say no more. But for her, I'd try to change and settle down. 'Darling. I've asked a few rogues to Sunday lunch.

No Kitchen Joyce says she'll weed the border, Maltese Laurie's going to mow the lawn and Norman says he'll carve the joint. We could play bridge in the evening and perhaps we might splash out on a bottle of sherry.'

MISTRESS: 'Oh Jeffrey, you're an absolute poppet. I'm so glad you've changed and settled down. You don't miss Soho and all those awful people, do you darling?

JEFF: 'Of course not, my angel. Take your knickers off. Oops, sorry. Forgot. We're married and settled down in Chislehurst.'

JEFF finds in his belongings a photograph of the MISTRESS. Smoking pensively he sets it on a table of its own and looks at it reflectively.

But if I never change, neither do they. When they leave you, for instance I wonder who writes their scripts?

MISTRESS: It's over. You've snapped at me for the last time. As far as I'm concerned, anything there was is finished.

JEFF: *(Still narrating.)* I can't say I was surprised but I still couldn't get on to her wavelength. You might know that strange process. It's got nothing to do with arrogance or conceit simply a dull amazement at the fact that someone can't see how truly wonderful you are. I mean, there you are, standing right in front of them, the never-to-be-repeated offer of a lifetime, in your prime and only a short climb away from your peak, and the fools can't see it. It never fails to amaze me.

MISTRESS: I don't mind going to the cinema with you, or going Dutch for a meal – but so far as anything else is concerned, it's over.

JEFF: She waited for me to say something. I stood there thinking of about six different things at once.

MISTRESS: Aren't you going to say anything?

JEFF: I couldn't. I was miles away. That business about going Dutch had really got to me. I had a vision of us drifting in and out of cinemas and restaurants, and me – or worse still, her – always saying to management –

MISTRESS: Do you mind if we separate bills? You see, I don't sleep with him anymore.

JEFF: Also, I was thinking how very hard she was going to be to replace. She still stood staring at me, her brown eyes flecked with malice and realistic thinking.

MISTRESS: Well?

JEFF: I still couldn't think of anything to say memorable enough to haunt her for the rest of her days, so I put on my mask of tragedy and went through the usual motions of offering up the late, late prayer. It's one all hopeless punters mutter in betting shops and it goes –

PUNTER: Please, God, let's start again. I know I've been a fool, but if this horse wins the last race I promise I'll never have another bet again. Ever.

JEFF: But it doesn't work with women. Come to that, it doesn't work with horses either...

MISTRESS: Very well...

JEFF: Suddenly I saw that picture from my schooldays of Napoleon on the deck of the *Bellerophon* saying farewell to Europe – only it wasn't Napoleon it was me. Actually, more post Charing Cross than post Waterloo so far as I was concerned. I was upset, yes – no one likes their sweets taken away – but I wasn't heartbroken.

MISTRESS: So it's goodbye, then.

JEFF: Then she shrugged her mouth and left. I found myself thinking: it's just like they say it is in novels. Women really do turn on their heels when they go. I watched her down stairs and heard the front door close and then I heard her nasty, tinny little Renault starting up below. I waited for her to crash the gears but she didn't. It's bloody fantastic, I thought while I made some tea. After a scene like that she remains so icy cold that for once she doesn't make a mess of the gears. I mean, I ask you – would a man remain so utterly cool after closing a rhapsodical chapter in life? Not him – he'd drive straight into a wall blinded by tears at a moderately safe fifteen miles an hour and she'd come running down the stairs and out into the street deliciously blaming herself.

The sound of screeching brakes. JEFF smiles malevolently.

That's better. I took my cup of tea into the sitting-room and sat there wondering at my own coolness. I felt quite ashamed at not being more upset so I put some Mahler on to see if he could provoke the appropriate misery. Nothing. In fact, I sat there listening to the syrup feeling distinctly irritated. She'd be on the phone now, I reckoned, to an old, reliable friend.

As we bring up the Mahler the Old Reliable Friend, filling his pipe, enters and sits on a table with a bottle of wine, where he is joined by the Mistress.

God, I hate those old, reliable, pipe-smoking friends who, of course, have never laid a finger on the lady in question – they lecture at some obscure university on Anglo-Saxon pottery and you can't get more decent than that. The bugger's just been waiting for her affair to go on the rocks. Up until then he's been hanging around like a non-functioning lighthouse but now he suddenly lights up.

MISTRESS: No, actually, I was very fond of him, Bob.

JEFF: They've always got old, reliable names like Bob.

MISTRESS: It's just that he needs more love than I can possibly give him.

OLD RELIABLE: I know, darling, I know...

JEFF: ...says Bob, patting her hand while at the same time catching the wine waiter's eye, filling his pipe with St Bruno, grinding the pepper mill over madam's artichoke and scribbling a note about a new find of sixth-century cocoa mugs near Winchester.

MISTRESS: I really was very attached to him. It's just that I couldn't take any more of his eternal snapping.

OLD RELIABLE: I know, I know. But you must have known it couldn't last.

JEFF: They always say that. I wonder they don't set themselves up as bloody fortune-tellers.

OLD RELIABLE: I could tell he was trouble from the moment I set eyes on him, but of course, one doesn't like to pour cold water on love's young dream.

JEFF: How about throwing up on it, then? So, after plying her with wine he wastes a good dinner by pouring her into a taxi with the words –

OLD RELIABLE: What you need, my dear, is a good night's sleep. Now you just try to forget all about him.

MISTRESS: *(Pecking his cheek.)* Dear Bob. I don't know what I would do without you.

JEFF: All that happened a long time ago. I haven't seen her since; the Mahler's well scratched by now and I've licked my wounds clean... Then two weeks ago she had the cheek to ring me up and ask me if I happened to know of a good plumber. Some people have no sensitivity whatsoever.

Delving into his belongings, JEFF produces a pair of tortoiseshell-backed hairbrushes.

(Staring at them.) Tortoiseshell hairbrushes. Now how did I acquire these? I know. In settlement of a bad debt by a very severe case of alopecia. *(A moment's brooding.)* I wonder what it's like to be a tortoise. Not a barrel of laughs, I shouldn't imagine. You can't be frivolous or facetious if you're a tortoise, can you? And you think of the danger of being turned into a pair of hairbrushes. But you do have a home to go to. Just pull in your head and there you are, all snug and cosy... God, I hate flat-hunting. And I hate staying with other people while I'm looking for somewhere to live. No matter how kind and generous they are, you can see them looking at you all the time, with their eyes pleading –

HOST: Please, please, Jeff, don't get pissed and set the flat on fire.

JEFF: One thing I know. I will never ever again live anywhere beyond staggering distance of the Coach and Horses.

During the following, he produces photographs from his belonging, looking at them and setting them up on the pub tables.

I pitched my tent in Soho at around thirteen and it's been a downhill struggle ever since. And if anyone wonders how much a dump could possibly have gripped me and seduced me, then they didn't know Soho when you could end up drunk, penniless and alone on less than a pound. To step out of both the classroom and mother's Dresden-littered drawing-room into the enchanted dung heap was like waking up in Disneyland, treasure Island, Pleasure island, you name it. And what an incredible mixture I've had the luck to stumble across mostly in the gutter where you find the best company. Poets, painters, prostitutes, bookies' runners, bohemians, bums, philosophers, crooks, cranks, Dylan Thomas, Francis Bacon, Lucien Freud, John Minton, Frank Norman, French Vera, No Knickers Joyce, Sid the swimmer, Ironfoot Jack, Nina Hammett, Muriel Belcher. Muriel Belcher! She ran the *Colony Room Club* or Muriel's as it was always known. I can see her now, sitting on her stool at the end of the bar, like a raven on its perch, and chatting up the punters.

MURIEL: Come on, cunty, spend up. You're not buying enough champagne. Are you a member, sir? Go on, then, fuck off. Members only.

JEFF: She did have her favourites, though. There was a charming old queen who worked in the City and drank scotch for England at Muriel's every evening. He was more or less a club hostess but it happened that he'd won the Military Cross in nineteen sixteen when he was a captain in the Guards, and whenever anyone asked Muriel why she put up with him, she always said –

MURIEL: She was a very brave little woman at the Somme.

JEFF: There was this bearded bugger, well known for his compulsive verbosity. One afternoon he walked into Muriel's and said –

BORE: Muriel, I'm worried. I've got to get to a fancy-dress party tonight and I can't think what to go as.

MURIEL: Why don't you put talc on your chin and go as an armpit?

JEFF: Of course, it was all too good to miss a moment of, so working for a living was out of the question. I did the odd job obligatory in the life of a bum – navvying, dishwashing, acting, even a spell down a coal mine and then in a boxing booth in a fairground. But I was always drawn back to Soho who was always there waiting with open arms and legs.

He takes out a collection of tapes from one of his carrier bags and browses through them.

Rosenkavalier. That must be when I was working at Covent Garden as a sceneshifter. Do you know – the flymen and sceneshifters at the Royal Opera House are the most discriminating critics you could wish to meet. I'd trust their judgement rather than those long-haired prats on Radio Three any day.

We hear a snatch of 'Der Rosenkavalier'.

SCENESHIFTER: Tell you what, Jeff. *(Spitting.)* I don't care who she is – I've better Rosenkavalier's than this one.

JEFF broods through the rest of the snatch until the music fades.

JEFF: I now realize it's highly likely that the two biggest of the many mistakes I've made in my life were to have moved from Soho to Suffolk in nineteen sixty-six and from Soho to Berkshire in nineteen seventy-eight, both times with new wives, in the pathetic belief that geographical change would solve all my problems. But any idea that living in the country is romantic is all romancing as far as I am concerned. The idyll is utterly without stimulus and all those trees and all that grass drain the spirit. I remember once foolishly suggesting to Francis Bacon that he could solve all his tax headaches by moving to Switzerland.

BACON: Are you crazy? All those fucking views – they'd drive me mad.

JEFF: And it's not only the views – it's the dreadful horse brassy pubs run by rude, jumped-up shoe keepers in blazers and cravats, and it's the bloody regulars – the Backbone of England and his lady wife, Mrs Backbone, Of Neck of the Woods.

MR BACKBONE wears an anorak, MRS BACKBONE a sheepskin coat and headscarf. They come in vigorously rubbing and clapping their hands.

They invariably make the same entrance wherever they go – I presume they're rehearsed in it as children. Then Mr Backbone says –

BACKBONE: Brrrr!

JEFF: And Mrs Backbone says –

MRS BACKBONE: Brrrr!

JEFF: Then Mr Backbone says –

BACKBONE: What'll you have, darling?

JEFF: And Mrs Backbone says –

MRS BACKBONE: Ooh, let's see. What shall I have?

JEFF: So Mr Backbone says –

BACKBONE: Why don't you have a whiskey mac?

JEFF: And Mrs backbone says –

MRS BACKBONE: Yes, why don't I have a whiskey mac?

JEFF: Good idea!

MRS BACKBONE: Good idea, darling. Yes, I'll have a whisky mac. What are you going to have, darling?

JEFF: – asks Mrs Backbone.

BACKBONE: Ooh, I'm not sure, darling. I know –

JEFF: – says Mr Backbone.

BACKBONE: – I think I'll have a nice bottle of Guinness.

JEFF: There! Then, when Mr Backbone dips into his pocket for change he drops a coin on the floor and quick as a flash the barmaid says –

BARMAID: Leave it for sweeper.

JEFF: Pause for laughter. Then, when the drinks have been savoured by our resident Bisto Kids –

BACKBONE: Mmmmm!

MRS BACKBONE: Mmmmm!

JEFF: – The Backbones of England smile knowingly at one another, and then Mr Backbone says to the barmaid –

BACKBONE: Busy Christmas?

JEFF: And the barmaid says –

BARMAID: Ooh, terrible. Packed all the time we were.

BACKBONE: Well –

JEFF: – says Mr Backbone

BACKBONE: – that's for another year, anyway.

JEFF: And Mrs Backbone, her nose dripping in unison with his, decides it's time for her to scintillate.

MRS BACKBONE: Yes, all over for another year.

JEFF: I know, deep down, that they're going to continue to plunder the calendar and I should leave now but I don't. I just wait for it. And Mr Backbone rubs his hands and asks the Still Life with Pineapple ice bucket –

BACKBONE: How was the New Year, then?

BARMAID: New Year?

JEFF: – squawks the barmaid.

BARMAID: Don't talk about it.

JEFF: But Mr Backbone does.

BACKBONE: Oh, like that was it?

JEFF: And Mrs Backbone echoes –

MRS BACKBONE: Like that, eh?

JEFF: To which she adds saucily, to My Backbone –

MRS BACKBONE: Ours was pretty hectic too wasn't it, darling?

BACKBONE: Always is –

JEFF: – concurs Mr Backbone.

BACKBONE: Always is –

JEFF: – concurs Mr Backbone.

BACKBONE: Still, you expect it, don't you?

MRS BACKBONE: Wouldn't be New Year if it wasn't would it, darling?

JEFF: – says Mrs Backbone, and I drink up and leave before they embark on their forecasts for Easter. *(He crosses towards the bar, then pauses as a thought strikes him.)* I do have one unfulfilled ambition as regards the country, though. I once remarked to Fred Winter on how healthy his horses looked.

WINTER: That's because they don't sit up all night playing cards and drinking vodka.

JEFF: And it occurred to me to wonder what would happen – just what would happen – if you fed into the average farm animal what some of us consume in the course of a single day. I'd very much like to wake up one morning with a cow of the Friesian variety and walk her down here to the Coach and Horses, stopping on the way to buy twenty Players, ply her with vodka until closing time, whip her off to an Indian restaurant, take her up to the *Colony Room* till five thirty and then on to the *York Minster, Swiss Tavern* and *Three Greyhounds*, get beaten up by Chinese waiters at midnight, have a row with a taxi driver, set the bed on fire, put it out with tears and then wake up on the floor. Could you then milk said cow? I doubt it.

Resuming his journey to the bar he pours himself a vodka, then picks up phone and dials.

(Drumming his fingers impatiently.) Norman – will you please answer the bloody phone? I am locked in your pub and drinking all your vodka. And another thing – there's no ice. *(Narrating again.)* Not that you'd move him, the ungracious bugger. Yesterday I asked him for the menu and he threw it at me. When he brought my cottage pie I thought he was going to throw that at me, too. Instead he said to the man sitting on that bar stool, 'Get off your arse and let Jeff sit down – he's fucking ill.' I am fucking ill, too. As the *Spectator* always puts it when I'm too fucking ill to write my column –

SPECTATOR: Jeffrey Bernard is unwell.

JEFF: I tell a lie – they don't invariably say that. They have been known to put it another way.

SPECTATOR: Jeffrey Bernard's column does not appear this week, as it is remarkably similar to that which he wrote last week.

JEFF is by now in bed – one of the Coach and Horses chaise longues – being tucked in by a NURSE.

NURSE: Why *do* you drink so much, Mr Bernhard?

JEFF: To stop myself from jogging.

As the NURSE departs with a sigh, JEFF unfolds the copy of the 'Sporting Life' she brought in for him. Forgetting the audience, he studies it for a while.

I'm about to do you a favour. I'm going to refrain from advising you what to back in the big race tomorrow. A tip is only an opinion and I'll give you a tip – the nearer the horse's mouth it is, the more it's worth ignoring. And that goes each way.

The trouble with betting is that if you lose you lose, and if you win you think about how much more you *could* have won if you'd doubled the stake. It's pathetic, really. I think a psychiatrist I know probably hit the nail on the head when he described punting as –

PSYCHIATRIST: Collecting injustices.

JEFF: This was when I was in a very curious establishment
in Surrey which was like a gambling research clinic. On
the third day of my confinement, the psychiatrist came
along and sat down beside my bed with a great wad of
papers, an instrument for measuring blood pressure, a
thermometer and the *Sporting Life*. I thought he was going
to delve into my childhood and establish whether I still felt
guilt at introducing the sport of masturbation to my prep
school – as a matter of fact I felt like Marco Polo returning
to Europe with the new invention of gunpowder, and
soon the whole school was rocked to its foundations both
metaphorically and physically. But not a bit of it. He went
straight to the point.

PSYCHIATRIST: Do you think King's Ransom has a better
chance than Baby Dumpling at York this afternoon?

JEFF: No. Looking at the weights, I'd say that Baby Dumpling
has a better chance than King's Ransom.

PSYCHIATRIST: You really are in a bad way, my friend. King's
Ransom will piss it.

JEFF: He then went off to back King's Ransom and thus prove
I was mad. But Baby Dumpling pissed it.

NURSE: I should be careful, Mr Bernhard. We had a man in
here who was such a good tipster the psychiatrist kept him
in for five months.

JEFF rises hastily as he continues his narrative.

JEFF: I became hooked on racing when I was about sixteen
and doing time at a disgusting naval college called
Pangbourne. A boy called Vickers got twelve of the
best – the maximum – for running a book. I was deeply
impressed. It put gambling in the same wicked league
as drinking and sex and if it was as bad as that I wanted
some of it. It took thirty-five years for retribution to set in.
Not twelve of the best, but an appearance at Bow Street
magistrates' court. After a long series of contributions to
the Joe Coral Benevolent Fund, my luck changed or so
I believed at the time. I had a yankee up and won over

two grand – a big win for a small punter. It was the sort of win that compensates for all the losses but then I began to reflect that since it had taken three and a half decades to arrive at that one big win, punting was indeed a mug's game after all. So I decided to open a book. Just among friends and acquaintances, in a small, fun sort of way. But the law didn't see it quite like that and my luck changed again.

A CUSTOMS OFFICER has appeared. He speaks in the sing-song tones of one giving evidence in court.

CUSTOMS OFFICER: On thirteenth of June, at approximately fourteen hundred hours, I entered the Coach and Horses public house, Greek Street, London, W1, as an officer of Customs and Excise. A television set was switched on showing racing from Sandown and York. A man who I now know to be Jeffrey Bernard said –

JEFF: Does anyone want anything on this?

There are now other people standing around the bar.

CUSTOMS OFFICER: – just as the three o'clock race from Sandown was starting. I asked a woman at the bar for the running number of a horse called Bonhomie. She consulted her newspaper and replied. At this point, Mr Bernhard said to me –

JEFF: Do you want a bet?

CUSTOMS OFFICER: I handed him two one pound coins and asked for Bonhomie. Two other customers handed Mr Bernhard coins and both asked for Bonhomie. Mr Bernhard turned to a female companion and said –

JEFF: If Bonhomie wins I'm fucked.

CUSTOMS OFFICER: Bonhomie lost and I left the premises at approximately fifteen eighteen hours.

One of the customers at the bar proves to be a CUSTOMS INVESTIGATOR. He draws up two chairs facing one another.

INVESTIGATOR: Would you care to sit down, Mr Bernhard? Just a few questions... *(He flashes his identity card.)* Now do you pay tax to the government on these bets you've been taking?

JEFF: How could I? I'm not a licensed bookmaker.

INVESTIGATOR: Do you think it's against the law not to pay tax?

JEFF: I do now.

INVESTIGATOR: Why do the regulars bet with you rather than go to the Mecca around the corner?

JEFF: They regard it as fun and are too lazy to walk to the betting shop and desert their drinks. It's a joke between us. I think they're fools and they think I'm one. We're taking the piss out of each other.

INVESTIGATOR: Do they bet with you because you don't charge tax?

JEFF: No, it's just a game. Nobody's that mean – at least, my friends aren't.

INVESTIGATOR: How well do you have to know someone before you take bets off them?

JEFF: They'd have to be friends or acquaintances, not strangers. Most of them are good mates.

INVESTIGATOR: Would you be surprised to know you've accepted bets from custom officers?

JEFF: *(To himself.)* Fuck.

Rising, he resumes his narrative.

It took nine policeman and three customs men in one wagon and one squad car to arrest me. Little me. At how much public expense I don't know, but they recovered the vital sum of thirty-one pounds twelve pence in evaded betting tax.

MAGISTRATE: Anything known?

JEFF: *(Still narrating.)* Not a lot. I was once nicked for going over the top with a rubber plant in the *Raj of India* restaurant. Then I collected another bit of a criminal record for kicking someone's car parked annoyingly on the pavement. A CID man arrested me here in the Coach and Horses and took me to Vine Street to be fingerprinted and photographed. But here's an extraordinary thing. As we were walking past a certain pub on our way to the nick, the detective suddenly said –

DETECTIVE: You screwed the landlord's daughter here in nineteen seventy-six, didn't you?

JEFF: I was amazed. How anyone but me and the party of the second part could have knowledge of what went on that Christmas Day on the saloon-bar when the guvnor went upstairs for his after-lunch nap, I'll never know. But I liked the magistrate. He looked up my previous form and said –

MAGISTRATE: The last time it was rubber plants, Mr Bernard. Now it's cars. What next?

JEFF: Keeping a book without paying better tax, that's what's next.

MAGISTRATE: Quite. Fined two hundred pounds and fifty pounds costs.

JEFF: Ah, well. A mere fleabite compared with what the sods did to Lester Piggott and as we always say around here, if you can't take a joke you shouldn't have joined.

He opens his suitcase, rummages about in it and produces a clean but crumpled shirt which he holds up for inspection.

Oh, dear. When Norman finally does surface he's going to think I look more dishevelled even than after that night I spent in the ditch of the celebrated Pond Fence at Sandown. I don't know how I got there, or who my companion was, but we got on famously.

Tossing the shirt on a chair he moves off with uncertain step – for the first time showing signs of drunkenness – to a back room where we hear him crashing and banging about. Unseen by JEFF, a folded page of the 'Spectator' has fallen out of the shirt pocket and now lies on the floor. ELIZABETH SMART enters and stands motionless in the

*same spot as formerly. JEFF staggers out of the back room with an
ironing board and an iron.*

(Trying to set up the ironing board.) People are always
surprised to find that I'm a domestic animal. Who the hell
do they think washes my glass up every morning if there's
no-one else there to do it? I cook, I sow, I reap, I...

*While he does not see ELIZABETH SMART, he does see the folded paper
on the floor and recognizes it. Leaving the ironing board to collapse
in a heap he crosses and picks it up and opens it out.*

Slightly rhyming verses for Jeff Bernard's fiftieth birthday,
by Elizabeth Smart.

SMART: Wilde would have smiled
and been beguiled
and bright enough to know
that *you* had a better
Muse in tow
than he.

Could he see
the angelic emanations
from gutters where we
all fall, while
trying to pee,
and rise, or try to rise,
unwisely, in majesty?

Your subject is not mean,
who's up, who's in,
or jockeying for position
(what a dreary sin).
Funny but kind,
your subject is justly seen
as the inexhaustible one
of nude mankind.

Yourself, in fact, drinking,
amidst the alien corn,

and explaining the amazing
joke of being born.

ELIZABETH SMART is lost in the shadows.

JEFF sits, lights a cigarette, and thinks about her.

JEFF: It's terrible to think that dear Elizabeth got me my first
job in journalism. We got drunk together one lunchtime
and she took me back to her office at *Queen* magazine and
said to the editor, 'Give him a job.' He did. Until then, I
was a reasonably happy, sane stage-hand. She's dead now,
like too many of my friends. God forgive you and rest in
peace, Elizabeth. And if anybody writes to tell me you only
get out of life what you put into it, I might just kill them.

*He closes his eyes, cigarette in hand, and for a moment seems to be
asleep. But then he opens them again.*

That was the most touching, but not the only poem I've
had addressed to me.

MISTRESS: With the crown of thorns I wear
Why do I need a prick like you?
If you choose to bugger off
It isn't going to spoil the view.

I've been put down by the best
And crucified by experts, dear,
And I really do not need
A friend like you to bend my ear.

You claim that generosity
Is something that I lack
May I suggest you've had from me
Much more than you gave back.

So don't think I'll mope and mourn
Because you tell me that we're through.
With the crown of thorns I wear
I sure don't need a prick like you.

But JEFF, lighted cigarette between his fingers, has gently nodded off.

Jeffrey, I want to know who wrote that poem to you and why. Jeff? Jeffrey! Oh – you make me sick!

CURTAIN.

Act Two

The same. Perhaps an hour later.

The light of dawn filters through the windows of the Coach and Horses, highlighting the wisps of smoke from the chair or sofa which has been set on fire by JEFF's cigarette while he was asleep.

Muttering oaths, he has been trying to extinguish the conflagration with a pair of old cricket flannels from his suitcase. He now acquires a soda siphon from the bar and applies it to the smouldering upholstery.

JEFF: *(Muttering to himself.)* This – is going to do – my reputation – no good – whatsoever... Such as it is. How absurd. How ridiculously absurd...

He surveys his flannels, which are badly charred, and tosses them aside.

Which makes me a survivor, I suppose. A good friend of mine, Eva Johansen, used to say you can't get through life without a highly-developed sense of the absurd. She could well have been here now to recognize the absurdity of my situation, but one night she went to bed drunk with a lit cigarette in her hand and in her case she was taken seriously. How inconsiderate, Eva. Soon there'll be no-one left to drink with at all... The rows we had, always in pubs. And if Norman or some other anxious landlord tried to intervene, she'd say with her winning smile –

EVA: Oh, it's quite all right. This is a friend of mine and I'm just trying to explain to him what a stupid bastard he is.

JEFF: Our longest standing row goes back to when I was living in the country and I asked her what she'd like for breakfast.

EVA: A slice of cold, rare, roast beef and a glass of Tio Pepe, preferably chilled.

JEFF: Why can't you have a fucking egg like anyone else, you flash cow?

EVA: Because I'm not anyone else.

JEFF: And she wasn't. One of these people she used to call 'these people' approached her here in the Coach and Horses with a view to picking her up.

BORE: Good-morning. Nice day.

EVA: Your place or mine?

JEFF: Exit frightened rabbit. Someone who did succeed in picking her up and became a close friend, one day said to her for some reason –

FRIEND: You know, Eva, if I hadn't met you I think I would have taken up keeping bees.

JEFF: He was known as The Beekeeper and Eva said –

EVA: The poor sod wanted to keep bees and he ended up with a hornet's nest.

JEFF: Some months before she set herself on fire she wrote to me and it was a case of like calling to like.

EVA: So I have no flat, no job, no lover, no income and as far as I can see no prospects. Even my cat has left me. I keep sitting around expecting fear and all I'm getting is exhilaration. Here I am, exulting in the clean dry air of absolute selfishness, secure in the knowledge that there's nothing more they can do to me. If it weren't so totally out of keeping with everything I've been told, I'd say it could only be described as happiness.

JEFF crosses to the telephone and dials.

JEFF: Wake up Norman! ... Engaged. At least that means he's stirring... *(Replacing the receiver.)* You won't begrudge me breakfast, will you. Norman?

Going round the bar he locates and plugs in an electric kettle, then forages for food.

Now shall it be tea and bikkies, tea and vinegar-flavoured crisps, tea and prawn crackers, tea and tortilla chips, tea and roasted peanuts or tea and pork scratching, and is it possible to boil an egg in an electric kettle? Tea and bikkies, I think.

He finds a square biscuit tin and struggles to open it. He is holding it upside down and the tinful of biscuits cascades to the floor, leaving JEFF holding the lid.

Fuck.

During the following, he produces the items named and lays them out on the bar counter.

Now what was that trick Keith Waterhouse used to do on the dance floor of the old *Establishment Club* with a biscuit tin lid and what else? A pint glass of water. A matchbox. His right shoe. And a raw egg.

He hobbles round to the front of the bar and, following his own directions, sets up the trick, C, on the floor.

And what you do is you set the biscuit tin lid-side up squarely over the pint glass, so. Then you make a funnel of the matchbox sleeve and you place it on top of the lid, bang in the centre. Then you perch the raw egg on the funnel and what you do then is, you give the biscuit-tin lid such an almighty thwack with the heel of your shoe that it flies off across the room and the egg plops into the glass. Or not, as the case may be. I've never seen the trick done unsuccessfully, but Keith tells me that when it doesn't work it's remarkable how great an area one little egg can splatter. He was in a hotel once in Birmingham for some reason, and doing the egg trick in the residents' lounge for some reason, and there was this young eighteen-year-old snooker champion in the bar, very high on the success he'd just had, so of course, he wanted to do the egg trick and he got Keith to show him how it was done. Then he tried it himself and the egg caused two thousand poundsworth of damage to the décor. And just before he was thrown out of the hotel the young man asked Keith where he'd gone wrong, and Keith said –

WATERHOUSE: I forgot to add that you've got to be at least fifty years old and pissed out of your brains.

JEFF: Well, I'm fifty years old and that's not tonic water I've been drinking all night... *(He positions himself for the egg trick.)* You need a good unsteady hand, Keith says. Here we go. One...two...

He does the egg trick which, it is to be hoped, works. If it does:

I wish I hadn't done that. I hate pub tricks. Next thing you know I'll telling Irish jokes.

If it doesn't work (and the egg should be hard-boiled just in case.):

Sorry about that, Norman. I was just about to scramble an egg for my breakfast when I saw your ugly mug leering at me from the doorway, and it slipped from my nerveless fingers...

He now sets up the ironing board and, during the following, proceeds to iron his clean shirt. Subsequently, he changes his shirt and socks. The set by now should be strewn with his possessions and look as if he has set up home in it.

But if memory serves me right, which it doesn't very often, we were talking about racing. At times, I think it would save me a lot of time and travelling expenses just to get up in the morning, shove fifty quid down the loo and pull the chain. But at other times I like to spin out the agony by going to the races. I once went to an evening meeting at Windsor, got absolutely arseholed, lost every penny in my pocket and had no idea how to get back to London after the last race. I was almost the only person left on the racecourse and, as I stood desolately in the car park, I suddenly saw this beautiful white Rolls Royce heading for the gate. I stood in its way and signalled it to stop. The owner, as suave as any film star, asked –

ROLLS' OWNER: Yes, what can I do for you?

JEFF: I said –

ROLLS' OWNER: *(Amused.)* He said, 'I'm pissed and potless. Please take me to the *Dorchester* immediately and buy me a drink.'

JEFF: I'd never seen him before and I've never seen him since, but he was absolutely charming. He recognized someone who'd done their bollocks and was feeling thirsty. He drove me straight to the American Bar of the *Dorchester* and stood me a huge one. We never introduced ourselves. He just filled me up then gave me my taxi fare back to Soho. And that's typical of what happens at the races. You wouldn't get it in a soccer stadium or at a cricket match. The racing world is stuffed with lunatics, criminals, idiots, charmers, bastards and exceptionally nice people. Like, for instance, Valentine Dyall, the actor – remember the *Man in Black* on radio? – who was responsible for a classic exchange in the Bankruptcy Court.

RECORDER: To what do you attribute your downfall, Mr Dyall?

DYALL: Two and a half mile handicap hurdles, sir.

JEFF: As for my own downfall, I attributed it to my parentage. I was sired by a scenic designer who was himself by a theatrical impresario out of an actress. My dam was an opera singer, who was by an itinerant pork butcher out of a gypsy. My father designed the Lyons Corner Houses, did you know that? And his son washed up in them. He also designed the entrance to the *Strand Palace Hotel* which was so brilliant it's now in the Victoria and Albert Museum. In any other country it'd still be outside the *Strand Palace*. He was an architect – well, he would be, wouldn't he? My mother was very beautiful. And she had style. She was once in court for non-payment of a debt – she must have taken after one of her sons – when she got into a slanging match with one of the lawyers. The judge intervened.

JUDGE: If you continue to speak in that vein, Mrs Bernard, I shall have to commit you for contempt of court.

MRS BERNARD: Make that *utter* contempt.

JEFF: She wanted to turn me into an officer and a gentleman, but at the same time she was throwing occasional cocktail parties for musicians, actors, actresses and similar interesting riff-raff. It didn't take me long to see that they were all getting a little more fun out of life than the Latin master at my prep school, or the local grocer in Holland

Park. At naval college I fell naturally into the company
of secret Gold Flake smokers and cherry-brandy swiggers
who got into trouble, and eventually the officer and
gentleman idea was knocked on the head by my being
asked to leave. The Captain of the college paid me the
greatest backhanded compliment I've ever received.

CAPTAIN: Dear Mrs Bernard, While I consider Jeffrey to be
psychologically unsuitable for public-school life, I believe
he has a great future as a seam bowler.

JEFF: And with that reference I set out on the great journey of
life in search of more trouble. I didn't have to look much
further than the racecourse.

*Changing his socks, JEFF unearths another photograph, of himself
with a trainer.*

(With a reminiscent smile.) Of all the lunatics I've known
in racing, one of the looniest was a brilliant trainer whose
wife had triplets – two boys and a girl. One night, after his
wife and kids had gone to bed, he was downstairs enjoying
a gargle with a merry band of punting-mad Irishmen when
he had a brilliant idea. He crept up to the nursery, came
back with the triplets in his arms, and dumped them in a
row on the sofa.

*THE TRAINER, carrying the babies – represented by dolls wearing
only nappies – enters and arranges them on a sofa.*

TRAINER: All right, gentlemen, now we're going to play Find
the Lady. Watch me shuffle the babies. No bamboozling
or trick babies involved, it is the quickness of the hand
which deceives the eye. Come along, Jeffrey, you look a
sportsman. Place your bet.

JEFF: I'll take a fiver on the middle one.

TRAINER: Jeffrey bets that the lady is the middle one. Is he
right or is he wrong?

He holds the right-hand baby aloft and whips down its nappy.

Sorry, my friend, on this occasion you lose. Now, give the
game another sporting try. Find the Lady. Now you see her

and now you do not. *(Shuffling the babies in the manner of a three-card trickster.)* I switch the babies so, and you place your bet. The quickness of the hand deceives the –

His WIFE appears in her nightdress.

WIFE: Would you put those triplets back where you found them, please?

The TRAINER scoops up two of the babies and she the other one, and he shamefacedly follows her off.

JEFF: The true gambler will, of course, bet on anything and there's no cure. When there's nothing to bet on I sometimes worry quite seriously about going mad. In fact, another winter might do it. The long-range weathermen say the athletes among us will be skating on the Thames come January and you know what that means, don't you? No racing.

CASPAR, with a cat in his arms, passes through the pub.

CASPAR: *(Cryptically.)* Not necessarily.

JEFF: That thin dividing line people are so fond of referring to, the one between sanity and insanity, was breached by that bloke there, and an equally mad bugger known as Tom the copywriter, plus my good self, the last time we had a surfeit of snow and ice. Caspar, his name is. He works, or did work until he was fired for spending too long in the betting shop, in one of the foreign embassies. Not exactly a career diplomat, but what's a career when there's racing at Doncaster.

CASPAR moves out, stroking the cat.

(Confidentially.) Caspar's wife left him after he told her, in a moment of intoxication and great frankness, that in his considered opinion, when it came to who had the strongest hold on his affections, his wife or the great Italian racehorse Ribot, Ribot won by a furlong. So there he was, living all alone in this enormous flat opposite Battersea Park with his two cats, Keir Hardy and George Lansbury –

because he was something of a socialist was Caspar – when it began to piss down with snow.

CASPAR and TOM enter from opposite directions, both reading the 'Sporting Life'.

TOM: Disaster. All racing cancelled.

CASPAR: Not necessarily.

JEFF: For three weeks we fidgeted here in the pub, re-living the glories of our past wins and near misses, nigh desperate for a horse to lose our money on. Then, on the twenty-second day of the great cold spell, Caspar walked in and said –

CASPAR: Who fancies coming racing tonight?

JEFF: Where? Australia or California?

CASPAR: Battersea.

TOM: There's no dog racing at Battersea for a month.

CASPAR: Not dog racing, my friend. Cat racing.

JEFF: *(Narrating.)* When I spoke of going mad, I didn't necessarily mean I would be the first in our little group to crack... *(To CASPAR.)* Cat racing.

CASPAR: Round at my place.

TOM: That'd be a flat race, of course?

CASPAR: Normally yes, but since we're in the middle of the National Hunt season I've had to build a hurdle course. Four jumps, and it's a good forty feet from the starting post at the kitchen end of the passage to the front door. So we get a run for our money.

We are by now transported to CASPAR's flat downstage. The 'course' is assumed to be up the aisle of the auditorium.

JEFF: What are the odds?

CASPAR: Even Keir Hardie, three to one in the field.

TOM: Both are under starter's orders, are they?

CASPAR: Well put it this way, Tom. I haven't fed these cats for two days. Now, I'm going to place a saucer of tinned salmon here by the front door, give them a sniff of it, bring them back to the kitchen and then – they're off!

TOM: But they're not.

CASPAR: Not yet they're not – hold Keir Hardie. It's a seven thirty meeting, isn't it?

JEFF: *(Narrating.)* Course it is – and it's only seven twenty-nine. You've got to do these things right. *(To CASPAR.)* George Lansbury looks a goer. I'll have a pound to win.

CASPAR and TOM are now crouching, holding their imaginary cats.

TOM: The same on this bugger.

CASPAR: And – let him go, Tom – they're off.

JEFF, TOM, and CASPAR watch the race – JEFF in silence, the other two urging the animals on.

TOM: ⎫ Come on, Keir Hardie. Come on – you can do it,
⎬ Keir Hardie – come on, my son!
CASPAR: ⎭ Jump, you bastards, jump!

JEFF: *(Narrating.)* Keir Hardie by three lengths. While he and the runner-up attacked their tinned salmon, Caspar, Tom and I retired to the sitting-room, herein referred to as the Steward's Room, to discuss the next meeting.

TOM: *I've* got a moggy I wouldn't mind entering, Caspar. A little tabby called Samantha.

CASPAR: Ah – a filly.

TOM: Two-year-old.

JEFF: *(To TOM.)* When can I see her gallops?

TOM: Mornings, in the back yard.

JEFF: Form?

TOM: She's never been in a cat race. But with the dog next door behind her, she's a goer.

CASPAR: She's entered.

JEFF: *(Narrating.)* Samantha missed the first race, being delayed on the tube due to incident on line at Earl's Court.

Some poor frozen sod threw himself under the train in a last desperate effort to get warm, I shouldn't wonder. Keir Hardie once again romped it and once again I went down on George Lansbury whose form I was led to believe had improved. I said to Caspar: This is not going to be a bundle of laughs if the favourite's going to win every race.

CASPAR: You're right. When Samantha turns up we'll make it a handicap race.

JEFF: How do you propose to do that?

CASPAR: With the weights off the kitchen scales.

JEFF: Of course. *(Narrating.)* We agreed that if the horses get three pounds for a length then cats should get an ounce for a length. Keir Hardie finished up carrying three ounces, stuck to his back with Sellotape. Then Tom turned up with Samantha, this evil-looking tabby outsider. Samantha was very much on edge and a few years in the racing game have made me easily suspicious. I was even more suspicious when Tom asked, all nonchalant –

TOM: Anyone care to lay four fivers on her?

JEFF: We declined and I had a quid at threes on George Lansbury, who I was convinced was improving with every race.

CASPAR: Under starter's orders.

The three of them crouch with the imaginary cats, releasing them at the cry of:

And they're off!

TOM: *(As a racing commentator.)* And it's Keir Hardie away first followed by Lansbury then Samantha. Samantha taking the lead, over the first hurdle, under the second and it's Samantha way in front and the rest nowhere as Samantha grabs the tinned salmon and tries to hurl herself through the fucking door. What a race! Samantha first, Lansbury second, Keir Hardy still struggling to the post.

CASPAR: Could I have a word with you, Tom?

JEFF: *(Narrating.)* You'd have thought Caspar was Lord Derby, the way he carried on. He actually pulled a red handkerchief out of his pocket, which I correctly guessed to be cat racing's equivalent of the red flag at Newmarket or Epsom, denoting a Steward's Enquiry.

CASPAR: You doped that cat, didn't you, Tom?

TOM: What are you talking about?

CASPAR: Come on, you gave it a Dexedrine or some sort of pep pill, didn't you?

TOM: You'd better watch what you're saying, Caspar. Nobody accuses me of cat-doping.

CASPAR: Well *I'm* accusing you, friend.

TOM: Right. Come outside.

They march angrily out.

JEFF: And that was the end of cat racing. Or was it? A few weeks later, chancing to wake up in Battersea, for reasons now lost in the mists of time, I was walking home through the park when who should I bump into but Caspar.

CASPAR has reappeared, with a pair of binoculars focussed on some distant object.

What are you doing, Caspar?

CASPAR: Cantering Keir Hardie.

JEFF: Oh, yes?

CASPAR: We could be in for a very hot summer. A drought, in fact. In which case, the going could be so hard that racing might be cancelled again. You never know, Jeff.

JEFF: You never do. *(Softly: observing the cat in the distance.)* Just wait till he gets the sun on his back.

Lighting a cigarette and enduring a coughing fit, he crosses to the phone and dials. After listening for a while, he slams down the receiver.

Oh, for God's sake! Talk about waiting for Godot – now the bugger's not there. He must have gone to Smithfield to select the savoury mince. Or New Covent Garden for today's dawn-plucked crop of frozen peas... *(Rubbing his chin.)* I need a shave. If I'd stayed in the French Pub last night, none of this would have happened. But I was driven out of the French Pub, wasn't I, by a man who walked up to me and said –

BORE: D'you remember Peter the Pole who worked in a dirty bookshop in St Anne's Court. You know, the bloke whose father is an ear, nose and throat surgeon in Warsaw? Well anyway, he's just moved to Hounslow.

JEFF: There's no answer to that. Not only do I not know Peter the Pole, have never even heard of him, nor care greatly about how his father scrapes a living, I also have very little time for a man who moves to Hounslow and wouldn't trust him an inch. So I repaired to the Coach and Horses, to ponder the meaning of life and man's incredible ascent from the discovery of fire and the invention of the wheel to the ability to move to Hounslow, who whispered in my ear –

NORMAN'S MOTHER: I bet you didn't know my grandfather had an umbrella shop in Gower Street.

JEFF: Oddly enough the possibility of Norman's mother's grandfather having had an umbrella shop in Gower Street had never crossed my seething brain, although God knows I'm a broad-minded man. Well, after a short but emotional discussion on the subject of the eighteen ninety umbrella boom in Gower Street I felt in need of a strictly medicinal drink, and in the hour or so it took to get served, it suddenly clicked. I was in the middle of some dreadful plot. These mad utterances were codes or ciphers like the Thirty-Nine Steps or the Five Orange Pips or the Dancing Men. Obviously, I was to meet a man with a Polish accent in Housnlow who would give me a message to deliver to an ear, nose and throat specialist in an umbrella shop in Gower Street. Nothing so extraordinary about that after all, is there?

JEFF fishes out an electric razor from his belongings. With it he unearths a dog-eared copy of 'Vogue'.

(Shaving.) Now what the fuck am I doing with last month's 'Vogue'? Perhaps I'm supposed to be writing something for them. Who's in and who's out in the drinking clubs. No Knickers Joyce is in, Herpes Henry is out, in fact barred for life. Or perhaps I'm in it. Jeffrey Bernard seen throwing up over a friend on Ladies' Day at Royal Ascot... Well, the sun ought to be well over the yardarm somewhere in the world by now. Time for a Bloody Mary. *(Mixing it with care.)* The merit of these things is that you can persuade yourself you're having breakfast, and a healthy one at that. Though it's possible to overdo the health angle. A bloke I know had fourteen healthy breakfasts on the trot and what with one thing leading to another didn't arrive home until six the next morning when he was totally legless and bursting for a pee. Falling out of his taxi, he was just about to urinate in desperation against the offside rear wheel, which like all of us he erroneously believed to be legal, when a dear old couple hove into sight very possibly on their way to early morning Mass. Some modicum of decorum prompted our man to do the decent thing and so he zipped up and bounded up the steps to his front door which he attempted to unlock. Unfortunately, his keys not being magnetic, he was unable to make contact. One knows the problem.

Having mixed his Bloody Mary, he now attempts to pick it up but his hand is too shaky. He tries to steady it by gripping his wrist with his other hand.

(Managing the manoeuvre.) Health hint. A good cure for shaky hands: grip the glass very firmly... So, our man can't get his key in the lock and by now he's at wits' end – no great distance to travel. There's only one thing to do. He inserts his member through the letter-box and proceeds to relieve himself. Now. It so happens that at this precise moment his landlord, a naturally angry young man who has been trying to evict our hero for some time, is coming

down the staircase with the not unreasonable intention of taking his dog for a walk. You can imagine his and Fido's bemusement when confronted, not with the terror of a buff envelope thudding through the letter-box, but with our man's cascading member. The hound backed away snarling and steaming, the landlord – one can only imagine – clasped his fluttering heart and our man politely turned his head to say good-morning to the churchgoing pair he'd originally tried to avoid offending. There has to be a moral there somewhere, but I'm damned if I can work out what it is. Cheers.

My own worst experience in the same direction was waking up in the bottom drawer of an Edwardian wardrobe dying to spend a penny. Imagine trying to open a drawer from the inside and you'll appreciate my predicament. But however desperate, I would never have done it through the keyhole. I mean, just imagine – if that dog had been of a more savage disposition. The eyes water just to think about it...

He freshens up his Bloody Mary with another vodka.

I need this, because I'm reluctantly reminded of the man in the paper who chopped off his own chopper and threw it in the fire so he could devote the rest of his life to God without any further distractions. With his wife's blessing, wouldn't you know – they've been discussing it for twelve years. She was probably a *Guardian* reader after her Jill'll Fix It badge. But what I want to know is why did the wretched man pick on his perfectly harmless cock? Surely he must have realized that sex is all in the mind that his dangler was merely his solo instrument in a far bigger concerto than you or I will ever comprehend. I mean, if I wanted to devote the rest of my life to any one thing at all without being distracted I'd cut off my head. And another thing. Why dispose of the blackballed ex-member on the fire? What on earth does he think wastepaper baskets are for? And then of course I can't help wondering what this couple's sex life must have been like during their twelve

years of disarmament talks. Pretty tentative, I should think.
The fact that God didn't intervene in the matter proves
my theory that He is a woman after all – probably another
Guardian reader. And who took the initiative? What a mug!
I mean, it so happens I don't have a wife at the present
moment but if there chanced to be a Mrs Bernard Mark
Five and she took to chatting me up on certain lines, I'd be
more than suspicious.

FIFTH WIFE: So why won't you?

JEFF: Why won't I what?

FIFTH WIFE: Cut it off.

JEFF: Why should I?

FIFTH WIFE: You never do anything for me these days. You
never do the shopping, you won't wash up, you don't ever
bring me a cup of tea in bed. I know you're a lazy, idle,
selfish brute, Jeff, but for heaven's sake – is it such a big
thing?

JEFF: *(Reflecting.)* Not really, no.

FIFTH WIFE: Then cut it off!

JEFF: No.

FIFTH WIFE: Please? Pretty please? For me, darling. Come on
– just be a love and cut it off.

JEFF: *(Narrating again.)* Do you know, there's a possible TV
sitcom in this.

FIFTH WIFE: Then I shall just have to cut it off for you!

JEFF: Or possibly a one-off video nasty. Not, despite these
occasional nightmares, that there's the slightest chance
of there ever being a fifth Mrs Bernard. I've learned
very slowly that for a boozer on my scale, marriage is
impossible. Drink is the other woman. *(Displaying his
shaking hands.)* With the evidence of the affair only too
visible.

A DOCTOR approaches him significantly and helps him into a dressing-gown.

DOCTOR: Come along, Mr Bernard. There's only one place for you.

JEFF suffers himself to be put to bed.

JEFF: At last, after years of trying, I'd finally landed the spring double. Pneumonia *and* pleurisy. So here I was back in the same hospital where I was first shown the yellow card in December nineteen sixty-five. But this was the first time I've ever been in hospital for something that wasn't self-inflicted and that made it seem a little unfair. I mean, they didn't *conscript* kamikaze pilots, did they, Nurse?

NURSE: Eat your mince.

JEFF: They put me in the Ellen Terry Ward just down the corridor from the Alfred Tennyson. The nurses were nice. It's not always the case and some of them can be right nutters, but then look who they've got to contend with. The patients never change. They must be provided by some sort of agency. There's always a Paisley dressing-gown sort of bloke with a jar of Tiptree jam in his locker and trouble with what he calls 'the old waterworks'. There's usually someone dying in a resigned sort of way... Otherwise it's the usual cast – *Sun* readers to a man, they stare vacantly at Hungarian children's cartoons on the box all afternoon, occasionally coughing and farting. And to think that's going to be the curtain-down scene for most of us. And the menu for the last supper will be brown Windsor soup and minced beef with cabbage and boiled potatoes.

A NURSE approaches with a syringe.

NURSE: Just a little prick, Jeffrey.

JEFF: They always say that. It's their joke. Little pricks please little minds, don't they, darling?

NURSE: Eat your prunes.

She injects him. During the following he becomes progressively more tired.

JEFF: Needless to say, in this situation one's thoughts tend to drift towards the Grim Reaper. There's a dreadful fellow in the French Pub who once tried to make a book on who would be next in Soho for the last jump and he made me five to four favourite, so he was pleased to tell me. But the long shots kept coming in and although I'm only too delighted to survive, it's a lousy race to have been entered for. Eva. Frank Norman. John Le Mes. Sean Lynch who ran *Gerry's Club*. Dennis Shaw even. And dear old Jeremy Madden-Simpson, rechristened by Eva Jeremy Madman-Simpleton, certainly won't be walking into the Coach and Horses come opening time. Old? He hadn't turned forty. We first got really friendly after I broke a bone in my right hand on him one night in the French Pub – for what reason neither of us could remember, but he'd say –

JEREMY: But if you can't hit a friend, who can you hit?

JEFF: Once when I was at death's door in this very hospital he used to visit me every evening with a croissant for tomorrow's breakfast. When a piss artist takes time off during licensed hours to visit you then you know you've got a friend. Sometimes, when I wonder whether this interval on earth might just be a bit of nonsense, I think about all those friends who've gone. And the lunchtime sessions in the *Coach* when they were all still here were worth all the trappings of all the success stories you've ever heard, and I'd rather keep down with the likes of Jeremy than up with the Joneses. I do worry about my own wretched mortality, though. Shuffling off this mortal coil it seems as though we're in a queue that's shuffling along towards a sort of bus stop. 'Who's next?' 'No, sorry chum. You was before me.' Maybe the party could go on, though. Different premises and no closing time. A kind of celestial and sterilized *Colony Room Club*...

He has fallen asleep, a lit cigarette inevitably between his fingers.

The DOCTOR enters and shakes him awake.

DOCTOR: Mr Bernard? Mr Bernard! Are you trying to set the hospital on fire?

JEFF: *(Sleepily.)* Just the bed, Doctor. I have no territorial ambitions.

DOCTOR: I'm discharging you, Mr Bernard. But I want you to do nothing at all for the next two or three weeks.

JEFF: That shouldn't be too difficult.

DOCTOR: By which I mean you're to stay at home.

JEFF: Yes, Doctor.

Discarding his dressing-gown, he heads straight for the bar and pours himself a drink.

Home is where the heart is... I wonder if Norman would let me live here – I mean considering I *do* live here he might as well be charging rent. What did once strike me, though, is that I could hang about in the window of the Reject Shop in the Kings Road. I mean I could actually get bought by someone quite nice. I see myself being bought by a tarty blonde who'd show me off to her friends in a sleazy afternoon drinking club in Sheperds Market...

TART: Yes, I bought him in the Reject Shop in Chelsea. Not bad for twenty-five quid, including VAT. He couldn't get it up, mind you, when I first got him home, but it's amazing what a couple of stiff vodkas will do. Have another, ducks.

JEFF: I can think of quite a number of personalities who could further their wilting careers in the Reject Shop. For instance –

The telephone rings shrilly and unexpectedly. JEFF stares at it. As it continues to ring, he approaches the phone warily, then gingerly picks it up.

Coach and Horses?... Norman! What the fuck do you mean, what am I fucking doing here?... How the fuck did you *know* I was fucking here?... Oh, I see... The cleaning lady – no, she's not arrived yet. Any messages?... It's a long story, Norman. No, in fact, it's a short story. I fell asleep in the bog and why the hell don't you call 'Time Gents,

Please' in the gents? I mean I would have thought there'd be some kind of legal requirement under the Landlords' Liability Act. Oh, and talking of the law, Norman, I appear to have caned the best part of a bottle of vodka. Does that count as drinking after hours, I mean given the circumstances? I'll tell you one thing, Norman, the service was a bloody sight faster than it usually is. If you made this Britain's first self-service pub you'd quadruple the takings overnight... Yes, Norman... No, Norman... I owe you for vodka, one tomato juice, a dash of Worcester sauce, one tea bag, a slightly cracked egg, oh, and a tin of biscuits which unfortunately became spilled... What do you mean, what have I been up to all night? I have been sitting here quietly nursing my drink and contemplating the meaning of life. It's all going to change, Norman, starting tomorrow... All right then, if you insist – to-fucking-day. Now how long are you going to be? ... Of course, I won't move until you get here – I'm hardly in a position to move, am I? ... No I won't touch anything, Norman, I'll just get on with my packing... My packing. It's another long story, mate. Just get off your arse and get down here...

He replaces the telephone. During the following he re-packs his scattered belongings.

He's coming. I've never seen Norman at seven in the morning before – it should be a fascinating if grisly sight. Come to that, he's never seen me at seven in the morning. People who say I'm not at my best, though they do generously add that I'm not at my worst, either.

JEFF now picks up the bundle of letters which he tossed down earlier.

(Leafing through them.) Dearest Jeff... Jeff dear... Dear Jeff...

He tosses the letters into his bag one by one as the MISTRESS appears and he hears fragments from the correspondence as it progresses.

MISTRESS: So looking forward to next weekend...

Wasn't last weekend fun...

Still missing you terribly...

So looking forward to Friday...

I waited and waited – where were you?...

We must try harder...

I'm tired of your excuses...

We can't go on like this...

I must have been mad to think it would work...

It's goodbye, Jeffrey. This time I really mean it. You've gone too far.

JEFF: And I make her sick. There's a bloke I know in what's left of Fleet Street who plans to sink his redundancy money in an establishment to be called the *This Time I Really Mean It Hotel*, specially designed for people who've just walked out on, or been walked out on by their spouses. You could check in at any hour of the night without luggage – there'd be a razor, toothbrush and change of clothes on every pillow along with the after-dinner Valium wrapped in tinfoil. And there'd be a twenty-four-hour bar known as the *Gone Too Far Bar* where you could drink yourself silly. And every night they'd have an Unhappy Hour when the drinks would cost double and you could tell the barman your troubles... I wish he'd get on with it – I'd book a permanent suite.

Towards the end of the bundle of letters he finds a dry-cleaning bill.

The things one keeps. An old dry-cleaning bill. To removing tartare sauce from top pocket... *(Screwing the paper up and tossing it away.)* I've no memory of that whatsoever but I do have unhappy memories of tartare sauce in general. I woke up in the *Groucho Club* one day thinking I'd gone blind. I was scared shitless. It turned out I'd been resting my head on a grilled turbot and I had tartare sauce all over my reading glasses...

Now turning up a buff envelope.

This is good. A demand from the Inland Revenue for one thousand seven hundred and sixty pounds. It's to be hoped they're pulling my pisser. One hundred and seventy quid would just about crucify me but one thousand seven hundred and sixty is a joke and utterly beyond me...

There's always suicide, of course. So many of us around here have contemplated it at one time or another that Dave in the French Pub once had the idea of us all hiring a coach and driving it over Beachy Head. Fifty-two seats only. Book now to avoid disappointment.

He has now completed his packing.

I'd better have the one.

As he pours himself a drink, there is a clinking sound from without.

(Looking towards the outer door.) Norman...? No, it's the milkman. Always the signal to the law-abiding citizen to be making tracks home...if he had a home to go to.

He moves back to his belongings and fastens up his suitcase, then sits down, nursing his vodka.

What the hell – this *is* home: – sitting by the bedside of dying Soho holding her hand but wondering wouldn't it be kinder to switch off the life-support system... *(Contemplating his drink.)* What an amazing jemmy to the door of the mind is a few large vodkas...

1ST FRIEND: Let's start a club for people who've been barred from all the others. Instead of throwing members out, we'll throw them in.

1ST GIRL: You don't bring me flowers any more.

2ND FRIEND: Don't worry, Jeff. Give it back to me when you win.

2ND GIRL: Couldn't you have telephoned?

3RD FRIEND: Now if I put you in a cab will you promise not to fall out the other door?

3RD GIRL: You only get out of life what you put into it.

4TH FRIEND: Fancy a spot of cat racing, Jeff?

4TH GIRL: You're a mean, alcoholic, diabetic little prick.

JEFF: And?

4TH GIRL: You make me sick.

JEFF, far away, sits in his chair, smoking.

ELIZABETH SMART appears.

SMART: But you're never snide
   and you never hurt,
   and you wouldn't want to win
   on a doctored beast,
   and, anyway, the least
   of your pleasures
   resides in paltry measures.

   So guard, great joker God, please guard
   this great Bernard...
   Let him be known
   for the prince of men he is,
   a master at taking out of
   himself and us the piss.

JEFF: *(Simply.)* Thank you.

   He stirs as he sees a shadow flit past a window.

   The bugger's here at last.

   He stands, picks up his suitcase and carrier bags, and faces the outer door.

   Come on, Godot...! *(Raising his voice.)* And I meant what I said, Norman! It's all going to change, starting to-fucking-day. It's new leaf time! From now on it'll be gin instead of vodka, Capstan Full Strength instead of Senior Service and the French Pub instead of the Coach and Horses... *(To himself, softly, as a key scrapes in the door lock.)* And life does go on, whatever proof there may be to the contrary. Last week...last week I had an erection. I was so amazed I took its photograph. Life after death! What more do you want? Come on, Norman!

   The outer door opens as –

   the CURTAIN falls.

GOOD GRIEF

A PLAY ADAPTED BY KEITH WATERHOUSE
FROM HIS OWN NOVEL

First performed on a UK tour in 1998, by arrangement with
Theatre Royal Bath Productions and Pericles Productions with
the following cast of characters:

JUNE PEPPER, Penelope Keith
PAULINE, Sarah Berger
THE SUIT, Christopher Godwin
ERIC GRANT, David Firth
BARMAN/TAXI DRIVER/POSTMAN, Christopher Hackett

Directed by Ned Sherrin
Designed by Tim Goodchild
Lighting by Robin Carter
Sound by Tom Lishman

Characters

JUNE PEPPER
the widow of a tabloid editor

PAULINE
aged about 32, her stepdaughter

ERIC GRANT
about 35, a tabloid executive

THE SUIT
mid-40s to early 50s, a new friend

SYNOPSIS OF SCENES

The action takes place in June Pepper's home in the London suburbs and *The Duke of Clarence* pub.

ACT ONE

Scene 1: The house. Late winter.
Scene 2: The house. Morning, a few days later.
Scene 3: The house. A late winter afternoon.
Scene 4: Outside and inside the pub.
Scene 5: The house. Immediately following.
Scene 6: The house. Morning.
Scene 7: Outside and inside the pub. Sunday.
Scene 8: The house. A short while later.

ACT TWO

Scene 1: The house. Early morning.
Scene 2: Outside and inside the pub. Lunchtime.
Scene 3: The house. Morning.
Scene 4: Outside and inside the pub. Lunchtime.
Scene 5: The house. Evening.
Scene 6: The pub. Late evening.
Scene 7: The house. Night.
Scene 8: The house. Evening.
Scene 9: The house and pub. Mid-morning.
Scene 10: The pub. Sunday evening.
Scene 11: The house. Immediately afterwards.

Time
A few months in the present.

The set comprises the living room, open-plan staircase and landing of a much-modernized Edwardian house in the prosperous outer London suburbs.

The action is set in the present, over a period of roughly nine months commencing in late winter and going through spring, summer and autumn. Thus the various scene changes are in fact time jumps, marked by June changing into appropriate costumes up in her room while she continues her linking dialogue.

The scene changes are also punctuated by various snatches from the memorial service at St Bride's, Fleet Street, of her late husband Sam, editor of a national tabloid, from which June is just returning as the curtain rises.

Act One

The living-room, hall, open-plan staircase and landing of JUNE PEPPER's much-modernized Edwardian house in the prosperous outer London suburbs. Another area represents the Duke of Clarence, a local up-market pub. Late winter. Immediately after the memorial service.

Off the landing two adjoining doors lead to JUNE PEPPER's bedroom and the spare bedroom, later to be occupied by her stepdaughter PAULINE.

As the Curtain rises there is a rousing organ voluntary.

JUNE PEPPER, the widow, a no-nonsense northern lady in her early 50s, enters, smartly but not funereally dressed, and carrying the Order of Service which she puts down on her late husband's desk. After a moment she rather self-consciously addresses him, perhaps directing her remarks to a framed photograph.

JUNE: Dear Diary. Got up. Grieved... That what you had in mind, pet? And when to start? You didn't say. As soon as I got back from the hospital? When? Straight after the funeral? I could never have managed that, Sam, too much to do, lad. You wouldn't know, you've never had to organize anything like that. Your mama's funeral, I had it all to do.

PAULINE, her stepdaughter, aged about 32, enters during the following. She too has been to the memorial service. She carries a handbag.

I can hear you now... *(In an approximation of her late husband's voice.)* "Get it bloody done! Don't come running to me over details – I wouldn't know fumed bloody oak from stripped pine." *(She tails off as she realizes PAULINE is there.)*

PAULINE: Are you all right?

JUNE: That's a daft question, Pauline, on a day like this. We've just come back from the memorial service – of course I'm not all right.

PAULINE: You know what I mean, June.

JUNE: I don't know what you mean, no.

PAULINE: You were talking to yourself.

JUNE: No I wasn't. I was talking to your father.

PAULINE: I see. *(She doesn't.)* Would you like another drink?

JUNE: Why not say *yet* another drink and be done with it? Yes. Please.

PAULINE: Vodka again?

JUNE: Again. Yes. Vodka.

PAULINE: You're sure you wouldn't prefer some tea?

JUNE: Vodka.

PAULINE goes reluctantly into the kitchen.

JUNE resumes her conversation with her late husband, Sam.

Anyway, you'll be glad to hear we did it your way. Regrets I've had a few, including going along with you on Frank Sinatra. How many Fleet Street memorial services have we been to where they had 'I Did It My Way'? Not to mention 'Death is nothing at all, I have only slipped into the next room'. Still, originality never was your middle name, was it, pet? You didn't get where you were before you started coughing up blood by being original, did you? The number of times I've heard you say, 'The thought that hasn't already been thunk, isn't worth thinking.' And even that wasn't original, you got it out of a fortune cookie. Still.

PAULINE returns from the kitchen.

PAULINE: There's no vodka in the fridge.

JUNE: No, I don't keep it in the fridge.

PAULINE: But you've always kept it in the fridge.

JUNE: No, your father kept it in the fridge – I prefer my vodka at room temperature.

PAULINE crosses to the drinks trolley.

You won't find it there – it's in the bedroom.

PAULINE: *(With a frown.)* Are you *sure* you're all right, June?

JUNE: I said I wasn't, didn't I?

PAULINE: But will you *be* all right? Should you be lying down? Would you like me to stay over with you while Jack's at his sales conference in Birmingham? Can I get you anything?

JUNE: Yes! You can stop being such a tower of strength and get me a drink!

PAULINE goes upstairs and, with a worried backward glance, goes into JUNE's bedroom.

JUNE resumes her conversation with her late husband.

Do you know what I miss? The office car. You'd think they'd have sent one round, though, on this of all days, wouldn't you? If only out of respect to you, Sam. I don't suppose it crossed anyone's mind. Or if it did, I bet Bob Carp's already on the same cloud nine you were on. You know he's your successor, don't you? Like you he'll believe he only has to think a thing and he doesn't have to put it into words, it gets done. Fleet street. Thank God none of you's running the government.

She glances at the ceiling.

She's moving about up there. She's found the vodka, no problem there, it's on my bedside table, but now she's looking for the brandy – she'll have noticed it was missing from the drinks trolley. *(Calling upstairs.)* You're getting cold – it's in the wardrobe...

During the following, PAULINE descends the stairs carrying a half-empty bottle of vodka and a nearly empty bottle of brandy. She is not privy to JUNE's conversation with Sam – JUNE speaks aloud only when she believes herself to be alone, otherwise it is all in her head. Nevertheless, PAULINE has good reason for giving JUNE a curious look as she very pointedly deposits the brandy bottle on the drinks trolley.

As it happens, what with Pauline's Jack having to be in Birmingham, Bob's sidekick Eric Grant ferried us there and back. Very kind of him to go out of his way, considering you couldn't stand the sight of him.

PAULINE pours a very modest measure of vodka with a good deal of tonic water. JUNE, impatient, reaches vainly for the glass.

PAULINE: Ice?

JUNE: Two lumps.

PAULINE: Cubes. Sugar *lumps* – ice *cubes*.

She carries JUNE's drink off into the kitchen.

JUNE: *(Calling.)* You could have brought the ice to the drink instead of the drink to the ice!

Crossing to the drinks trolley JUNE takes a swift, furtive swig from the vodka bottle.

(Addressing SAM.) It was a very good turnout. Better than some we've been to. Two thirds full, I'd say – more than half, anyway. Lots of old faces. As you'd expect. Tricia was there, obviously. Your brother Derek was ever so funny – he was a sidesman or usher or whatever they call themselves, as he would be. Apparently Tricia trolls into the church, makes a beeline for him and says, 'Which side am I supposed to sit, Derek?' He says, 'It's not a wedding, Tricia, you sit where you like!' She goes, 'But which side is our family and which is hers?' Hers is me, of course. But I mean to say, Sam. Twenty-five years you'd been divorced and she still calls herself your family. In the end she sits next to Pauline across the aisle from me. It went very smoothly, considering. Tommy Little was half-cut, it goes without saying, but you would have him read the Lesson, so there we were. I don't think any of the relatives noticed – they don't, outsiders, do they, they just think he's got a naturally thick voice. Then the readings – I'm afraid your Derek made a complete cock-up of not being dead but only in the next room. Honestly, you'd have thought he was dyslexic. Turns out he's forgotten his reading glasses. Typical.

PAULINE returns with the vodka and tonic.

JUNE almost grabs the vodka and tonic from PAULINE.

PAULINE: I thought I'd make some sandwiches. You ought to eat something, June.

JUNE: I will – later.

PAULINE: There's a chicken roll, Kraft cheese slices, Brussels pâté…

JUNE: I'm aware of the contents of my own fridge, Pauline!

PAULINE: Then you'll be aware that every time you open the fridge door it is scraping a dent in your kitchen wall. As well as grazing the back of my hand.

JUNE: Mine too. It faces the wrong way. Your father was going to fix it but he never got round to it.

PAULINE: So what you would like?

JUNE: I would like, Pauline, for you to stop fussing!

PAULINE: I'll make you a chicken sandwich.

PAULINE makes for the kitchen. JUNE resumes her conversation with Sam.

JUNE: So then we had 'To be a Pilgrim'. You've got some very good voices on that staff of yours – whatever his faults Eric Grant's a lovely baritone, did you know? No, you were never on singalong terms, were you…

PAULINE: *(Turning back.)* White or brown?

JUNE: Whatever there is.

PAULINE goes into the kitchen.

JUNE continues, while topping up her glass with a guilty glance towards the kitchen.

The Address. Charlie Whittington did it, and *he'd* had a few, as well. After saying you didn't suffer fools gladly but that you'd helped many a lame dog over a stile – kicked would have been a better word – he gets going down Back Memory Lane and launches in to the tale about you and him in that hotel in Nottingham when you were both on the road. Yes, that one. Where one of you was peeing in the sink – you always said it was him, but he says it was you – when you lost your balance and brought the fitting down from the wall and flooded the place. Now if he had to tell that story at all in a place of worship he should have left it at that, but no, he has to go into all that stuff about the plug chain getting caught in your zip – I thought he'd never stop. Honestly, you would have thought he'd rented that lectern for the morning.

PAULINE returns from the kitchen.

PAULINE: There's no bread.

JUNE: So there isn't.

PAULINE: Are you eating enough, June?

JUNE: If I've eaten all the bread, I'm obviously eating enough, aren't I?

PAULINE: I could pop out for a loaf – or shall I get you a plate of chicken?

JUNE: I don't want anything, thanks.

PAULINE: I'll do you a plate of chicken.

Heading back from the kitchen, PAULINE glances at JUNE to check she's not looking, and then slyly confiscates the vodka bottle. She goes into the kitchen. During the following she returns with a tray on which there is a cloth, salt and pepper, cutlery, a glass of water and a small salad. This she sets down on a side table.

JUNE: *(Resuming.)* Didn't suffer fools. You were a fool to yourself, Sam. I wish I'd been at that lectern instead of Charlie. I could have said a thing or two. Because do you know what I thought when you went, Sam? I thought, you silly sod. Fifty-three years of age, sixty a day, bottle of Bells a day, and that's only counting what you admitted to, three stone overweight, no exercise. And you were told and told, but you wouldn't *be* told, would you? 'I Did It My Way'. Thank you very much.

PAULINE: You've got some ham, if you'd prefer it.

JUNE: No, thank you.

PAULINE: I'll do both. You've got to keep your strength up, June…

She returns to the kitchen. JUNE, her vodka glass being empty, picks up the glass of water and takes a sip with distaste.

JUNE: *(Calling after PAULINE.)* There's some chardonnay in the fridge! Bottlescrew in the cutlery drawer! *(Addressing SAM.)* Fat chance!… Then after the Reading it was 'Let all the World in Every Corner Sing My God and King' – but bugger me as you would have put it, Sam, if the organist wasn't playing the wrong tune. None of us knew it! I was that cross with myself, it was the one thing I hadn't thought of, to check that we had the traditional hymn tunes and none of these new-fangled arrangements. You'd have been livid – it's a good job you weren't here. Still, we struggled through it, then it was the Blessing, and then out we all troop to the strains of Vera Lynn singing 'We'll Meet Again'. At least *she* got the tune right. Then everyone charged up to El Vino's, shouting 'It's what he would have wanted.'

PAULINE enters with an opened bottle of wine and a glass.

PAULINE: Now if I pour you one glass, will you promise to eat something?

JUNE: When I'm hungry.

PAULINE pours a careful measure.

And it's not a glass, it's half a glass.

PAULINE: *(Clutching the bottle.)* And how many of these are you getting through in a week?

JUNE: *(Ignoring the question, continuing to SAM.)* Then I got to thinking about this diary you want me to keep.

PAULINE: Because there must be a dozen bottles under that kitchen sink. Of course, we don't know how long they've been there.

JUNE: No, we don't, do we?

During the following, PAULINE surreptitiously examines the bottles on the drinks trolley, holding them up to check how full or empty they are.

(As to Sam.) I was going to get one of those big desk diaries from Smith's, but then I thought, hang on a sec, June, he never said anything about writing it down. Because you didn't, did you, Sam? I can remember word for word what you said in between your fits of coughing and spluttering – 'Now listen, girl. Once I'm gone I want you to start keeping a diary. Just let it all pour out, what you're thinking day by day, how you're coping, what it's like to be left on your own, the bloody lot.'

In disapproving triumph, PAULINE finally holds up a near-empty whisky bottle.

PAULINE: *(Accusingly.)* June!

JUNE: Evaporation.

PAULINE: I'll get your food.

PAULINE returns to the kitchen, taking the wine bottle with her.

JUNE: *(Continuing to Sam.)* Then you said, 'Oh, and by the way, this isn't my idea.' No, pet, I didn't think it was. 'No, it was a piece I read in the *The Guardian*, how that bloody woman writer, what's her name, complete pain in the arse, coped with losing her husband. *She* kept a diary. For a wholed year. And that's what I want you to do. Get it out of your system.' But you never said to write it down. So I'll keep it in my head, if you don't mind…though what good it'll do either me or you, God only knows.

PAULINE enters with a plate of chicken and ham. Unseen by JUNE, she stares at her with concern.

I'll tell you when I will give it up, though, and that's if people start noticing my lips moving. I don't want them thinking poor June Pepper's gone round the twist at last.

PAULINE: Your lips are moving.

JUNE: The time to worry is when you see me in the middle of the High Street, directing traffic.

PAULINE: *(Putting the plate on the tray.)* Now I don't want you leaving this, June.

The doorbell rings.

JUNE: That'll be the Oxfam chap – I've been sorting out some of your father's clothes.

PAULINE goes to answer the door.

(Calling after PAULINE.) They're in two tea-chests in the garage, tell him.

The moment PAULINE is in the hall, JUNE leaps to her feet and tips the contents of her plate into a drawer of the desk.

ERIC GRANT, a youngish (35) executive on SAM's paper, is at the front door.

During the following, we can hear the indistinct sound of PAULINE in conversation with ERIC.

(Returning the empty plate to the tray.) And what your Pauline's banging on about I do not know. Eating? I do eat. Do you know that Baskin Robbins across from the health food shop? Very Berry Stawberry, three pounds twenty-five. Comfort eating. But it won't do, Sam. I've gained four pounds since you left us, do you know that? Go on, say it – it's the booze. And it's not only the booze and the Baskin Robbins, it's the chocolate. I'm on Mint Aero at present, just the one bar a day. No, because I was determined to get myself off Rolo, they're habit forming if you ask me anything, and I thought the bubbles in Aero have got to mean it's less fattening. But now I'm hooked. Booze, chocolate and Very Berry Strawberry. They never said death was addictive.

ERIC, a snappy dresser with a foxy expression, now enters the room with PAULINE, who now carries a copy of the Order of Service.

PAULINE: I've talked Eric into coming in for a drink.

JUNE: *(Coldly.)* There's brandy, scotch, gin, sherry – or there's vodka in the kitchen, probably behind the gas cooker.

ERIC: Just something soft. I'm driving, remember.

PAULINE: *(Pouring a mineral water; to JUNE.)* Eric thought you'd left your Order of Service in his glove compartment.

JUNE: As if I'd do such a thing!

PAULINE: It must be mine, then. I thought it was in my handbag.

JUNE somewhat detaches herself from her guests as she addresses her late husband. While PAULINE and ERIC cannot hear what JUNE is saying, they are aware that she has gone into a reverie.

JUNE: That Order of Service never left my hands, Sam, and I was careful to keep it pristine, no folds or creases and no wine glass stains. It goes with the obituaries I clipped out – the *Telegraph* did you proud, then column inches: 'He was a larger than life figure, perhaps the last of the Fleet Street buccaneers...' I wonder who wrote it. Charlie, most likely. Larger than life, what does it mean? Shouting a lot and getting pissed every night...

ERIC: Is she all right?

PAULINE: Well she *says* she is.

JUNE: I said no such thing – I said I wasn't.

ERIC: *(Regarding the empty plate.)* At least she's got her appetite back. She ate nothing at El Vino's.

PAULINE: *(Accusingly at JUNE, picking up the empty plate.)* June! *(To ERIC.)* She's hidden it!

JUNE: Who's 'she' – the cat's mother? Why don't we have a game of hide and seek – you look for the chicken and ham and I'll look for the vodka.

ERIC: Actually, June, I should be on my way in a minute. Would you like a lift, Pauline, or are you staying on?

PAULINE: Ready when you are, Eric, if it's not taking you out of your way.

During the following, ERIC and PAULINE start preparing to leave.

JUNE: *(As to SAM.)* But of course it's taking him out of his way! And that's twice in one day! There's something going on here, Sam, mark my words. Or is there? You go looking for mischief in widowhood, I'm finding it. It gives you something to do.

Again ERIC and PAULINE notice that she is in a reverie.

ERIC: Now are you sure you'll be all right, June? Left here on your own?

JUNE: Oh, I'm not on my own, Eric.

ERIC: *(Uneasily.)* No…in a sense, no… It's going to be bit big for you now, this place, isn't it, June? A bit empty? Pity the property market's not more buoyant.

JUNE: *(As to Sam.)* What a gloompot he is. *(To ERIC.)* It's no bigger now than it was with just the two of us here, and as for empty, Sam was more often out of the house than in it, as you'd know more than most, Eric, being as you were supposed to be his night editor.

ERIC: *(With a little hurt laugh.)* Supposed to be, June? Oh, I wouldn't say that. Compared with some editors I've known, Sam usually got himself off in very short order. No, he wasn't one for breathing down our necks, June.

JUNE: But I know very well that he was, Eric. Once he was installed in that office it was like prising barnacles off a ship's bottom, trying to get him out of it. He was never back before midnight.

ERIC: Ah, now I'm not saying he came straight home, June.

JUNE: *(Sharply.)* Then *what* are you saying?

ERIC: Nothing at all, June. Just that when the day's work was done he liked to have a jar with his particular cronies.

JUNE: Yes – in his office. Like King's Cross Station, that office was – while yours, I've heard him say, was like the Tomb of the Unknown Warrior.

PAULINE: *(Hastily intervening.)* Now can I make you some tea before we go?

JUNE: Pauline, when I want some tea I'm quite capable of making it myself. It's a bereavement I've suffered, not a stroke.

ERIC: Is there anything else we can do? Anything at all? Anything you want, anything you need, anything we can get you, anything we can do for you?

JUNE now ushers them towards the front door.

JUNE: Nothing at all, thanks. Now off you go, or you'll be running into the rush hour.

PAULINE: I'll drop round again.

ERIC: Don't forget, June – anything at all, give us a ring…

ERIC and PAULINE go.

During the following, JUNE opens the drawer in which she has deposited the ham and chicken. She takes out the file of papers on which the food has landed and tips it back on to the plate. She picks up the tray.

JUNE: What's Eric's game, eh? Just what is he driving at – do you know, Sam? Or is paranoia another of the side effects of grieving?

She carries the tray through into the kitchen.

We hear a snatch of 'Let All the Word in Every Corner Sing' from the memorial service as the light darkens into evening and the kitchen light is switched on.

JUNE, a little unsteady on her feet, returns, clutching the now nearly empty vodka bottle and a glass. She switches on the light and drains the bottle into the glass.

It's gone down like lemonade, has this. Reaction, I expect, after the memorial service. I hadn't realized how tensed up I've been, wanting it all to go off all right, thinking what kind of fools we should both look if hardly anyone turned up. But it's got to stop, lad, now it's over and done with. The parade's gone by, eh? Until today I've had to look forward to. Yes, look forward to. I suppose some folk dread it, but not me. It was – how can I say this without sounding… It was my due, Sam. Look at it this way – it isn't everyone merits a memorial service, not even in Fleet Street where there's some would turn out to bury the office cat so long as there was a drink in it. But we did you proud,

Sam. I was going to say I wish you'd been there but of course you were there, all through the service, still making the arrangements, still stage-managing. Because when they put on 'My Way' I wasn't hearing Sinatra, I was hearing you saying, 'Of course the bloody rector won't mind, why should he. Bloody hell, woman, when we saw off Ted Rawcliffe from the *Express* they had "The Teddy Bears" Picnic'! Because all through the service and in all the days leading up to it I could hear your voice dictating how it was going to go and what had to be done, and that kept you alive for me, Sam, do you know what I mean?

She drains her glass, switches on the landing light and switches off the living-room light. Then she begins to move slowly upstairs.

And you didn't die in that hospital and you didn't die at the funeral, you didn't die until right at the end of your memorial service when the rector gave the Blessing and they all waited for me to walk up the aisle like some raddled old bride before filing out of the church and up the pub. The Grace of our Lord Jesus Christ be with us all evermore, and then you were gone. G'night, Sam.

She is at the door of her bedroom. She enters the room, switches off the landing light and closes the door.

We resume the memorial service congregation singing 'Let All the World in Every Corner Sing.'

SCENE 2

The same. Morning, a few days later.

As the Lights come up the hymn fades.

JUNE, dressed for the day and clutching a toothbrush, appears at the door of bedroom.

JUNE: I've bought a new toothbrush. A green one, the first green one I've had for years and years and years. It's always been blue for me, red for you. We were colour-coded. No need to bother now. Bar giving your clothes to Oxfam, it's the first thing of yours I've thrown out, your toothbrush. I just couldn't bear facing it in the tooth mug each morning and night – but then I couldn't bring myself to toss it in the bin. In the end I slung both our old toothbrushes out together. You've got to start somewhere, rebuilding your life. If that's what I'm supposed to be doing.

Discarding the toothbrush, JUNE comes downstairs to a choral rendering of 'Jesu, Joy of Man's Desiring.'

SCENE 3

The same. A late winter afternoon.

As the Lights come up the choir fades.

JUNE does some tidying up during the following.

JUNE: True to her word, your Pauline keeps dropping in. Would I like any shopping done, can she make some tea? She's getting to be a right little meals on wheels. Do I want any soup heating up? You'd think I needed nourishment. What is it with being widowed – do we look as if our little legs want building up? *(With a chuckle.)* Which reminds me, Sam – I had to go to the medical practice yesterday – did I tell you? The health centre, whatever it calls itself...

PAULINE, wearing her outdoor coat, comes through from the kitchen with two bowls of soup on a tray.

PAULINE: What was that again?

JUNE: *(Drawing her into the conversation.)* The health centre. That Dr Colefield's gone, did you know? It was a Dr Shilholm who saw me, silly cat that she was.

PAULINE: I've never used the health centre, I have my own doctor.

JUNE: She says, 'Yes, I know all about you, Mrs Pepper, I'm putting you on Prozac.'

PAULINE: *(Setting a bowl of soup before her.)* It's carrot, is that all right?

JUNE: I says, 'You're what, doctor?' She says, 'I'm prescribing Prozac, I'm surprised you're not on it already.'

PAULINE: I'm surprised myself, though I suppose they had their reasons.

JUNE: She says, 'Though I'm sure Dr Colefield had her reasons – do you have a heart condition that I wouldn't know about?'

PAULINE: It would have been in your notes, June. But there's a lot to be said for Prozac.

JUNE: I says, 'What do I want with Prozac, that's the so-called happy pill, isn't it?' She says, 'Well, that's what the gutter press call it, but it's to handle depression, really.'

PAULINE: Which it is. Would you say I've over-peppered this soup?

JUNE: I says. 'Yes, I know all about it, my late husband ran a big series about it in his newspaper.'

PAULINE: I remember it. June – have you started clearing up yet?

JUNE: Clearing up?

PAULINE: After my dad.

JUNE: Clearing up after him? He's dead, Pauline. Cremated. There's not much left of him to clear up.

PAULINE: I mean his things.

JUNE: I know you do – it's just me.

PAULINE: His possessions.

JUNE: His effects, as the hospital calls them. Anything of your dad's you want to take, Pauline, you're welcome to look around.

PAULINE: I might just do that, one day.

JUNE: But getting back to this doctor, I says, 'I'm very sorry, Dr Shilholm, I am not suffering from depression.'

PAULINE: You don't know that, June.

JUNE: She says, 'You'll excuse me, Mrs Pepper, but you don't know what you might be suffering from. Now Dr Colefield had you on tranquilizers, didn't she?'

PAULINE: Which ones?

JUNE: I couldn't tell you which ones, because they finished up down the loo.

PAULINE: You should pay more attention to your doctors, June. They know what's good for you.

JUNE: She says, 'And did Dr Colefield ever discuss grief counseling I says, 'She tried to. Once.'

PAULINE: As it happens, I know someone who's done a course in grief counseling. There's a lot in it, June, believe me. I could bring her round for coffee.

JUNE: Don't you dare.

PAULINE: But you won't mind me coming round? To look through –

JUNE: His effects. Not at all.

PAULINE: When convenient. You couldn't let me have a front door key, could you?

JUNE: *(As to Sam.)* She's a cheeky cat! *(To PAULINE.)* I don't think so. I don't have a spare.

PAULINE: What about Dad's key? In the effects?

JUNE: Stop pressurizing me, Pauline! What do you want it for, anyway? What are you looking for?

PAULINE: You *should* be on something, June.

JUNE: I should not!

PAULINE: You're edgy.

JUNE: I am not edgy. *(As to Sam.)* Am I edgy?

PAULINE: Why did you go to the doctor's in the first place, then?

JUNE: I'm about to tell you, Pauline! She says, 'I'm giving you a leaflet, with a twenty-four-hour helpline number you can ring, it's entirely up to you.' And she says, 'I'm going to give you a prescription, and I want you to come back in four weeks.'

PAULINE: Have you done with your soup?

JUNE: I says, 'Well, doctor, I knew Prozac was the latest miracle drug, but I can't see it doing much for my ingrowing toenail!' *(A triumphant cackle.)*

PAULINE: I'll take these through.

She takes the soup bowls into the kitchen.

JUNE: I felt much better for that... She doesn't have much of a sense of humour, your Pauline, does she?

She follows PAULINE into the kitchen.

Continue the choir rendering of 'Jesu, Joy of Man's Desiring.'

SCENE 4

Outside and inside the pub.

The Lights come up and the singing fades.

A man in his mid-to-late forties wearing an ill-fitting grey check suit and with a newspaper under his arm, crosses slowly on his way to the pub, looking in (imaginary) shop windows en route. His name is Douglas, but he will be known to JUNE always as THE SUIT.

JUNE herself, now wearing outdoor clothes and carrying a shopping bag, enters from the same direction. She takes in the back view of THE SUIT and reacts in surprise.

JUNE: *(As to Sam.)* I'd ever such a shock a few days ago. I'd just come out of the Minimart when who should I see but you. No, I know it wasn't really you, you silly article, but at first glance, from the back, he looked like you – although thinner, which doesn't take a lot of doing. So much so that I galloped along to where he was looking in a shop window so I could study his face.

She does just that.

THE SUIT, nonplussed by this total stranger craning her neck to gaze at him, moves off and saunters away.

And of course he looked nothing like you. But he was wearing one of your suits. That light grey check job you had to buy after that pissed MP knocked a bottle of red wine over your jacket at the Tory party Conference. Or was it Labour? Anyway, considering you bought it up in Blackpool it isn't a bad suit. He shows good taste. It didn't fit him, but then it didn't fit you either. Not after you put on all that weight.

Now, carrying half a pint of beer, THE SUIT sits at the pub table and reads his newspaper.

And after that, I've kept on bumping into him. I've been on the verge of speaking to him once or twice. I've felt like saying, 'Excuse me, but that's my husband's suit you're wearing, do you like it?' But who wants to be reminded he's wearing charity clothes? He'd have thought I was barmy.

With a deep breath, JUNE plucks up the courage to pursue THE SUIT into the pub. Carrying a glass of Guinness, she crosses to his table, where he is rubbing at a Lottery scratch card.

Excuse me, if anybody sitting here?

THE SUIT: Not unless it's the Invisible Man!

JUNE: *(As to Sam, sitting.)* You laugh, don't you, even when you've heard the joke a thousand times.

THE SUIT looks at his scratch card and discards it.

THE SUIT: Do you ever have any luck with these things, because I'm sure I don't. Complete waste of money so far.

JUNE: *(As to Sam.)* So there he is, Sam, sitting in your suit that he's bought from Oxfam, nursing half a pint when everyone around him's on pints, empty packet of ten in front of him but no dog ends in the ashtray, and he's moaning about having just lost a pound. I didn't have to be one of your crack reporters to work out that he has count the pennies. *(To THE SUIT.)* I'll tell you what *is* a waste of money. The Minimart only selling their cinnamon crumpets in packets of twelve. Because if you're on your ownsome they go stale.

THE SUIT: You don't have to tell me. It's the same with their individual bannans – they have them all done up in plastic bags now.

JUNE: Same thing. They'll only sell them in dozens.

THE SUIT: Tens, actually. They've metricated their bananas.

JUNE: *(As to Sam.)* So then I knew he was on his ownsome too. Turns out he's divorced, has been for two years, his wife ran off with his best friend, or who he thought was his best friend until that fateful moment. Duggie it seems his name is – though Duggie what I didn't catch. It doesn't matter, I shall always think of him as The Suit. *(Rising, to THE SUIT as she picks up her empty glass.)* Can I get you one while I'm up?

THE SUIT: *(Unconvincingly.)* Oh, no, thanks very much, I'm not half-way through this one yet.

JUNE: Go on – by the time I've fought my way through to the bar you'll have finished it.

THE SUIT: Well, that's very kind of you, I'll consider my arm twisted.

JUNE: *(As to Sam, moving off.)* Of course, he could have said, 'No, sit down, let me, I'll get them.' But he didn't. He probably doesn't have two halfpennies left to scratch his bum with, as we used to say.

JUNE moves off.

THE SUIT drains his glass and self-consciously straightens his tie.

JUNE, waiting to be served, momentarily appears.

He lives in that little block of flats over The Parade, which is why I've kept seeing him round here. And the only other thing I know is he worked for a building society, something managerial although he was nowhere near being top dog, more bottom dog I should imagine, and he was made redundant when they merged with some other building table.

JUNE moves off and then reappears with a half-pint of beer and a glass of Guinness.

(Carrying over the drinks.) So what are you doing now, Duggie?

THE SUIT: Looking around, as they say. By the way, what we were saying about cinnamon crumpets and individual bananas equally applies to their blueberry muffins...

JUNE: *(As to Sam.)* And that was that, Sam. We had our drink, we had our chat, and because I thought he might be embarrassed wriggling out of getting another round in if he hadn't the wherewithal, I got up and said – *(Rising, to THE SUIT.)* 'Well, it's been very nice talking to you but it's high time I wasn't here – I've got a lot to get through today.' *(As to Sam.)* Which is true – getting those piles of books you had stacked all over the house sorted out. All those review copies you'd fetch home and never read but wouldn't let me give away.

THE SUIT: *(Rising.)* I should be making tracks too.

JUNE: *(As to Sam.)* Where he should be making them to he didn't say. Nowhere in particular, I shouldn't wonder. He looked lost. *(To THE SUIT.)* If you don't mind my saying so, that's a very nice suit you're wearing. It's a very good piece of cloth – could I ask you where you got it?

THE SUIT: Oh, that Oxfam shop on the corner of Chapel Street – you can get some very good stuff there, real bargains.

JUNE: *(As to Sam.)* Now if he'd said, Oh, Marks and Spencer's, or Oh, Burton's, I should have left it at that. But as he came right out with Oxfam I could see no harm in saying – *(To THE SUIT.)* Yes, I thought so – it used to belong to my late husband.

THE SUIT: *(After an embarrassed pause and with a nervous snigger.)* I wish you hadn't told me that.

JUNE: Why? It's nothing to be ashamed of. People do die, and their clothes have got to go somewhere. I'm glad you bought it – it suits you.

THE SUIT: Well, I did need something for everyday wear, and I've often fancied a check but I can never find anything approaching my size round here, let alone anything I really want, so of course when I noticed this suit in the window…

JUNE: *(As to Sam.)* He was just burbling, till he screwed up the courage to say what he'd got to say.

THE SUIT: If you don't mind me asking, what did he die of?

JUNE: *(With a giggle.)* Nothing contagious, if that's what's worrying you. If you must know, it was what he always used to call the Big C. Or the dread lurgy. So it was nothing catching.

THE SUIT: Thank you, I hope you didn't mind me asking. Only I must say, and don't take this the wrong way, I do wish you hadn't told me.

JUNE: What do you mean? You just asked me.

THE SUIT: No, I mean that he was dead. Your late husband. It feels – how shall I put this? – a bit spooky. Dead men's shoes.

During the following, they move outside the pub.

JUNE: *(As to Sam.)* I could have taken offence at that but I didn't – he meant no harm. *(To THE SUIT, glancing down at his scuffed suede shoes.)* You should have treated yourself to a pair of dead men's shoes while you were about it, because I sent six pairs down there.

PAULINE enters purposefully, then falters as she sees JUNE talking to a strange man. She pretends to be looking in a shop window while glancing covertly at the pair.

THE SUIT: I did try on one or two but I couldn't find anything in my size.

JUNE: He was a size nine, broad fitting.

THE SUIT: I'm an eight and a half.

JUNE: *(By now she has noticed PAULINE.)* Well, nice talking to you.

THE SUIT: You too. I hope we bump into one another again some time.

THE SUIT moves off, passing PAULINE.

PAULINE stares after him.

JUNE: *(As to Sam, with a nod at PAULINE.)* What's the betting she'll be round before the day's out?

As JUNE moves off we hear the memorial service congregation singing 'Fight the Good Fight.'

SCENE 5

The house. Almost immediately afterwards.

JUNE, now minus her outdoor coat, enters from the kitchen, clutching a large vodka and tonic.

JUNE: And I was right. I wasn't wrong. Just as I'm settling down to watch Gina Lollobrigida in *Go Naked Into The World* as a good way of not having to sort all those books out for a while longer, who should troll up the garden path but you know who.

The doorbell rings. JUNE takes a swig of her vodka, then tips the rest into a plantpot. Crossing to answer the front door, she rehearses her conversation with PAULINE.

No, I'm not neglecting myself, Pauline, yes, I have had a proper lunch, no, I'm not caning the vodka at this time of day, now what else do you want to know?

PAULINE sweeps into the room.

PAULINE: Who is he, what does he do, and where did you find him?

JUNE: Who do you mean by he?

PAULINE: You know very well who, June – him that you were chatting up outside that public house. I just happened to be walking along the street when you came out.

JUNE: Yes, we know you did, Pauline, and I saw you just happening to watch us and wishing you could lip-read. If it's any of your business, he's a gentleman I *just happened* to call in for a half of Guinness.

PAULINE: It's not like you to go pubbing of a lunch-time, June. At least I'm sure you never did when Dad was here. Are you sure it was only Guinness?

JUNE: Excuse me, Pauline, but it's nothing to do with you whether it was Guinness, rum, lager, brandy or what it was. And another thing – it's none of your business where I go or when I go or who I'm with. I don't want to sound rude, Pauline, but can we just be clear about that and leave it?

PAULINE: I'm sorry, June. I didn't mean to intrude, but can you tell me one thing? How does he come to be wearing Dad's suit?

JUNE: Who says he was wearing your father's suit?

PAULINE: Well if he wasn't, it was one very like it.

JUNE: Oxfam.

PAULINE: And then you just happened to come across him wearing it.

JUNE: That's right.

PAULINE: Quite a coincidence.

JUNE: There was no coincidence about it. If you'd seen your father's suit going into a pub, maybe you'd have gone in after it too.

PAULINE: Oh, so you're admitting you followed him?

JUNE: I'm saying nothing more, Pauline. Now can we just drop it, once and for all?

PAULINE: I'll put the kettle on.

JUNE: It's on.

PAULINE: Then I'll make some tea.

Picking up JUNE's empty glass and sniffing it suspiciously, she goes into the kitchen.

JUNE: Honestly, Sam! Is that what it's all about, then, being in mourning? The corners they push you into! Having to be careful who you're seen with, having to hide your vodka glass *(She notices that her vodka glass is gone.)*, having to justify your behavior. I mean to say, here you are, Sam, not cold in your grave – well, you're not in a grave, you're in an urn, but you know what I mean – and already I'm having to put up with these sly innuendos from your own daughter.

PAULINE returns from the kitchen, carrying the tea things on a tray.

PAULINE: I'm sorry if I got you all upset, June, but none of that was what I came round about.

JUNE: *(As to Sam.)* She could have fooled me.

PAULINE: You might as well hear it from me before you hear it from everybody else. I'm, thinking of leaving Jack.

JUNE: *(Flatly.)* Oh dear. *(As to Sam.)* I was furious. I thought. That's your problem, sweetheart. At least you've still got a husband to leave. *(To PAULINE.)* So what's triggered this off, then?

PAULINE: The usual story. Bit of spare at the office.

JUNE: Oh, I am sorry. How long has it been going on? *(As to Sam.)* Why do we ask these questions?

PAULINE: The usual way, these days, so I'm told, June. Itemized phone bill. He's been ringing her every chance he got, four or five times a day sometimes, every time I was out of the house.

PAULINE pours the tea during the following soliloquy to SAM.

JUNE: Silly sod. They never learn. I mean he works with the woman, and anyway if he does have to ring her up what does he imagine phone boxes are for? With you, of course, it would have been your office mobile, crafty bugger that you are. Were. Not that you were ever much of a womanizer, were you? Too fat, too pissed, too bone idle. I know that from when *I* was the other woman. It was me that had to do the chasing. But if it isn't a woman, what is it? Because it keeps on nagging away at me that there's got to be something, some guilty secret. I know very well that's why I keep on turning out cupboards and emptying drawers of your old pill bottles and cheque stubs and God knows what else, as if death was the occasion for a spot of spring cleaning. I'm looking for something, aren't I? Skeletons.

PAULINE: Biscuit?

JUNE: *(Shaking her head.)* So what are you going to do then, Pauline? Is it the big showdown, the big ultimatum, or what?

PAULINE: Oh, no, June, we've been through that stage, ten times over. I would have told you before but you'd enough on your plate with Dad. It's a case of him wanting his cake and eating it – he swears blind he's going to stop seeing her but then he says he's got to take her out for one more lunch so he can tell her properly. *(Tearfully.)* I mean would you stand for that, June?

JUNE: *(As to Sam.)* If there's a God up there with you, Sam, will you plead with him not to let her turn on the waterworks?

PAULINE: *(In tears.)* Do you know what I can't get over, June? Do you remember the day of Dad's memorial service?

JUNE: *(Sharply.)* No, Pauline, it's gone clean out of my mind.

PAULINE: I'm sorry, June, you know what I mean. Well, you remember he couldn't get to the service because he had to be in Birmingham? He was with her. I found the bill. Mr and Mrs.

JUNE: *(As to Sam.)* That's what we get, for going through pockets.

PAULINE: How could he, June, on that day of all days? I mean imagine, the planning that must have gone into that, while you were planning the memorial service, the scheming bastard. Doesn't it just make you sick?

JUNE: *(With a shrug.)* At least he turned up for the funeral.

PAULINE: How can you be so forgiving, June? Because I know I'll never forgive him, never.

JUNE: *(Stifling a yawn.)* So how have you left it, then?

PAULINE: I shall go round to see her.

JUNE: Why – to see what she looks like, or to scratch her eyes out, or what?

PAULINE: To tell her to leave my husband alone, June. Because if she doesn't, she can have him, and I do mean that.

JUNE: And does that mean you'd leave him or that you'd throw him out, which would it be?

PAULINE: Oh, I should be the one to leave, June – make a clean break of it. Because if I stayed in that flat I know what would happen – he'd be round after a fortnight begging me to take him back, and then it'd all start again. No, it'll be me that packs my suitcases, and we can work out the finances with the divorce.

JUNE: *(As to Sam.)* Oh, my godfathers – you know what she's leading up to, don't you? She wants to move in with me.

Rising with a falsely winning smile, she removes PAULINE's teacup from her grasp.

Well, I'm sorry to rush you, Pauline.

PAULINE: *(Confused.)* What?

JUNE: I'm expecting the damp-proof specialists in to look at the spare bedroom. Because talk about condensation, it's like Lake Geneva in there.

PAULINE, rising, finds herself being ushered to the front door.

PAULINE: Sorry to moan and groan at you, June.

JUNE: My pleasure. I hope you work something out, the pair of you.

PAULINE: I'll keep in touch.

JUNE: I'm sure you will.

PAULINE goes.

Closing the door on PAULINE, JUNE, returns to the living-room in relief.

(Stacking the things back on the tray.) I'll get those books of yours sorted out. The rubbish I've unearthed already, though. Michael Dukakis, *The Man Who Would Be President*. What were you hanging on to that for – did you think he'd make a come-back? I'll get them boxed up and send them back to the office.

JUNE carries the tray into the kitchen.

The Lights fade. We hear the congregation singing 'The Lord's My Shepherd'.

SCENE 6

The same. Morning.

The Lights come up and the singing fades.

JUNE, wearing a house coat, emerges from her bedroom on to the landing. She carries a duster.

JUNE: *(As to Sam.)* My aching back, what with all this bending and stooping! Do you know what, Sam? Clearing up after the dead is worse than clearing up after a party. But what do I think I'm doing, Sam? Am I trying to exorcise you or what? And answer came there none. Death is nothing at all, I have only slipped into the next room. But there's no one in the next room, that's the trouble.

JUNE goes into the kitchen.

In JUNE's absensce, ERIC noses around SAM's desk, opening drawers, picking up letters and holding them up to the light, and revealing a generally snoopy nature. JUNE returns with the coffee things.

(Pouring coffee.) So what's this something or nothing you wanted to have a word about?

ERIC: All in good time, June. How's Pauline? *(He sits.)*

JUNE: Very well, so far as I know. *(As to Sam.)* I could have shook him.

ERIC: Very nice coffee. What blend is it?

JUNE: St Michael Medium Roast, decaffeinated. Sam always liked it, he wouldn't have any other kind. But in all these years I never told him it was decaff, because he wouldn't have drunk it. *(As to Sam.)* And you wouldn't, would you, stubborn pig that you are?

ERIC: Do you miss him?

JUNE: Yes, of course I miss him.

ERIC: But you'll have got over the worst of it by now?

JUNE: How do you mean, get over it? It's not like measles, Eric, it's something you have to live with.

ERIC: *(With a doleful nod.)* He's much missed at the paper, you know. He's often talked about.

JUNE: Oh, yes – who talks about him, for instance?

ERIC: We all do – some more than others. I wish I could have got closer to Sam, you know, June.

JUNE: Well, he was always approachable.

ERIC: To some, yes.

JUNE: *(As to Sam.)* Is he just insensitive, or what?

ERIC: Now don't get me wrong, June. No-one had more respect for Sam than me. But if you don't know anything about how he used to run the paper, it can't be denied that he did have his coterie, and unfortunately I wasn't one of their number.

JUNE: That I wouldn't know, because Sam didn't bring his work home with him. But if you weren't one of his closer circle I'm sure he had his reasons.

ERIC: I'm sure he did, June, I'm sure he did.

JUNE: Just what is it you're driving at, Eric?

ERIC: Only that Sam was playing favourites. He was blind to the present Editor's faults and blind to my virtues.

JUNE: Right. Now I can see what's upsetting you, Eric, but I'm not having you coming here and upsetting me, because

I'm not up to dealing with it. And now I'd be glad if you'd please go.

ERIC: *(Rising.)* I'm sorry, June, I'm afraid I'm out of order.

JUNE: You are out of order.

ERIC: It's just that –

JUNE: It's just nothing, Eric, now leave it. And you yourself, I want *you* to leave. Thank you for picking up the books. They're in the garage in black plastic sacks.

ERIC: I'll get them in the boot.

JUNE: You said you'd been wanting to have a word with me. That was it, was it?

ERIC: *(Slapping his forehead.)* Thank goodness you reminded me, June, it had gone clean out of my head. The letters!

JUNE: What letters, what are you talking about, letters?

ERIC: First can we get one thing straight, June – I didn't come here to slag off Sam – that was just something I had to get off my chest and I see now it wasn't the right time.

JUNE: Eric, what are these letters?

ERIC: *(Taking his time.)* Well, I don't know whether you remember, no reason why you should, but way back when Sam worked out in the newsroom he had a locker, as we all did.

JUNE: *(As to Sam.)* I'll strangle him, I will.

ERIC: Only we've just taken on a new chief sub, Tom Stanton from the *Sun*, don't think you know him, and he was looking for somewhere to put his gear.

JUNE: Can we get on with it, Eric? You'll be late for work at the rate you're spinning it out.

ERIC: So. We get security to open Sam's old locker, and of course, there's still some of his things there.

JUNE: *(Sharply.)* What things?

ERIC: Nothing much, June, few bits and pieces. Couple of paperbacks, empty Bell's bottle, three or four packets of

Silk Cut, gone dry by now I should think. And this bundle of letters.

JUNE: Yes?

ERIC: Tied up with blue ribbon.

JUNE: *(As to Sam.)* So this is it, is it? The skeleton. What we've been waiting for. The Big One. *(Calmly, to ERIC.)* Do you think you should be telling me this, Eric?

ERIC looks elaborately blank-faced, then makes a great show of the penny dropping.

ERIC: Oh, there's nothing to get yourself het up about, June, nothing at all. I can see the way your mind's working, but I can promise you they're not what you're thinking. Not that anybody's read them, of course.

JUNE: Oh, no, of course not, it's never even crossed their seething minds. What – bundle of letters tied up with ribbon, newsroom full of slavering tabloid hacks, and nobody thinks to open them? Perish the thought.

ERIC: But going by the childish writing on the envelopes, I'd say they were from a little girl, and going by the postmark I'd say that little girl was Pauline, when she was about what – eight? Nine?

JUNE: *(As to Sam.)* Or at least we hope they're from Pauline. If not, Sammy lad, you're in big trouble. *(Angrily, to ERIC.)* And couldn't you have told me that straight away, instead of coming round here playing cat and mouse games?

ERIC: I don't know what you mean, June.

JUNE: You know very well what I mean. So where is this bundle of letters, then?

ERIC: Locked in my office, just at present. I wasn't at all sure you'd want to see them – some things can bring back painful memories.

JUNE: For once in your life you've got something right, Eric. I do not want to see them, they're not mine to see. But I'm sure Pauline would like to have them.

ERIC: *(Cryptically.)* Ah, but we don't know that for sure, June.

JUNE: *(As to Sam.)* He has read those letters, I know he has.
And there's something in those letters to open old wounds.

ERIC: I'd better stash those books.

JUNE: I should.

ERIC goes out.

(Sitting, addressing SAM.) But what old wounds? There's
no old wounds to open. If he means the divorce, if that's
what the sly little sod's been driving at, he wasn't around
at the time so he can't know it passed off without too much
rancor as these things go. It isn't as if we ran off together
– Tricia found out and threw you out and that was that.
She didn't keep you but she kept her pride. As for Pauline,
you always said she took it reasonably well. But she never
wanted to meet me. Well, that was her privilege. Didn't get
to meet me until she was what, sixteen she must have been,
when she was thrown out of that tin-pot la-di-da boarding
school you sent her to.

ERIC, carrying a paperback, enters to retrieve his coat.

ERIC: Enough to stock a small library there, June. But we'll see
they get good homes.

JUNE: I think you'll find the nearest good home is that second-
hand bookshop across the street from the office.

ERIC puts his coat on.

(To SAM.) She didn't take to me and quite frankly I didn't
take to her, little sulkpot that she was. Thank God Tricia
got her on that beautician's course and found her a job,
and at long last she turned into the Pauline we know and
love today.

ERIC: About those letters, June. Now are you sure Pauline will
want them back?

JUNE: They're a little girl's letters to her Daddy, Eric, why
wouldn't she want them back?

ERIC: It's not for me to say.

JUNE: *(As to Sam.)* Not only has he read them himself but for some warped reason of his own he wants me to read them. *(To ERIC.)* Just get them back to their rightful owner.

ERIC: It'll be easier to drop them round here, June, then you can hand them over.

JUNE: Post them.

ERIC: It's no trouble.

JUNE: Recorded delivery.

ERIC: *(Brandishing his paperback.)* Oh – do you mind if I hang on to this biog of Michael Dukakis? He was something of a hero of mine.

ERIC departs.

JUNE heads for the kitchen.

JUNE: Ooh, he's such a slimy bugger, Sam, and that's swearing.

Bring up a snatch of 'All People That on Earth Do Dwell'.

SCENE 7

Outside and inside the pub. Sunday.

The Lights come up.

THE SUIT sits at the pub table nursing an empty half a pint and reading an unidentified Sunday tabloid.

JUNE, dressed for outdoors, addresses Sam as she crosses and enters the pub.

JUNE: I've started going into the *Duke of Clarence* of a Sunday morning, did I tell you? No, only they do a nice snack-type lunch – Yorkshire pudding with savory fillings style of thing. Not up to my standard – but I do miss my Yorkshire puddings. Because I've given up making Sunday lunch, I've stopped bothering, there's no pleasure in cooking for one, not on that scale.

Having entered the pub she joins THE SUIT with a glass of Guinness.

THE SUIT: Well well well, you're the last person I'd expect to see in here on a Sunday. I pictured you round with your children.

JUNE: I don't have any. And it's news to me that you picture me doing anything.

THE SUIT: Oh, not being personal – it's just that all the widowed people I know, they seem to spend weekends with their families. Because they reckon that's the worst time.

JUNE: It is and it isn't. *(As to Sam.)* Though what I mean by that, Sam, I've no more idea than you. *(To THE SUIT.)* I see you read a particular Sunday paper.

THE SUIT: What's particular about it?

JUNE: It's particular to some people, all newspapers are. Do you take it every week?

THE SUIT: Only when I can't get a *News of the World*.

JUNE: What do you think of it as a paper, then? And before you answer I should mention that my late husband used to work on the daily.

THE SUIT: Oh yes and what did he do then? Printer?

JUNE: Goodness me, no, they don't have printers in this day and age, you're out of touch. No, he was the Editor. *(To Sam.)* And do you know, Sam, I still get a thrill when I hear myself saying that. My husband the Editor.

THE SUIT: Well, I suppose someone's got to edit these things.

JUNE: *(As to Sam.)* At least he's honest. *(Rising, she picks up THE SUIT's empty glass.)* I'll get you one in.

JUNE moves off.

THE SUIT picks up his tabloid and shakes his head disbelievingly at a headline.

JUNE, returning with half a pint, addresses Sam before returning to the table.

Now how the thump did we get on the subject of fridges? Oh, I know – I was asking if he always ate out, or could he cook for himself?

THE SUIT: Oh, I can boil the usual egg but I don't stray too far from Sainsbury's microwave bags, culinary-wise. Anyway, talk about room to swing a cat round, I've got a kitchenette about the size of this table.

JUNE: Well, I haven't seen your kitchenette, but in nine cases out of ten it's not the size, it's the design. Take my kitchen – it stretches from one end of the house to the other, yet every time I open the fridge door I graze my knuckles against the wall.

THE SUIT: So why don't you move it, then?

JUNE: Can't be done. It's built-in, it's part of a fitted unit, so we're stuck with it. *(As to Sam.)* Funny how I can still say we, isn't it?

THE SUIT: Sounds to me as if they should have put a bit more care into the design – you ought to write to them. But why don't you reverse your fridge door?

JUNE: Reverse the fridge door, how do you mean?

THE SUIT: Reverse the fridge door, so *(Demonstrating.)* instead of opening this way it opens that way.

JUNE: *(Also demonstrating.)* But it doesn't open that way, it opens this way.

THE SUIT: Same difference.

JUNE: In any case, it's not just like changing round any old door, it's a flipping refrigerator.

THE SUIT: It doesn't matter what it is, whether it's a fridge or a front door or a back door or a rabbit hutch, a door is a door, take my word for it. Now are you the proud possessor of a screwdriver?

JUNE: Of course I've got a screwdriver – don't take me for one of those women who can't use their hands. I've had to, because my husband never could. *(As to Sam.)* Could or wouldn't.

THE SUIT: Well this is what you do, after you've taken all your food items out and allowed it to defrost. What model is it?

JUNE: Ooh, let me see, it's that Dutch lot that make tellys.

THE SUIT: Right – that's the make, but what's the model?

JUNE: I've absolutely no idea.

THE SUIT: Well has it got a door-fitted egg rack?

JUNE: Yes, as a matter of fact.

THE SUIT: Now we're getting somewhere, now with that particular model it's simplicity itself. You should find two screws on top of your door, one on either side, right, and what you do, you unscrew these and put them somewhere safe, say in a saucepan lid.

JUNE: A saucepan lid, why a saucepan lid?

THE SUIT: Or a cup, or a saucer, or an ashtray, anything that's handy. And then what you do, you unscrew your level adjuster assembly.

JUNE: My what?

THE SUIT: What they call your level adjuster assembly. I only know this because I've had occasion to read the instructions. It's what you and I would call the handle.

JUNE: Right, I've unscrewed the handle and put it in a saucepan lid – now what do I do?

THE SUIT: Then there's two more screws to remove, there might be more on your model. Just remove all the screws in sight.

JUNE: And put them in the saucepan lid.

THE SUIT: Then very carefully lift the fridge door away from the cabinet with a downward motion to disengage it from the middle hinge pin.

JUNE: Middle hinge pin, I'm afraid you lost me.

THE SUIT: It's simple really. I'm making it sound more complicated than it is.

JUNE: No, I'm sorry, I can't take it in – it's not you, Douglas, it's me.

THE SUIT: Duggie. You've to call me Duggie.

JUNE: If you call me June.

THE SUIT: June.

JUNE: Duggie then. *(As to Sam.)* But he'll always be The Suit to me… It's the same with anything technical, Duggie, my mind blanks off. Like the instructions for the video recorder – they might as well be in Japanese.

THE SUIT: They usually are. Well, it's up to you, June, if you don't mind grazing your knuckles every time you open the fridge door. Of course, you could always wear an oven glove.

JUNE: *(Archly, as to Sam.)* He has quite a sense of humour. *(To THE SUIT.)* Well, they must have a maintenance service – I suppose they're quite capable of changing a fridge door round.

THE SUIT: Cost you an arm and a leg, love. Beside, how old is it? Because they'll probably try and sell you a new one – don't forget they're all on commission, this day and age. Tell you what, though, if you'd like me to come over and do it for you one of these days, I'd be only too happy.

JUNE: Oh, I couldn't put you to the trouble.

THE SUIT: Are you going back home after this? I'll just pop round the back, then I'll walk back with you – honestly, there's nothing I like to do more after my lunchtime sheperd's pie than take a fridge door off its hinges.

Rising and moving off, he turns back with a wink.

Mark you, there's no guarantee I can get it back on again!

JUNE: You'd better!

THE SUIT goes.

(Rising, as to Sam.) Talked me into it, didn't he?

A snatch of 'Amazing Grace' as she moves off.

SCENE 8

The house. A short while later.

JUNE comes through from the kitchen, carrying THE SUIT's jacket. She presses a lapel fondly to her cheek and then hangs the jacket over a chair.

JUNE: Do you remember the last time you wore this suit, Sam? Because I do. It was the last time we ever went to bed together, before you were carted off to hospital. Two weeks before, must've been, maybe three. God knows we were never at it like knives, apart from the few months before we started living together, when I was still the newsroom secretary and if you recall you had permanently grazed knees from us doing it on your office carpet. But after we got together, we settled down rather quickly, didn't we, pet? Perhaps too quickly.

THE SUIT, holding a screwdriver, comes in from the kitchen.

THE SUIT: Well, I don't know whether it's your thermostat playing up or what, June, but I don't reckon that unit needs defrosting at all.

JUNE: Probably not, it's not all that long since it was done.

THE SUIT: And there's practically nothing in your freezer, apart from – what is it?

JUNE: *(Sadly.)* A Waitrose mixed vegetable flan. The last supper.

THE SUIT: Pardon?

JUNE: Nothing.

THE SUIT: Even so, you can't be too careful, keeping frozen goods at too low a temperature, because there is such a thing as salmonella, or do I mean listeria?

JUNE, lost in her own world, vaguely shakes her head.

I'll get on with it, then.

JUNE, recollecting herself, calls after him as he moves back to the kitchen.

JUNE: There's the remains of a six-pack in the fridge, if you feel like a drink. I don't suppose that'll give you salmonella.

Giving her a thumbs-up, THE SUIT goes into the kitchen.

(As to Sam.) Yes, Waitrose's mixed vegetable flan. And that fridge. This particular night I didn't know when to expect you. So I thought, if I'm waiting up, I might as well defrost the fridge, it'll save me a job tomorrow. And I'd just got everything out when you came rolling in. I hadn't even heard the car. Naturally, you were half-cut – some scoop you were celebrating. You were that good humoured , I thought you'd brought someone home with you. You were practically singing. I asked if you'd had any supper and you roared, 'Supper! Supper! I'll tell thee what I want for my supper!' You always lapsed into broad Lancashire when you'd anything vulgar to say. I says, 'What's got into you tonight, then?' And you went, 'It's not what's got into me, lass. It's what's going into thee!' Not that I minded. It saved me heating up that mixed vegetable flan. So you poured us a drink apiece and we went upstairs. And I'll say this: considering the state you were in, it was very good. I won't say the earth moved, but that bed did. And that was the very last time, and I'm glad to have the memory of it.

THE SUIT enters from the kitchen, clutching a can of beer.

THE SUIT: Right – how would you like to test-drive the latest model left-handed fridge?

JUNE: You've never done it already!

She is about to look into the kitchen when THE SUIT dons his jacket. JUNE looks disappointed.

Oh, you're putting your jacket on again. *(As to Sam.)* I must say that should bring my pulse rate down, because having a man in his shirt-sleeves wandering around the house after all this time fair set my blood racing, I don't mind telling you.

THE SUIT: Is there anything else you wanted doing?

JUNE: No, no. And I can't thank you enough, Duggie. Will you let me give you a drink for your trouble?

THE SUIT: If by a drink you mean a drink, June, fair enough, but offer me anything else and I shall be mortally offended.

JUNE: *(As to Sam.)* And I nearly said, 'It depends what's on offer.' But I didn't. Credit yourself with just that little bit of dignity, June.

THE SUIT: Now are you sure there's nothing else I can do for you while I'm here, June, any other little task – you've only to say the word, leaking taps our specialty.

JUNE: And I said it, Sam. I'm sorry, but I did. *(Directly to THE SUIT.)* I suppose a fuck's out of the question?

THE SUIT, mouth open, gapes in astonishment.

(Addressing Sam.) Why I had to put it like that I shall never know. Either it was a compulsion, like that swearing disorder I've read about, somebody's syndrome. Or I wanted to shock The Suit into doing something about it without any gooey preliminaries. Or I wanted to shock myself – maybe out of a deep sleep. Anyway, I said it.

THE SUIT: Would you mind repeating that, June?

JUNE: I don't chew my cabbages twice.

THE SUIT: Are you serious?

JUNE: Never more so.

THE SUIT: But are you sure?

JUNE: No, I'm not sure at all, so don't push your luck, lad – I'm not exactly begging for it, do you want to come upstairs or not? *(As to Sam.)* All words that came out wrong – I must sound like a Manchester Piccadilly brass.

THE SUIT: Yes, of course I do – it's been a long time for me too, you know.

JUNE: How do you know it's been a long time for me?

THE SUIT: Because I do know it, you're not that kind of –

JUNE: That kind of girl? No, you're right there, and I don't usually come out with what I've just come out with, so don't think I do. Now let's just go up before I change my mind.

THE SUIT: Which you can do at any time you like, June. Now you know that, don't you?

JUNE leads the way upstairs.

JUNE: *(As to Sam.)* Now is he being considerate or just covering himself in case I turn round and accuse him of rape? The former I hope.

The doorbell rings persistently.

Either way, it doesn't matter. There's a happy ending, Sam – at least for you. Talk about being on cue.

THE SUIT: Don't answer it.

JUNE: No, I must – it could be one of my nosey neighbours with a parcel or something, and they would have seen us coming in.

Leaving THE SUIT on the staircase, JUNE descends and crosses to open the front door as the bell rings again.

PAULINE is at the front door. She has two bulky suitcases.

JUNE returns, followed by PAULINE carrying her suitcases.

JUNE: *(As to Sam.)* Saved by the bell, eh? Still – who's to know, Sam, I might not have fancied him once he got your suit off.

To the strains of Vera Lynn singing 'We'll Meet Again' –

The CURTAIN falls.

Act Two

SCENE 1

The house. Early morning.

The CURTAIN rises to a choral rendering of 'The Hallelujah Chorus'.

JUNE, wearing a man's plaid dressing-gown far too big for her, comes through from the kitchen clutching a mug of coffee.

JUNE: I did ever such a silly thing yesterday. I bought your tartan dressing-gown back from the Oxfam Shop. Only £2.15 – quite a bargain, considering what I paid for it in the first place. No, only I'd steeled myself to go in and ask if they wanted any part-time help – because it's time I was doing something, Sam, something to take me out of myself, stop me slummocking about the house. And there was your dressing-gown, on its wire coat hanger, all on its lonesome against that bare distempered wall. I just had to touch it, feel it, smell it – tobacco and rancid bacon – but I never meant to buy it. I mean, what would I want with it – why did I give it away in the first place? It's far too big for me, and the only constructive thing I could do with it would be to take it up to the street to the Sue Ryder charity ship, which would be downright bloody ridiculous. But then the lady came up behind me, and I said how much, and here we are.

PAULINE, also wearing a dressing-gown, comes downstairs and heads for the kitchen.

'Morning.

PAULINE: I wish you'd get that damp patch in my room seen to, June – I'm sure it can't be healthy.

PAULINE goes into the kitchen.

JUNE: *(As to Sam.)* *Her* room, do you notice – she hasn't been here ten minutes and it's her room. *(Calling after PAULINE.)* I'll get it fixed while you're on holiday – when do you say you're going again?

PAULINE: *(Calling back.)* Next weekend.

JUNE: *(As to Sam.)* I'll be glad to see the back of her for a fortnight. I will. Now I don't want you to think I've got it in for your daughter, Sam, but there is such a thing as waiting for an invitation before moving into someone's second bedroom.

PAULINE emerges from the kitchen, carrying a mug of coffee and bowl of cereal. She is on her way upstairs.

PAULINE: Your fridge door's wonky, do you know that?

JUNE: Wonky?

PAULINE: It's practically hanging off its hinges, June – if you have an insulation problem, you'll know about it, when it comes to food going off. Especially in your freezer.

JUNE: I'll keep it in mind, Pauline. You'd a call from that Eric Grant last evening – I did leave a note.

PAULINE: I know – I saw him later on.

JUNE: Oh, yes? I didn't know you were seeing him.

PAULINE: I didn't say I was seeing him, I said I saw him.

JUNE: *(As to Sam.)* It doesn't matter two shakes of a pig's bottom who she's seeing or who she's not seeing.

PAULINE proceeds upstairs.

I wonder if it's him she's going to Spain with next weekend – could be.

PAULINE pauses on the half-landing.

PAULINE: Oh – and Eric tells me he's in possession of a bundle of letters that I wrote to Dad.

JUNE: *(As to Sam.)* She *is* seeing him. *(To PAULINE.)* I should've mentioned it, Pauline.

PAULINE: You should have done, June, yes.

JUNE: For one reason or another it slipped my mind. *(As to Sam.)* Or I let it go, more likely. But ooh, she can sound nasty when she likes, your Pauline. *(To PAULINE.)* So I can leave it to you to get them back, can I?

PAULINE: Leave it to me? But of course – they're my letters, June.

JUNE: And off she trolls upstairs. But being creepy-crawly June and just to keep in with her, I have to call – Oh, Pauline!

PAULINE: *(On the upper landing.)* Yes, June?

JUNE: I don't suppose you know of any part-time work going?

PAULINE: I could ask at the Nail Boutique. They sometimes need a relief receptionist.

JUNE: No, it's voluntary work I'm looking for, Pauline, something to take me out of myself. Because it'll do me good to know I'm helping some of those more fortunate than myself.

PAULINE: You mean less fortunate, don't you, June?

PAULINE moves into her bedroom.

JUNE: *(As PAULINE goes.)* It must be the way I tell 'em.

JUNE carries her coffee mug through to the kitchen.

We hear a choral rendering of 'Dear Lord and Father of Mankind'.

SCENE 2

Outside and inside the pub. Lunchtime.

THE SUIT is sitting at a table in the pub, reading the small ads in the 'Evening Standard'.

JUNE crosses on her way to the pub, with a bit of shopping.

JUNE: *(As to Sam.)* Your Pauline's right – that fridge door *is* working loose. I should've left it well alone. I shan't mention it to The Suit though, we don't want to go through all that again. But the good news is that I've found that part-time job. Advert in the council newsletter, which I was reading as a change from counting the flowers on the bedroom wallpaper.

She enters the pub. With her glass of Guinness, she joins THE SUIT at his table.

THE SUIT tosses aside his newspaper at JUNE's entrance.

THE SUIT: So you're not avoiding me after all.

JUNE: Of course I'm not avoiding you, why should I? *(As to Sam.)* I have been, though. I hope he doesn't want an inquest into that Sunday. *(To THE SUIT.)* I've been too busy stuffing.

THE SUIT: Pardon?

JUNE: Envelopes. My new part-time job – with the Animal Trust. Three mornings a week – stuff stuff stuff. Me and a girl called Helen, she spends all her time crying in the loo. Man trouble, I expect – I haven't asked, I've got enough man trouble of my own, in a manner of speaking.

THE SUIT: Stuffing envelopes. That won't pay much.

JUNE: It doesn't pay at all. It's a charity.

THE SUIT: Oh, I see. You don't know of any paid jobs going spare, by any chance?

JUNE: I'm afraid not. Nothing in the situations vacant.

THE SUIT: Not for me. They might as well print a big notice on this page saying 'No over forties need apply.'

JUNE: Bad as that.

THE SUIT: Worse. Do you know how many job applications I've made so far, June?

JUNE: A good many, I shouldn't wonder.

THE SUIT: Would you believe getting on for a hundred?

JUNE: You don't surprise me, Duggie. You'll just have to persevere and plug away at it until you strike lucky.

THE SUIT: Not this chicken, June. Enough is enough.

JUNE: What *are* you going to do then – throw yourself in the river?

THE SUIT: It's not come to that yet, but I'll tell you what it has come to. June, let me know if you think this is a good idea or a bad idea, because I'd value your opinion. The thing is, I'm considering abandoning looking for desk work altogether and striking out on my own.

JUNE: You mean self-employed style of thing?

THE SUIT: Got it in one, June. Self-employed handyman.

JUNE splutters over her Guinness.

THE SUIT: Have I said something funny?

JUNE: *(Straightening her face.)* No, no – on the contrary I think it's a good idea. There must be lots of work in that line, if people know where to find you.

THE SUIT: Leaflets through letterboxes, trade cards in newsagents' windows, word of mouth – there's got to be scores and scores of households around want little jobs doing. Shall I tell you what put the idea into my head, June?

JUNE: Go on.

THE SUIT: It was when I came to switch your fridge door round.

JUNE tries, and fails, to restrain pearls of laughter.

What *is* the joke, June? Come on – I could do with a laugh.

JUNE: I'm sorry, Douglas – I was just remembering how we were nearly caught red-handed by Pauline coming in. Five minutes later and I shouldn't have known where to put my face.

THE SUIT: Can I say one thing and one thing only about that day, June?

JUNE: It depends what the one thing is.

THE SUIT: Whatever could have happened that Sunday didn't happen, and that's that. There's no going back on these things, June, take my word for it.

JUNE: Thank you for saying that, Duggie. We'll just put it behind us and forget the whole episode.

THE SUIT: Good.

JUNE: *(As to Sam.)* Now why am I disappointed?

THE SUIT: *(Rising.)* And now I'll get them in.

JUNE: *(Also rising.)* I won't have another, Duggie, I've some more shopping to do.

THE SUIT: But you think I should give the handyman venture a whirl?

JUNE: Go for it, Duggie.

THE SUIT moves off to have his glass replenished.

(As to Sam.) But for God's sake keep away from refrigerators.

Laughing to herself, she moves off.

Bring up the memorial congregation singing 'He Who Would Valiant Be'.

SCENE 3

The house. Morning.

JUNE, wearing a housecoat, enters from the kitchen as we hear the sound of the post arriving. Still speaking to Sam, JUNE goes into the hall and retrieves a thin batch of mail and a picture postcard.

JUNE: *(As to Sam.)* Postman – late again. And I can just hear you saying, 'Why did they ever invent postcodes, girl, just tell me that. Because the post's slower with new technology than if it was being carried through the jungles of Borneo by cleft stick.' *(Glancing at the postcard.)* Card from your Pauline on the Costa del Vomit as you used to call every Spanish resort. Having good time. I bet she is – and I bet I know who with. You and your sayings. How many times a week do I hear you saying, 'Age before beauty, Better out than in, Rather you than me, What a bugger, and Why do they make sliced bread that won't fit in the bloody toaster?' It's nice to hear your voice, Sam, but I do sometimes wish you'd put a sock in it.

Putting the morning post on the desk, JUNE glances at the postcard again.

I wonder if she *has* gone with that Eric Grant. I wouldn't put it past either of them.

The doorbell rings. JUNE goes to answer it.

ERIC GRANT is there.

She returns, followed by ERIC.

No, she hasn't. *(To ERIC.)* If it's Pauline you're looking for, she's on holiday.

ERIC: Yes, I know that – I've deliberately been waiting until Pauline was out of the way, because it's you I wanted to see, June.

JUNE: You've barely got your feet across the threshold yet, Eric, and already you're building up a mystery. Do you do it on purpose for the thrill of it, or is it that you've got such a devious corkscrew mind you can't help yourself? *(As to Sam.)* That's telling him.

ERIC: There's no mystery, June, but do we have to conduct our business standing up?

JUNE: I didn't know we'd any business to discuss.

ERIC: I think we have.

JUNE moves into the living-room and sits down. ERIC follows suit.

JUNE: I suppose it's about those letters.

ERIC produces a stack of old letters and seaside postcards with which he toys.

ERIC: *(Weightily.)* The letters, June, ah yes, the letters.

JUNE: You've taken your time about delivering them, haven't you – I mean how many weeks, months even, must it be since you came round and admitted you'd got them?

ERIC: Admitted's a strange word, June. I simply dropped in to say I'd taken possession of them. I don't suppose there's any coffee on the go, is there?

JUNE: *(As to Sam.)* Talk about the hide of a rhinoceros. *(To ERIC.)* No, there flaming is not. And by the way, can we get one thing straight – are you seeing Pauline at all?

ERIC: I think that's my affair, June.

JUNE: It's certainly not mine. But I believe you are seeing her, or how would you have known she's gone on holiday?

ERIC: Oh, nice one, June, but the fact that we keep in touch doesn't mean to say we're quote seeing each other as you put it – that's if I understand the phrase right.

JUNE: It doesn't matter a toss to me whether you're seeing each other or not seeing each other, or what the phrase means or what it doesn't mean. What I want to say to you, Eric Grant, is I never want you ringing my number and asking for Pauline every again – you can ring her at work. And I don't want you ever turning up on that doorstep asking for Pauline, because I shall slam the door in your face.

ERIC: June, June, we don't have a problem. Now can we get down to business?

JUNE: Business, business, why do you keep on calling it business? You sound like a bloody blackmailer.

ERIC: Oh, come on now, June, calm down, calm down. I've brought the letters, haven't I?

JUNE: Yes, I can see that, but why have you waited till Pauline's out of the way, and come to that why have you never given them to Pauline herself? I mean how many times must she have asked for them?

ERIC: I'll surprise you now, June. She's never asked for them at all.

JUNE: Don't be ridiculous!

ERIC: I'm going to be frank with you now, June.

JUNE: *(As to Sam.)* It's unbelievable, isn't it?

ERIC: We have two problems here, June. The first is that regardless of the ins and outs of the situation, Pauline didn't want the letters brought round here. In fact she specifically asked me to hang on to them. But the question is, was I in a position to do what Pauline wished – to which the answer is I'm afraid not.

JUNE: What do you mean?

ERIC: Because legally – and I've checked this out with a newspaper lawyer – these letters belong to you, as part of Sam's estate. And it's my bounden duty to deliver them to you, otherwise I could be in hot water.

JUNE: Hot water my eye – I know what you're up to.

ERIC: *(Rising.)* Up to, June? All I'm up to is handing over your property, which I now formally do.

JUNE: *(Accepting the packet of letters.)* Right. And now you can formally push off. And if you're still here on the count of ten you'll get that vase of flowers over your head.

ERIC, departing, turns to deliver one last shaft.

ERIC: One thing, June. Don't blame the messenger for the message.

ERIC goes.

JUNE: *(As to Sam.)* What message, though? He wants me to read those letters, we know that. What I didn't realize is that Pauline very badly *doesn't* want me to read them. I wonder why. Do you know, Sam? *(Riffling through the sheaf of letters and postcards.)* About fifteen of them, and half a dozen picture postcards from her holidays with Tricia. Cornwall, Isle of Man, Guernsey. 'Wish you were here, Dads, this morning went shrimping, have made a friend called Karen, swam three lengths.' They're harmless enough, but I shan't read the letters. I want to but I won't.

Rising, she moves upstairs, carrying the letters.

They go up to Pauline's room, in her underwear drawer. And there they stay till she gets back.

She enters PAULINE's room.

As she does so 'He Who Would Valiant Be' continues.

SCENE 4

Outside and inside the pub. Lunchtime.

JUNE crosses on her way into the pub, carrying some shopping. She speaks to her late husband.

JUNE: Right. I am now the proud possessor of a brand-new fridge. Came down in the middle of the night for a glass of mineral water and wouldn't you just know it – the flaming fridge door came away in my flaming hand. Thank God your Pauline's not back yet – I'd never hear the last of it. And thank you for nothing, The Suit. Why do we always imagine that people who volunteer to do things know what they're doing? Still, he meant well.

JUNE enters the pub, gets her customary glass of Guinness and goes to the table.

THE SUIT is not at his usual table, although there is a half-pint on the table and a supermarket carrier bag of groceries underneath it. JUNE sits down and extracts a travel brochure from her own shopping bag.

Oh, and another bit of news, Sam – as soon as your Pauline gets back from holiday, I'm going on mine. Dublin. *(Looking around her.)* He's a long time in that loo, if that's where he is. I wonder if he's constipated. *(Prying into THE SUIT's shipping bag.)* He deserves to be, what he lives on. Melton Mowbray pork pie...scotch egg...chicken and sweetcorn microwave dinner... packet of custard creams... sliced loaf, white... All human life is there. Or all bachelor life.

THE SUIT comes up behind her and catches her poking into his bag.

THE SUIT: Anything there you fancy for tea, then, June? You've only to say the word.

JUNE: *(Flustered.)* I can see you're not a big believer in getting what you might call a balanced diet down you, are you?

THE SUIT: So long as I get my roughage and I'm not still hungry when I get up from the table, I don't worry, June.

JUNE: Well, you don't look as if you're fading away on it.

THE SUIT: I should be, I've been that busy.

JUNE: How's the handyman business coming along?

THE SUIT: It's all go, June, touch wood. Yesterday I had two tap washers, a sash cord and a broken loo window. Day before I had a jammed fluorescent light tube, some loose bathroom tiles that needed gluing and what else, oh yes, an old lady who wanted her kitchen floor scrubbing. I got down to it – I'm not proud.

JUNE: Great oaks, Duggie.

THE SUIT: There's just one snag, June. I've got to have wheels. I'm having to turn work away on account of I just can't reach it in the time available. It's ridiculous.

JUNE: Get yourself a van, then. I'm sure there's plenty of cheap second-hand ones going.

THE SUIT: Oh, there are, June, there are, most definitely, but unfortunately there's a certain shortage of this...

He rubs thumb and forefinger together to simulate peeling off banknotes.

JUNE: *(As to Sam.)* Just the faintest feeling of uneasiness there, Sam. *(To THE SUIT.)* Have you tried the bank?

THE SUIT: Won't touch me, June, they're not interested in the little man. Oh, and in case you're thinking I'm working my way round to asking you to tide me over till I win the Lottery, put it out of your mind, because that's not what friends are for. In fact, it's the best way to lose them. Now let me get you another drink.

THE SUIT goes off with their empty glasses.

JUNE: *(As to Sam.)* So that's all right. He's got a little oil stain on his sleeve, have you noticed? I wonder why The Suit always wears the suit – it can't have been to the cleaners since he got it. I mean it's not as if he can't have any other clothes, but I've never seen him wearing anything else – although I did come damn close to seeing him not wearing it. Sorry about that, lad. Joke.

THE SUIT returns with their drinks.

Cheers, Duggie. Do you mind if I ask you something?

THE SUIT: Fire away.

JUNE: If you think it's too personal, don't answer, but I can't help wondering why you always wear the same suit?

THE SUIT: I thought you liked it, June, it's a suit that means something to you. I thought you'd be glad to see it being worn.

JUNE: Oh, I do, and it does, and I am, if I've got all that in the right order.

THE SUIT: No, but seriously, I'm a blazer man, actually. I've got three blazers, so before this one came into my life I'd hardly ever wear a suit. But I'll tell you the truth now, June, since you put the question. I wear this suit because it brings me luck.

JUNE: It doesn't seem to have brought you much luck so far, all the jobs you've been after and they never even had the decency to reply.

THE SUIT: It's brought me two pieces of stupendous luck, June. Number one, it's set me on the road to running my own successful business because this is going to work, June, I've got a good feeling about it. And number two and even more stupendous, having the privilege of wearing this suit was instrumental in meeting one of the nicest and most delightful persons I've ever come across, and I do mean that.

JUNE leans over and gives THE SUIT a peck on the cheek.

JUNE: Thank you, Duggie, and I couldn't imagine that suit going to a nicer man... This van, Duggie. It means a lot to you, getting hold of transport of some kind, doesn't it?

THE SUIT: Put it this way, June. With wheels I can operate, I can expand. You'd be amazed at the amount of work there is out there, just begging to be done. Without wheels, I might just as well have a lie-in every morning and live on social security.

JUNE: And have you worked out how much you'd need to get these wheels?

THE SUIT: I could give you very precise figures, June.

During the following, THE SUIT riffles through a sheaf of papers from his pockets.

JUNE: *(As to Sam.)* And I'm thinking, Hang on, chum, not so fast. But widows can't be choosers – not if they're looking for company.

THE SUIT: No, I don't seem to have the paperwork on me, June. But I did work it out in detail for the bank, much good it did me. Capital cost, running costs, taxation, et cetera – then on the other side of the ledger my potential turnover, increased business, et cetera. I've done all the projections and I could have any loan repaid with interest within eighteen months to two years.

JUNE: *(As to Sam.)* You don't have to tell me, Sam – this man is a fantasist. *(To THE SUIT.)* So what sums are we looking at?

THE SUIT: It depends on the type of vehicle, how old she is, what state's she's in – you can get a second-hand Austin Maestro 500 van, one owner, for ooh, two and a half thou trade price, or you can get a clapped-out one, F registration, for less than a thousand. What you buy is what you get, but you see the lower the asking price the more you've got to bear in mind your escalating repair bills.

JUNE: Yes, I can see all that. Look – Duggie, I'm going on holiday in a few days.

THE SUIT: *(Not very interested.)* What – on your own?

JUNE: *(Nettled.)* No, not on my own! You've heard me speak of Helen, the girl I stuff envelopes with? Well, she was hoping to go away with her chap, but he's dumped her. And not only that, he's left her pregnant, which is why she's always in the loo, snivelling – I think I told you...

THE SUIT looks bored.

THE SUIT: So when do you get back, June?

JUNE: Oh, I'm only gone a week. Now while I'm away I want you to get some proper figures drawn up and then we'll go into the whole thing.

THE SUIT: Shall be done.

JUNE: And then we'll see. Mind you, it's got to be done properly – agreement drawn up, sign on the dotted line.

THE SUIT: Oh, most definitely, I wouldn't have it any other way. You won't regret this June.

JUNE: *(As to Sam.)* I will. I know I will and you know I will. *(To THE SUIT.)* Well, we'd best have a drink on it.

THE SUIT: Allow me, June – least I can do. *(About to move off, he turns back with an afterthought.)* Where did you say you're going?

JUNE: I didn't, but it's Dublin.

THE SUIT moves off.

Thank you, The Suit. Thought you'd never ask.

Bringing up the memorial service congregation singing 'All Things Bright and Beautiful'.

SCENE 5

The house. Evening.

Wearing her smartest outdoor coat and carrying two hats, JUNE comes downstairs. During the following as she addresses Sam, she tries the hats on at various angles in front of a mirror.

JUNE: I suppose you'll want to know where I'm going, all dolled up. If you must know, I'm taking myself out to dinner. That new Frenchified place in the alley by the old public library. You won't know it but I've been once or twice now and they're very nice to me, apart from the manager or maître d' or whatever he calls himself, and he can be a bit snooty. I don't think he approves of unattached women. There's quite a few places like that. But I need a little treat after last night, Sam. I had one of my panic attacks that I get every once in a while. I'm saying last night, it was more like three in the morning.

I should have told you about it there and then but what could I have said? I'm frightened, Sam, I'm frightened? And what could you have said, if you could have said anything? What am I going to do? It can't go on yet it will go on. I can't take any more of it yet I have to. It's got to have all been a big mistake yet there's no rubbing out and starting again. Onwards and downwards. And then comes the panic. It's like being buried alive. I try to get out of it by taking deep breaths and thinking how much worse it could be. I could have murdered you and have you buried in the garden. Or you could have lingered on helpless and speechless for years and years. Is that worse? At least it'd give me something to do, somewhere to go. And if I did have you in bin-liners under the compost heap at least I could pass the time building a rockery. What am I going to do? What am I going to do about the compost heap, it just keeps on mouldering, am I supposed to turn it over with the garden fork or what? And the grass keeps on growing and I haven't the first idea how to start the mower. And the house insurance, when is it due, do they send you a reminder or what? And how do I claim if the house catches fire? They should have a school for widows. Maybe I should start it myself. What am I going to do? What if I'm found dead and eaten by maggots? Do you know, Sam, it's almost worth having your Pauline here not to have to face that prospect. *(Adjusting one of the hats to a perky angle to her satisfaction.)* What do you think? This one? Come on, lass, get yourself out.

The congregation singing 'All Things Bright and Beautiful' resumes.

SCENE 6

The pub. Late evening.

THE SUIT sits with a pint, correcting some handwritten sheets of paper.

JUNE enters unsteadily, her hat askew and somewhat the worse for drink.

THE SUIT: June, I was just thinking about you! We don't often see you here at this time of – Are you all right, June?

JUNE: I'm not all right. Do I look all right?

THE SUIT: Let me get you a brandy.

JUNE: That's the last thing I need. Go on then.

THE SUIT goes to get JUNE a drink.

(Calling after THE SUIT.) None of your small ones! *(As to Sam.)* What a night! It's been worse than last night, and that's saying something. That bloody restaurant, Sam – I'm going to write to the local paper about it! 'Oh, have you a reservation, madam?' That's the snooty bugger I told you about. I've never had a reservation, never – they've always been half-empty. Tonight, as it happens they're nearly full. 'Is it just the one, madam?' 'Yes,' I says, 'just the one.' There should be a widows' national anthem called Just the One. We go through life being just the one. Just the one glass, is it, madam? Just the one ticket, on the edge of the back stalls, behind a pillar? So where does he put me?

THE SUIT returns with her brandy.

(Addressing THE SUIT.) I say where does he put?

THE SUIT: *(Humouring her.)* Who's that, June?

JUNE: The snooty bugger who runs that French restaurant near the old public library. I was telling my Sam. Even though there's other places vacant, he puts me at a little rickety table no bigger than this, wedged between the swinging doors of the kitchen. Then he has the cheek to take the other chair away. And I'm sitting there for all the world as if I'm the flipping cloakroom lady. I tell you, with a saucer of change and a book of raffle tickets, I could have cleaned up.

THE SUIT: Have you had a bad evening, June?

JUNE: The special is duck with pear and a Madeira sauce so I order it – Sam knows why. *(As to Sam.)* Yes you do, it was what we had at the *Connaught* on our last anniversary. *(To THE SUIT.)* He does remember – he just cracks on he doesn't. Cheers, Suit. Duggie. I need this. So. I polish off my crab and prawn tartlet then here comes the duck.

THE SUIT: I've never got on with duck. I like goose, though. Within reason.

JUNE: I cut into it and I kid you not, it's raw. And by raw I mean raw. It didn't look like a meal at all, it looked like what it was – a dead duck. As the chef would have known if he'd cut into it himself and arranged the slices like a fan like what they do at the *Connaught*. I felt really queasy.

THE SUIT: I called over Snootychops and I says, 'Excuse me, I'd like to send this duck back, please, I'm sorry but it's not cooked properly.'

THE SUIT: So what did he say?

JUNE: He picks up the plate and looks into the duck's innards as if searching for shotgun pellets. Then he says, 'This is just as it should be madam, crisp on the outside, the flesh moist and pink.' I say. 'Moist and pink? It's red raw!' He says, 'No, it's not raw, it's rare.' I says, 'That's not how they serve it at the *Connaught*.' He says, 'It doesn't concern me how the *Connaught* serves its duck, but this is how we serve it here.' I says, 'What, running in blood?'

THE SUIT: You were holding your ground, then?

JUNE: So do you know what he had the cheek to come out with then? He says, 'That's not blood, madam, it's the sauce, be assured by me, this is how duck with pear and Madeira sauce should be brought to the table.' He says, 'As you'd know if you had an escort to advise you.'

THE SUIT: You should have sent for the management.

JUNE: He *is* the bloody management, listen to what I'm telling you! I says, 'I'm not even going to dignify that outrageous remark with an answer.' But I says, 'You can bring me some coffee and the bill, because I've lost my appetite now.' He says, 'There's no charge, if you're not entirely satisfied with your meal.' But he says, 'May I ask if you'll be coming here again?' I says, 'If I do, I shall stick with the fish.' But I says, 'Why do you ask?' He says, 'You see, it's very difficult, trying to cater for parties of one person.'

THE SUIT: What you want to do, June, you should write to the *Good Food Guide*.

JUNE: I says, 'Your party of one has been no trouble to anybody, she's just been sitting quietly drinking her glass of wine and reading the *Evening Standard*.' So do you know what he says then?

THE SUIT: No, what does he say?

JUNE: He clears his throat and he says, 'That's another thing, madam, now how can I put this, chef doesn't encourage our patrons to read at the tables, he likes to feel they'd prefer to give their full attention to the enjoyment of their meal.' I said, 'Oh, does he, well you can forget the coffee, take that bloody duck back into the kitchen and stick it down the chef's throat.'

THE SUIT: Did you say that, June?

JUNE: I could feel tears scalding my eyes. He says, 'If you're going to be abusive, I must ask you to leave, madam.' I says, 'Don't fret, I'm off.'

THE SUIT: Only thing you could do.

JUNE: I blunder out, and there's a pub two doors down. Do you know where I mean, Duggie?

THE SUIT: It's called *The Grapes*, June.

JUNE: It's not called *The Grapes*, it's called something else. And so I went in there, and ordered a large brandy.

THE SUIT: To steady your nerves. Best thing you could do.

JUNE: Then I felt better.

THE SUIT: As you do.

JUNE: Till they very kindly asked me to leave.

THE SUIT: They did what, June?

JUNE: I fell down the steps, didn't I, on the way to the Ladies? With having nothing to eat.

THE SUIT: Happens to us all, June.

JUNE: So effectively, in effect, I was chucked out.

THE SUIT: Never mind, June, you're among friends now.

JUNE: I know I am, Duggie. Shall I get you one in?

THE SUIT: I'd advise against it, June. I think we should both be making tracks.

JUNE: *(As to Sam.)* He's right, Sam, he's not wrong, he's a good friend. *(To THE SUIT.)* Do you think you could ring for a taxi?

THE SUIT: I'll do that, June, with great pleasure, and I think I should.

He produces a sheaf of papers he was poring over before JUNE's arrival.

Afore ye go, though, as they say, while I've got your ear, I wonder if you'd like to cast your eye over this?

JUNE: What? What what?

THE SUIT: That agreement we were talking about. For the loan. It's all drawn up and verified.

JUNE: Verified?

THE SUIT: You just have to read it through and sign.

JUNE: Oh, not now, Douglas! Come on – time and place! I said after I come back from Dublin!

THE SUIT: You're right, June, I'm out of order. I'll call that minicab.

Hastily, he withdraws.

JUNE: *(As to Sam.)* Sign, when he knows I'm pissed? Ratarsed, as you would say? Am I doing the right thing, Sam? I'm not, am I?

Bring up a snatch of 'Lord of the Dance'.

SCENE 7

The house. Night.

In darkness.

The hall light snaps on as JUNE blunders in, goes to the living-room, switching on the light, and helps herself to a large shot of neat vodka.

JUNE: It doesn't get any better, Sam. Do you know what the taxi driver had the nerve to say? She's not going to be sick, is she? And I was... And I am again.

Clutching her mouth, JUNE staggers upstairs to the bathroom.

Bring up another snatch of 'Lord of the Dance'. Under it we hear the sounds of retching, and then the lavatory flushing.

The Lights fade up to morning.

JUNE emerges from PAULINE's room, wearing Sam's dressing-gown and clutching the bundle of letters. Addressing Sam, she descends the stairs and goes into the living-room.

And how I finished up in your Pauline's room I shall never know. I know it was Pauline's room because mine goes round and round in the opposite direction. God, it was like being on a carousel lying on that bed. But I remembered the cure for it. You showed me. 'You don't close both eyes, lass, that makes it worse. You close one eye, then you focus on some piece of furniture until it stops going up and down.' And I found that the piece of furniture I was focussing on was the chest of drawers, and in particular the underwear drawer where I'd put Pauline's letters.

She sits and riffles through the pile of letters.

(Extracting a letter.) It's no use, Sam, I've got to go. Sorry, Pauline.

Taking the letter out of its envelope she begins to read.

JUNE: 'Dearest Daddy, How are you, we are well...'

PAULINE emerges from her bedroom wearing a pristine, ankle-length white nightdress. Standing absolutely still, she recites in a clear, little girl voice the letter that JUNE is reading.

PAULINE: How are you, we are well. Bobby send you all his love and kisses...

JUNE: Who Bobby? Dog? Teddy bear? Rocking horse? Kid next door? You never mentioned a Bobby. But then you never mentioned very much at all about your home life. With good reason, as I'm beginning to see.

PAULINE: I like the new cartoon strip in the paper, The Muddles. I think you should make Mr Muddle go to the office without his trousers, he has forgotten to put them on. Then he fall in a puddle. You could call it Mr Muddle fall in a puddle. I love you, Daddy. Daddy, when are you coming home? You said you would but you have not. It is not good for you to sleep at the office because you so busy, you will get a sore back sleeping on the sofa. We both miss you so much. Mummy cries every night and this make me cry. I sleep in Mummy's bed now to keep your place warm, and she wake me up with her crying. She think you do not love us but this cannot be true, I know that you love us and that you will come home as soon as ever you can. Uncle Derek took me to the waxworks on Saturday but he did not let me see the murderers. I wish you had come with us, you would have let me see the murderers because I know you like murders, you should make Mr Muddle do a murder only he murders the wrong person. But I do not understand why you do not come on Saturday any more, the paper does not come out on a Sunday. Please come home, Daddy. Have we done anything wrong? If I have been making too much noise I will not, I will be quiet as mouse if only you will come back to us. Love and kisses...

PAULINE goes back into her room and closes the door.

JUNE: 'PS. Some of these kisses are from Mummy.'

She puts the letter back in its envelope and stares into space.

Sam, Sam, Sam. You lied to me. You said Tricia was glad to see the back of you, that you didn't even pack your own bags, she packed them for you and threw them down the stairs. And then what's all this about you said you would come home but you haven't? Am I to understand that you didn't have the courage to tell the child you were off for good, that you deliberately encouraged her to believe you'd be coming back to her? And then there's that stuff about missing you and crying every night. You assured me, over and over again, that Pauline wasn't over-bothered about your absence, that she'd hardly ever seen you during the working week anyway and that so long as you turned up of a Saturday with a prezzie and a treat in store she was happy enough. But here she is saying she can't understand why you don't come on Saturdays anymore. It's easy to see why, though, isn't it? It's all in this one letter. Because you were too much of a coward, Sam Pepper. You couldn't face a wife and little daughter begging you to come back to them and turning on the waterworks. You never did like scenes. That'll be why you packed her off to boarding school. You know, it's not opening old wounds we're talking about here, it's ripping in with the knife and starting new ones, do you understand that? You've deceived me, Sam. You let me down badly.

JUNE rises and begins to climb the stairs, carrying the bundle of letters.

Why couldn't you have come clean? I'll tell you why, shall I? Because if I'd known the truth of it, it'd be Tricia wearing the widow's weeds today, not me. And she'd be bloody welcome to them.

She goes into PAULINE's bedroom, returns minus the letters and enters her own bedroom.

Bring up 'O for the Wings of a Dove' by a boy soprano.

SCENE 8

The house. Evening.

The sound of a taxi stopping.

PAULINE enters from the street, carrying a suitcase, plus a duty-free bag which she puts down by the drinks table.

PAULINE: *(Calling into the kitchen.)* I'm back, June!

JUNE, wearing a housecoat, enters from the kitchen.

PAULINE is taking her suitcase upstairs.

JUNE: No delays, then. Have you had a nice time? You haven't caught much sun.

PAULINE: You don't get a suntan in night clubs, June. There's some duty-free Spanish brandy in that bag if you want to open it. I'll just dump my suitcase.

PAULINE goes into her room.

JUNE: *(Calling after her.)* Do you want anything to eat?

PAULINE: *(Off, from her room.)* Yes – Spanish brandy.

JUNE retrieves the bottle of Spanish brandy from the duty-free bag, opens it, and pours two large shots.

PAULINE emerges from her room holding the bundle of letters.

When did these turn up?

JUNE: He brought them round, a few days ago.

PAULINE: You've been reading them, haven't you?

JUNE: Only one, Pauline.

PAULINE: *(Descending the stairs.)* One's enough. They all say the same thing.

She takes the drink which JUNE proffers and takes a big gulp.

So now you know, June.

JUNE: Yes. Now I know.

PAULINE: Or did you know all along?

JUNE: I hadn't the faintest glimmering, Pauline. I'd been led to believe it was all amicable and that you'd taken it in your stride style of thing. Maybe that's what I wanted to believe, but if you'd written to him at home instead of the office I might just have learned otherwise.

PAULINE: *(Staring.)* I didn't know where he was living, did I? I thought he was staying at the executive flat at the office while he worked on something to do with the paper. That's what he said, anyway.

JUNE: So how often did you see him?

305

PAULINE: Not very often. I don't think he liked facing my mother.

JUNE: That figures.

PAULINE: And when he did take me out, June, he'd never mention you. I never knew of your existence. Not till after the divorce, a good year later.

JUNE: *(As to Sam.)* That figures too. It's all piecing together. *(To PAULINE.)* So who broke the news to you in the end, your father or your mother?

PAULINE: A girl at school, as a matter of fact. She'd heard her parents discussing the divorce – it had been in the *Evening Standard.* She came up to me in the playground and sneered, you know how horrid kids can be, 'Your mother and father are divorced, that makes you illegitimate nyah nyah nyah.' So then it all came out. Mother explained it to me when she found me in the linen cupboard, crying.

JUNE: *(As to Sam.)* Poor child. The hoops we put them through, and then we wonder why they turn out as they do. *(To PAULINE.)* What can I say, Pauline?

PAULINE: Not a lot.

JUNE: I'll ask you to believe one thing, and that's that if I'd known the effect it was having on you, I would have finished with him. *(As to Sam.)* Like a shot. Because what difference would it have made to me? I'd have got over you. I was young, someone else would have come along. And I wouldn't have had that bloody funeral to go through. But then who knows, I might have had someone else's bloody funeral.

PAULINE: It's all water under the bridge now.

JUNE: I'm afraid your father made a complete hash of it, Pauline. He should have told me about you and he should have told you about me.

PAULINE: It wasn't his way.

JUNE: No, we know. *(She pours them both another stiff drink.)* But once you'd heard about me, didn't you ever want to meet me?

PAULINE: No, of course I didn't.

JUNE: Oh, I see, didn't want anything to do with Daddy's fancy woman.

PAULINE: Something like that.

JUNE: *(As to Sam.)* Walked into that one, didn't I?

PAULINE: Come to that, didn't you ever want to meet me?

JUNE: Yes, I did, very much, but he always said he didn't want to mix his two lives.

PAULINE: Yes, he would do.

JUNE: So going back to when you did get to meet me, Pauline, after that you must have decided to accept me?

PAULINE: *(With a shrug.)* To tell the truth, June, by that time I didn't care about you one way or the other – if you want me to be brutally frank.

JUNE: It's quite understandable, Pauline. You'd been through a lot by then.

PAULINE: I know I had. Did he tell you about my anorexia?

JUNE: No, he didn't. Never a word. When was this?

PAULINE: When I was fourteen. In that case I don't suppose he told you about my pregnancy. That was when I was fifteen. It was terminated.

JUNE: Oh my God. *(As to Sam.)* You see what you get for dying? It all comes out. *(To PAULINE.)* Pauline, if only we could turn back the clock.

PAULINE: But we can't, can we?

Sadly, she takes her drink upstairs to her room.

JUNE watches her go and then, carrying the bottle of Spanish brandy and her glass, goes into the kitchen.

SCENE 9

The house and the pub. Mid-morning.

JUNE, dressed for outdoors, comes out of her bedroom carrying a small suitcase. She comes downstairs.

During the following, THE SUIT enters the pub and sits at his table, carrying the customary half-pint, produces a mobile phone and punches out JUNE's number.

JUNE: *(Addressing Sam.)* You won't be surprised not to have heard from me of late. I'm sorry, Sam, but I've had nothing to say to you. What's been done's been done, and there's no discussing it. And now if you'll excuse me I'm off to Dublin with my pregnant envelope-stuffing friend Helen. *(With a glance at the clock.)* That's if the minicab turns up. Another ten minutes and he'll be late.

The telephone rings.

(Answering the phone.) Three-seven-four-one, hallo?

THE SUIT: June! I've caught you in!

JUNE: You have, but only just, Duggie.

THE SUIT: Listen – any chance of a quick one down at the *Clarence*? Afore ye go?

JUNE: None whatsoever, Duggie, I'm on my way to Heathrow.

THE SUIT: I'll tell you what it is, June – I've seen this immaculate red Ford Transit van, F-reg dropside, one owner, only forty-three thousand on the clock, excellent nick, I've test-driven it, only it belongs to this bloke I've been laying a stair carpet for, not a scratch on it, it's a steal, June.

JUNE: How much?

THE SUIT: Let me tell you this in my own way, June. I said to him, 'I see you want to sell that Ford Transit out there, what's the asking price?' He said, 'A lot less than you'd imagine, my friend, in that condition and with that low mileage.' But he said, 'I've got an eye on a Dodge four-berth motor-home that's even more of a bargain, but there's no way of buying that without selling this.'

JUNE: How much?

THE SUIT: But he said, 'It's only fair to tell you, I've already had an offer.'

JUNE: They always say that, Douglas.

THE SUIT: Of course they do, June, of course they do. But in this case it happens to be true. Because he said to me, 'I'm really worried about that caravanette slipping through my fingers, do you think you could raise the money by tomorrow?' I said, 'I'll have a damn good try.'

JUNE: How much does he want?

THE SUIT: Two-four-nine-five, June, and she drives like a dream.

JUNE: So why are you in such a hurry to tell me all this – I thought we were going to work it all out when I get back from holiday?

THE SUIT: It won't wait for that, June. If he doesn't have the cash by tomorrow it goes to this other bloke – all he's got to do is drive the van out to New Cross and there's a cheque waiting for him on the other bloke's mantelpiece.

JUNE: Two-four-nine-five you say, I seem to remember you telling me you could get an F-registration van for around a thousand.

THE SUIT: Not in this class, June, it's cheap at the price – I could re-sell it tomorrow for three grand and we'd be five hundred in profit before we've even started.

The doorbell rings.

JUNE: My minicab's here, Duggie – are you sure he won't take less?

THE SUIT: I'll try and beat him down, June, but I highly doubt it. Look – you couldn't pop into the *Clarence* on your way to Heathrow, could you?

JUNE: No, I could not, but I'll tell you what I'll do. I'll leave a cheque here for you in an envelope.

THE SUIT: Made out to cash, if you would. And we'll talk about running costs when you get back.

JUNE: Pauline doesn't work on Saturdays so you should find her in. But there's no need to tell her what it's all about, in fact I'd rather you didn't.

THE SUIT: Trust me, June. And I'm very grateful. Tell you what, soon as you get back I'll take you for a spin down to Brighton.

JUNE: In a van? No thank you.

She hangs up.

THE SUIT reacts with satisfaction and departs.

JUNE sits at the desk, writes a cheque and puts it in an envelope. The doorbell rings again.

(Calling.) Yes, I'm coming!

She picks up her suitcase and goes out.

Bring up the choir singing 'God Be in My Head'.

SCENE 10

The pub. Sunday evening.

JUNE, carrying her suitcase in one hand and a half of Guinness in the other, enters wearily and sits down.

JUNE: *(As to Sam.)* I need this. What a washout. First off it's pissing down, as you would say, from morning till night. The hotel's a top. And that Helen! We're no sooner there – hadn't even had a meal – than she insists on dragging me from one folk music pub to another in the pouring rain, until at last the penny dropped. She was looking for her chap, wasn't she, the one who left her in the family way. She'd told me he was Irish but I'd never made the connection – not until she found him, scraping away on the fiddle in this back-street bar. He seemed pleased to see her, so I left them to it. I says, 'You two have got a lot to talk about.' I wonder where The Suit is. Maybe he doesn't get in on Sunday evenings. Anyway, an hour after midnight I'm woken up by the phone and it's Helen. 'Ooh, June, do you mind if I don't come back tonight, only I'm over at Sean's and there's no taxis.' Next morning – this morning – there's still no sign of her. I wait and I wait, I go out in the rain for a coffee, I come back, still no message. I'm getting quite annoyed by now, because we were supposed to be having brunch at the *Shelbourne*. No, Helen. Well, I did have brunch at the *Shelbourne* – brunch for one. But it's still raining stair rods and I thought, What do I do now? And a little voice said, Take yourself home, June, you're not wanted here. So I did. I left a note for Helen and took a cab to the airport, and here I am. Didn't cross my mind to ring Pauline, so she's in for a surprise...

JUNE goes out, taking her suitcase with her.

Bring up the conclusion of 'God Be in My Head'.

SCENE 11

The house. Immediately afterwards.

Only the landing and PAULINE's room, the door of which is ajar, are lit.

JUNE enters and glances upstairs.

JUNE: In fact I think we're both in for a surprise.

PAULINE, in a fetching silk kimono, appears in her doorway.

PAULINE: *(Sharply.)* Who's down there?

She flicks on the light.

So it *is* you, June. What brings you back – you weren't expected?

JUNE: No, I can see that. You've got someone up there with you, haven't you? Now if it's that Eric Grant –

PAULINE: No, it isn't Eric Grant, June. I'm sorry.

The lavatory flushes and THE SUIT emerges from the bathroom. He is wearing Sam's plaid dressing-gown. He stares down at JUNE.

JUNE: *(As to Sam.)* You know how your mind sometimes takes a photograph but doesn't develop it till later. I'd seen, but I hadn't registered till now, a red Ford Transit van parked outside, F-registration. *(Quietly to THE SUIT.)* You bastard. Get out of that dressing-gown and out of my house.

THE SUIT darts hurriedly into PAULINE's bedroom.

(To PAULINE.) And you! You can get out too! Pack your bags and go!

PAULINE: June, if you'd just calm down for a second and let me –

JUNE: Explain? What is there to explain? I've got eyes to see with, haven't I? You'd screw anything in trousers that comes through that front door! God almighty, aren't you ashamed of yourself? Sleeping with your father's suit. It's practically bloody incest!

PAULINE retreats into her bedroom.

JUNE wheels round to harangue her late husband.

Oh, yes, har har, very comical. I can just hear you saying, 'Hee hee, she does come out with them, our June.' But I mean it. And I'm done. I'm finished. And I'm going to tell you something now, Sam Pepper. I blame you for all this. I blame you for the state I'm in.

During the following, PAULINE and THE SUIT emerge from the bedroom and come downstairs. PAULINE is carrying a small suitcase.

What a bloody brilliant idea it was, I don't think. Keep a diary, let it all pour out, what you're thinking, how you're coping, month after flaming month. It's been like treading water at the top of Niagara Falls. And for what? 'I Did It My Way'! How could I get on with my life when I was so busy getting on with yours? Because that's what I've been doing, Samuel Herbert Pepper – getting on with your life, keeping you alive, stoking up the flaming fires of remembrance. Well, you've had your last shovelful of coke from me. It's done. It's over.

PAULINE and THE SUIT pose awkwardly in the hall.

They're going now. They pause to stare at this weeping, ranting woman.

THE SUIT: June, if I could say just one thing and one thing only –

JUNE: You can piss off, that's what you can do.

PAULINE: I'll come over for my things tomorrow.

JUNE: You'd better, or they'll go to the skip.

THE SUIT and PAULINE leave.

The door slams. In a minute, the sound of a red van starting up, a snip at two-four-nine-five. I shan't hold it against Pauline for long, not with the screwed-up life she's been made to lead. I shan't even hold it against The Suit – if I'd bedded him when I had the chance instead of reporting back to you all the time, this probably wouldn't have happened. But I do hold it against you, Sam – trying to be immortal, that's what you've been doing. No more. From now on, you'll have to do the same as I mean to do. Get a life – you know how the saying goes. A life, did I say? You've had your life, now let me get on with mine. Get a death! Do you hear me? Get a death!

Sinatra's recording of 'I Did It My Way' plays as –

The CURTAIN falls.

MR AND MRS NOBODY

AN ENTERTAINMENT DEVISED BY KEITH WATERHOUSE
FROM *THE DIARY OF A NOBODY* BY GEORGE AND WEEDON GROSSMITH
AND *MRS POOTER'S DIARY* BY KEITH WATERHOUSE

The play was first presented by Michael Redington at the Yvonne Arnaud Theatre, Guildford, on 8 October 1986, and subsequently at the Garrick Theatre, London, with the following cast:

CARRIE POOTER	Judi Dench
CHARLES POOTER	Michael Williams
SARAH The Maid	Penny Ryder
FACTOTUM	Gary Fairhall

Musicians Michael Haslam and John Bergin
Directed by Ned Sherrin
Designed by Julia Trevelyan Oman
Music Arranged by Peter Greenwell

The play is set in The Laurels, Brickfield Terrace, Holloway 1888-9, with brief excursions to Islington, the City of London, Broadstairs and Peckham.

Characters

CARRIE POOTER

CHARLES POOTER

SARAH The Maid

FACTOTUM

Prologue

The curtain is up. We see the outside of The Laurels, Brickfield Terrace,
Holloway – the POOTER home. As the play begins we hear lively period
music from our musicians who will be discovered in a kind of minstrels'
gallery as and when required. The music fades as we hear the voice of
CHARLES POOTER.

CHARLES: Why should I not publish a diary? I have often seen
    reminiscences of people I have never even heard of, and
    I fail to see – because I do not happen to be a 'Somebody'
    – why my diary should not be interesting. My only regret
    is that I did not commence it when I was a youth. Signed:
    Charles Pooter, The Laurels, Brickfield –

    (Before CHARLES has finished, the voice of CARRIE POOTER is
    superimposed.)

CARRIE: If my husband can entertain hopes of publishing
    a diary, then so may I. After all, it is not as if my dear
    Charlie were a 'Somebody'. He is, alas, thanks to the good
    nature that holds him back, no more of a 'Somebody' than
    is – Mrs Charles Pooter, The Laurels, Brickfield Terrace –

    (The front section of the house flies out, revealing the POOTERS'
    cluttered front parlour. Folding doors separate it from the back
    parlour, which lies behind.)

Act One

SARAH – who as CARRIE constantly reminds us is the housemaid – is tidying up. Apart from bobbing obsequiously at every mention of her name, she should be on stage, SARAH takes no part in the action except to act as our production's skivvy – fetching and carrying, turning up the gas, drawing curtains and so on.

As SARAH departs, CHARLES enters. Solemnly, flicking back the tails of his coat, he seats himself at his desk. He dips a penholder in the inkpot and chews it thoughtfully.

Then CARRIE enters, carrying a portable ladies' escritoire which she sets down on a table and opens. Pressing a lace handkerchief to her face, she makes a fastidious show of beating away the smoke that billows into the room as a train passes.

Except when they bring their diaries to life and speak directly to one another, CARRIE and CHARLES act as if alone with their own thoughts – though either one may react sharply to the thoughts of the other.

They begin to write.

CHARLES: My dear wife Carrie and I have just been a week in our new house, the Laurels, Brickfield Terrace, Holloway…

CARRIE: *(Simultaneously.):* My hear husband Charlie and I have just been a week in our new house, the Laurels, Brickfield Terrace, Holloway…

I hate it.

CHARLES: A nice six-roomed residence, not counting basement, with breakfast-parlour and a nice little back garden.

CARRIE: The back garden runs down to the railway. Every time a train passes by, the windows rattle – there's hardly a one that doesn't need new sash-cords – smoke billows in through every crack, and every stick of furniture is coated in cinder-dust.

CHARLES: After my –

CARRIE: As if that were not enough, there is evidence of rising damp in the scullery. All Charlie has to say on that score is –

CHARLES: *(Directly to CARRIE.)* When we are settled in, Carrie, I may well try my hand at growing mushrooms.

CARRIE: They'll come up toadstools.

CHARLES: After my work in the City, I like to be at home. What's the good of a home if you are never in it? 'Home, Sweet Home', that's my motto.

CARRIE: For a pound a week more we could have had a pretty villa near our old home in Peckham, *and* with a bay window. But no, nothing would do but that my lord and master must be near to his precious City, at Mr Perkupp's beck and call. I wonder he doesn't take his bed down to the office and be done with it.

(CHARLES, after lighting his pipe gets up and straightens the pictures on the wall.)

CHARLES: I am always in of an evening. There's plenty to be done: a fan to nail up, a blind to put straight –

CARRIE: *(Pointedly.)* A sash-cord to mend.

CHARLES: All of which I can do with my pipe in my mouth. Then our old friends Gowing and Cummings may drop in without ceremony – Carrie and I are always pleased to see them.

CARRIE: When all's said and done, Charlie is a good husband, and unlike other men does not pass the evening at his Club, but prefers to be at home with his pipe. *(She makes a face at the stench of it.)* entertaining his friends – who call far too often for my liking – or doing jobs about the house. I must count my blessings. *(For CHARLES's benefit.)* I know he will mend those sash-cords as soon as he has a mind to…

(He nods his assent.)

I shall continue to be a dutiful wife and make the best of things.

CHARLES: *(Back at his desk.)* April third. Tradesmen called for custom. Carrie being occupied, I ordered a shoulder of mutton from Horwin – he seems a civil enough butcher. Memo: the bells must be seen to. The parlour bell is broken, and the front door rings up in the servant's bedroom, which is ridiculous.

CARRIE: April third. I was writing my bi-weekly letter to our dear boy Willie, who is doing very well in the Bank at Oldham – he has all the drive his dear father lacks – when Sarah (my maid) brought in a card 'what a lady 'ad left'. Our very first caller, and my domestic staff turn her away! Had the parlour bell not been broken *(With a vicious glance at CHARLES.)* like much else in this house, I should have been aware that we had a visitor and given instructions that I was at home. *(Consulting the visiting card.)* It is one of our neighbours, a Mrs Borset, who so honours us. I shall return Mrs Borset's call at the earliest convenience.

CHARLES: April fourth. Gowing called, and fell over the door scraper coming in.

(CARRIE restrains a titter.)

Memo: have it mended.

(CARRIE consults a stack of 'part-work magazines in the bookcase. CHARLES, during the following, crosses to the window, sees something to interest him in the street below, and goes out of the room.)

CARRIE: Consulted 'Lady Cartmell's Vade mecum for the Bijou Household', which is appearing in weekly parts, upon the etiquette of returning a call in a new locality. Unfortunately, since the last number brings the work only up to 'Ventilation, necessity of', Lady Cartmell's observations on Visiting are yet to appear. I dressed suitably and sallied forth to the address printed upon her card...

(CARRIE, having put on a bonnet, looks around as if for the address on the card which she holds between finger and thumb.)

This proved to be the Welsh Dairy on the corner. I ordered some butter and eggs. *(Discarding her bonnet.)* So ended my first social engagement in Holloway.

CHARLES: *(Returning.)* April fifth. Two shoulders of mutton have arrived, Carrie having arranged with another butcher without consulting –

CARRIE: *(Interrupting.)* It is too bad of Charlie. *Two* shoulders of mutton arrived, he having arranged with another butcher. The piece ordered by me being the less fatty of the two, and not a few pence cheaper, his shall go back.

CHARLES: Cummings called, and fell over the scraper going out. *(Another suppressed titter from CARRIE.)* As I said to Carrie, I must get the scraper removed, or else I shall get into a *scrape! (He laughs inordinately.)*

CARRIE: Yes, dear.

CHARLES: *(Wiping his eyes.)* Oh dear, oh dear… *(Composing himself.)* I don't often make jokes.

CARRIE: *(Writing.)* April sixth, Charlie, in a filthy mood at breakfast, took it into his head to declare his egg uneatable. He was adamant that the eggs must be returned to Borset's, including, if you please, those already boiled and even our half-eaten ones! This is how he pays me back for ordering a shoulder of mutton over his head.

CHARLES: In the evening, hearing someone talking in a loud voice to the servant, I went down to see who it was and was surprised to find Borset, from the Welsh Dairy. He was both drunk and offensive.

CARRIE: Charlie came back looking very flushed but would say no more than –

CHARLES: *(Pointing a finger.)* Caroline, Mr Borset is to be given no further custom.

CARRIE: I held my peace.

CHARLES: April seventh.

CARRIE: Being Saturday, I was surprised when Mrs Borset was announced by Sarah (my maid), for I have always understood that ladies do *not* pay calls at weekends. However, I soon learned that this was not, after all, a visit of a social nature. Mrs Borset had come to prepare the ground for Mr Borset, who wishes to make amends to Charlie with a pound of fresh butter and a sample packet of breakfast cocoa.

CHARLES: Arriving home, found Borset waiting. He begged me to accept his apology, and a pound of fresh butter.

CARRIE: But not the packet of breakfast cocoa.

CHARLES: He seems, after all, a decent sort of fellow, so I gave him an order for some fresh eggs – *fresh*, mind!

CARRIE: Good humour restored, Charlie set to laying the old stair carpets we have fetched with us from Peckham. Now he will see for himself that –

CHARLES: I am afraid the old stair carpets are not wide enough to meet the paint on either side. There is nothing for it: we shall have to buy new ones.

CARRIE: As I have been telling him all along, they are too narrow. He will have to match the paint.

CHARLES: Unless, that is, I can match the paint.

CARRIE: April ninth. Engaged a charwoman, a Mrs Birrell, on references supplied by Mssrs Teale (late Moxon) painters' sundrymen. So continues my daily struggle to prevent the house from resembling a coal siding. *(She slams down a window as smoke billows in from a passing train.)* I have arranged a series of bell-signals: one ring for Sarah, two for Mrs Birrell. *(After pulling ineffectively on the bell-rope, and glaring at CHARLES.)* That is, when the bells have been mended.

CHARLES: April eleventh. Slight smell of –

CARRIE: The house reeks of paint, Charlie having been elected to have the stairs entirely repainted by Mr Putley the decorator. He tells me that –

CHARLES: *(To CARRIE.)* Mr Putley could not match the colour that is down, as it contains Indian carmine. He has spent half a day calling at warehouses.

CARRIE: Since it is dark chocolate, one of the commonest colours to be found, I begged leave to doubt this. I asked Charlie: *(To CHARLES.)* Has Mr Putley tried Messrs Teale (late Moxon), painters' sundrymen? By the look of their letterhead, they seem very reliable.

CHARLES: Matching paint is men's business, Caroline. *(To his diary.)* Gowing dropped in after tea –

CARRIE: – to use my parlour as his smoking-divan. I am pleased to say that for once he had his comeuppance from Charlie. Both he and Mr Cummings have been very tiresome about the smell of paint. On this occasion, as he began his usual sniffing, Charlie said –

CHARLES: 'You're not going to complain of the smell of paint again, Gowing?'

CARRIE: Mr Gowing said –

CHARLES: *(As GOWING.)* 'No, not this time, but I'll tell you what, I distinctly smell dry rot.'

CARRIE: To which Charlie retorted -

CHARLES: 'You're –

CARRIE: – without pausing for an instant to compose his reply –

CHARLES: 'You're –

CARRIE: It seemed to trip off his tongue! He said –

CHARLES: 'You're talking a lot of dry rot yourself!'

(Both CHARLES and CARRIE collapse with laughter.)

CHARLES: *(Composing himself at last.)* April fourteenth. Sowing some half-hardy annuals in the garden this afternoon, I thought of *another* joke, and called out to Carrie. *(Calling.)* Carrie!

CARRIE: My home-made ladies' fingers are a particular favourite with Charlie, who will often take them with his tea in preference to Marie Louise biscuits. It was contentedly enough that I was applying myself to turning out a batch this afternoon, when –

CHARLES: *(Calling.)* Carrie!

CARRIE: Thinking him to have had an accident I abandoned my whisking. All Charlie wanted to say was –

CHARLES: *(With a snigger.)* I have just discovered we have got a lodging-house.

CARRIE: *(Sharply.)* How do you mean?

CHARLES: Look at the *boarders!*

CARRIE: The borders? Yes?

CHARLES: No, *boarders.* Don't you see, Carrie – flower borders, lodging-house boarders!

CARRIE: Is that all you wanted to say to me?

CHARLES: *(Sulkily.)* Any other time you would have laughed at my little pleasantry.

CARRIE: Certainly – at any other time, but not when I'm busy in the kitchen. (*Writing again.*) My ladies' finger mixture was as custard. It is my own fault: I should not have encouraged him by laughing at his joke about dry rot the other day. Now he considers himself a wit.

CHARLES: April sixteenth.

CARRIE: Reminded Charlie that the sash-cords remain unattended to. He made a great show of examining the cords on the parlour windows, then said –

CHARLES: *(At the window.)* Yes, I'm *afraid* they're *frayed.*

CARRIE: *(To CHARLES.)* That's what I keep telling you.

CHARLES: No, I'm *afraid* they're *frayed.*

CARRIE: *(Writing.)* He repeated this several times with increasing emphasis, then took himself off into the garden, where I heard him writing to himself. I sometimes wonder if my husband is a secret drinker. (*A cackle from CHARLES.*) April nineteenth.

CHARLES: Cummings called, bringing with him his friend Merton, who is in the wine trade. *(CARRIE sniffs.)* Gowing also called. *(She sniffs again.)* I fear Carrie is in for a cold...

CARRIE: For which he took a third of a bottle of whisky last night, aided and abetted by Mr Cummings.

CHARLES: Merton made himself at home immediately, saying, 'You must take me as I am,' to which I replied: 'Yes – and you must take us as we are. We're homely people, we are not swells.' He answered 'No, I can see that.'

CARRIE: Mr Gowing laughed fit to burst his – fit to burst.

CHARLES: Only to be reproved in a most gentlemanly fashion by Merton, who said *(As Merton.)* 'Mr Pooter prefers a simple, wholesome life to gadding about to twopenny-halfpenny tea-drinking afternoon...'

CARRIE: Et cetera, et cetera. After a few more pleasantries of the most effusive, buttering-up variety, Mr Merton avowed that –

CHARLES: – he should treat me as a friend, and put me down for a dozen of his 'Lockanbar' whisky. Thirty-six shillings and cheap at the price.

CARRIE: Half a dozen would be even cheaper – and to anyone seeing double, they would still look to be a dozen.

CHARLES: *(Ignoring this.)* Merton further said that at any time I wanted any passes for the theatre I was to let him know. His name stands good for any theatre in London.

CARRIE: April twentieth. To tea with my old school friend Annie Fullers.

CHARLES: Now Mrs James, of Sutton.

CARRIE: Distressed to find Annie in straightened circumstances, being reduced to taking in sewing – 'obliging friends so as to keep my hands busy', as she puts it. I gather that Mr James's venture into the field of Bronchial Cigarillos for the relief of *(A delicate cough.)* –

CHARLES: PHLEGM.

CARRIE: – have not been the success he hoped for.

CHARLES: Carrie reminded me that as her old school friend, Mrs James of Sutton –

CARRIE: Annie Fullers as was.

CHARLES: – had come up with her husband for a few days, it would look kind to take them to the theatre, and would I drop a line to Mr Merton – my wine merchant – asking him for passes for four, either for –

CARRIE: The Italian Opera...

CHARLES: The Haymarket...

CARRIE: The Savoy...

CHARLES: Or the Lyceum.

CARRIE: April twenty-first. He has sent us four seats for the Tank Theatre, Islington.

CHARLES: And his bill for a dozen 'Lockanbar' whisky.

CARRIE: April twenty-third. Spent the entire day attending to the arrangements for our first dinner party in our new home, to which Annie Fullers –

CHARLES: Now Mrs James, of Sutton.

CARRIE: – and her husband are invited before the theatre this evening. After consulting my 'Lady Cartnell' I arranged the following menu. First course, gravy soup. Entrée, croquettes of mutton. Second course, cold broiled beef with oyster sauce, mashed potatoes, bottled beetroot, boiled onions. Third course, compote of rhubarb, ladies' fingers. Dessert, *Café*.

CHARLES: Carrie made a nice meat-tea before the theatre.

(As CHARLES and CARRIE emerge from the front door, donning evening cloaks, the parlour trucks upstage. Well downstage a theatre box office, flanked by a poster, trucks on to the sound of appropriate theatre music. It is manned by FACTOTUM.)

CARRIE: The dinner party was a great success. I wish I could say as much for the theatrical portion of the evening.

Having reached the Tank Theatre, Islington – a low place, so I feared Annie and Mr James would regard it, little better than a music hall – there was a mix-up over the tickets.

CHARLES: The man looked at them, then called out a Mr Willowly, the manager, who said: 'Who gave you these?' I said : 'Mr Merton, of course.' He said: 'Merton, who's he?' I answered, rather sharply: 'You ought to know, his name's good at any theatre in London.' He replied: 'Oh, is it? Well it ain't no good here.'

CARRIE: While Charles was arguing fruitlessly with the manager, Mr James slipped away and returned with tickets for Box H.

CHARLES: I said to James: 'Why, how on earth did you manage it?' To my horror he replied: 'Why, paid for it, of course.'

CARRIE: I was never so humiliated.

CHARLES: This was humiliating enough, and I could scarcely follow the play, but worse was to come. I was leaning out of the box, when my patent bow tie fell into the pit below. To my horror, a clumsy man –

CARRIE: *(Overriding him.)* Worse was to come. Reaching the box, we found that Mr James had purchased silk programmes for all. I tried to signal Charlie to offer at least to pay for these, but he was too occupied with his ridiculous patent bow tie which had fallen into the pit –

CHARLES: *(Overriding her.)* – where a clumsy man, I say, put his foot on it!

CARRIE: Serve him right.

CHARLES: *(Petulantly.)* To hide the absence of the tie I had to keep my chin down the rest of the evening, which caused a pain at the back of my neck.

(The box office trucks off. The parlour set trucks downstage. CARRIE takes off her cloak and speaks as CHARLES lets himself in through the front door carrying two tins of Pinkford's red enamel paint.)

CARRIE: April tenty-fifth. Beside myself with rage. His lordship came home bearing two tins of Pinkford's red enamel paint, as advertised.

CHARLES: I hastened through tea, went into the garden and painted some flowerpots.

CARRIE: *(Ironically, to CHARLES.)* If there was one job about the house I wanted you to do above all others, it was to paint the flowerpots.

CHARLES: Your wish is my command, Carrie dear.

CARRIE: As usual, he took my sarcasm for praise, and looked so pleased with himself that my heart melted. I said: 'Oh, Charlie, you've always some newfangled craze.' Then I returned indoors, leaving him painting a brick.

CHARLES: Went upstairs into the servant's bedroom and painted her washstand –

CARRIE: Her towel-horse –

CHARLES: And her chest of drawers.

CARRIE: Red, if you please!

(SARAH, having angrily cleared the tea things, goes out, slamming the door.)

CHARLES: As an example of the ignorance of the lower classes in the matter of taste, Sarah –

CARRIE: My maid.

CHARLES: – couldn't see any improvement. She thought –

CARRIE: *(As SARAH.)* 'They looked very well as they was before, sir.' If that girl gives notice I shall paint his head.

CHARLES: April twenty-sixth. Got some more red enamel paint, and painted the coal-scuttle and the backs of our *Shakespeare.*

CARRIE: April twenty-seventh. Sharp words with Charlie, who has painted the bath vermilion without consulting me. I have never heard of such a thing as a red bath.

CHARLES: It's merely a matter of taste, Carrie.

CARRIE: However, it is quite obvious to me – as it would be to him if he would only read the instructions on the tin before painting everything in sight – that Pinkford's paint must either flake or dissolve when introduced to scalding water. Whereupon Charlie will have to ask Farmerson's to come in and paint the bath white – exactly as he should have done in the first place.

CHARLES: April twenty-eighth. Cummings dropped in, but he said he couldn't stop – he had only called to leave the *Bicycle News*, as he had done with it.

CARRIE: No sooner had he departed than Mr Gowing arrived – again.

CHARLES: I said, 'A very extraordinary thing has struck me.'

CARRIE: Charlie made ever such a droll observation.

CHARLES: *(Smirks.)* I said –

CARRIE: *(Smiles.)* He said –

CHARLES: *(Sniggers.)* I said –

CARRIE: *(Giggles.)* He said –

CHARLES: 'Doesn't it seem odd that Gowing's always coming and Cummings always going?

(While CHARLES is convulsed in silent laughter, CARRIE notes the joke as she remembers it.)

CARRIE: 'Doesn't it seem odd that one of you is always arriving while the other is always leaving?'

(CHARLES' laughter tails off into a philosophical sigh.)

CHARLES: April twenty-ninth. Woke up with a fearful headache and symptoms of another cold.

CARRIE: Painter's colic.

CHARLES: Decided to take a bath as hot as I could bear it.

(CARRIE hugs herself in anticipation as CHARLES mimes stepping into the bath.)

Got in – very hot, but very acceptable. I lay still for some time. On moving my hand above the surface of the water I experienced the greatest fright I ever received in the whole course of my life – for my hand, as it seemed, was full of blood. My first thought was that I had ruptured an artery and was bleeding to death, and should be discovered looking like a second Marat, as I remember him at Madame Tussaud's. My second thought was to ring the bell, but then I remembered –

CARRIE: No bell to ring.

CHARLES: My third was, that after all it was nothing but the enamel paint, which had dissolved with boiling water.

(CARRIE smiles with self-satisfaction.)

I stepped out of the bath resembling a Red Indian. Determined not to say a word to Carrie, but to tell Farmerson to come on Monday –

BOTH: And paint the bath white.

CHARLES: April thirtieth!

CARRIE: The proudest day of my life.

CHARLES: Perfectly astounded at receiving an invitation for Carrie and myself from the Lord and Lady Mayoress, in the Mansion House, to meet –

(CARRIE has risen and is reading the card with him.)

CARRIE: The representatives of trade and commerce!

CHARLES: *(Taking her hands.)* Carrie, darling, I was a proud man when I led you down the aisle of the church on our wedding day. That pride will be equalled, if not surpassed, when I lead my dear pretty wife up to the Lord and Lady Mayoress at the Mansion House.

CARRIE: Charlie dear. It is I who have to be proud of you. And I am very, very proud of you. You have called me pretty; and as long as I am pretty in your eyes, I am happy. You, dear old Charlie, are not handsome, but you are good, which is far more noble!

(CHARLES kisses her tenderly.)

(Briskly, back to her diary.) I shall want a new silk dress, court gloves, fan, Dolly Varden dress shoes, stockings, evening bag from Shoolbred's, but otherwise I shall make do with what I have got.

CHARLES: *(To CARRIE, looking over the invitation.)* There will be dancing, I see.

CARRIE: Oh, Charlie, I have not danced with you for years! *(Writing.)* Asked Charlie if I might send the invitation to my mother, to look at.

CHARLES: I consented.

CARRIE: Putting his arm around my shoulder he said –

CHARLES: Of course you may! I want all the world to know that my little wife is invited to the Mansion House... Why Carrie, my love, you're crying!

(Giving him a hug, CARRIE takes the invitation and hurries out of the room. CHARLES dabs an eye and then coughs self-consciously and pulls himself together.)

Told Mr Perkupp, at the office, that we had received an invitation to the Mansion House. He said, to my astonishment, that he himself gave in my name to the Lord Mayor's secretary. I felt this rather discounted the value of the invitation.

(During the following, CHARLES produces a tin of Pickford's enamel paint and very carefully paints his opera hat a shiny black.)

In the luncheon hour, bought picture postcards of the Mansion House and sent one to Gowing, advising him not to call next Monday, as we are asked to the Lord Mayor's reception. Sent the other to Cummings, similarly phrased.

May first. While speaking incidentally to Spotch, one of our head clerks, about the Mansion House ball, he said: 'Oh I'm asked, but don't think I shall go.' When a vulgar man like Spotch is asked I feel my invitation is considerably debased.

(CARRIE re-enters wearing an all-concealing cloak and with her hands behind her back. She is at pains not to let CHARLES see what she is hiding from him as he goes out to change.)

CARRIE: May second. Devoted much of the day reading up 'Lady Cartmell' on matters of dress, etiquette, forms of address and so on.

(She now reveals that she has been holding the invitation behind her back – now blemished by a port-wine stain.)

(Ruefully.) Alas, Lady Cartmell is silent on the subject of removing port-wine stains from pasteboard. *This* is how the invitation came back from my mother's!

(During the following she rubs at the invitation with various preparations brought in by SARAH.)

Cold water applied with a handkerchief would not remove the blemish – nor hot water applied with butter muslin – nor chloride of soda – nor common soap – nor Neave's Varnish Syain remover – nor purified bullock's blood – nor essence of lemon – nor Fuller's earth – and rectified spirits of wine only made the wine stain worse! *(Examining her handiwork.)* Oh dear!

(In trepidation, she props the card on the mantelpiece. CHARLES returns, wearing full evening dress but still attempting to tie his white tie.)

CHARLES: At long last, May the – *(His eye falls on the disfigured invitation card.)* Carrie's mother returned the Lord Mayor's invitation with a port-wine stain over it. I was too angry to say anything. *(Nevertheless, after a moment's fuming.)* Caroline!

(CARRIE has removed her cloak to reveal her ballgown.)

CARRIE: Yes dear?

CHARLES: Never have I seen my little wife look so lovely.

CARRIE: Thank you, dear.

CHARLES: I thought perhaps the dress was a little too long behind and decidedly too low in front, but Carrie and Mrs James –

CARRIE: Who came from Sutton to assist with my toilette.

CHARLES: – assured me with one voice that –

CARRIE: It is à la mode!

(She takes over the task of tying CHARLES's tie, he having fudged it.)

Now as you were saying dear – at long last...

CHARLES: May seventh. A big red-letter day – viz...

CARRIE: Engagements for this evening: Ten o'clock –

CHARLES: Reception –

CARRIE: By the Worshipful the Lord Mayor and the Lady Mayoress of London –

CHARLES: At the Mansion House –

CARRIE: To meet the representatives of trade –

CHARLES: And commerce!

(Polka music. Arm in arm, they sally forth to the Lord Mayor's Ball, which is represented by the musicians in their minstrels' gallery, cut-out Du Maurier figures of other guests, and, downstage, a sumptuous Victorian buffet table, impossibly elaborate with vulgar confections and ice sculptures.

The FACTOTUM takes their cloaks.)

CARRIE: Bewigged footman looked sneeringly at port stain on invitation.

(They look around anxiously for familiar faces.)

CHARLES: We arrived at the Mansion House too early, which was rather fortunate, for I had the opportunity of speaking to his lordship, who graciously condescended to talk with me some minutes – but I must say I was disappointed to find he did not even know Mr Perkupp. I felt as if we had been invited to the Mansion House by one who did not himself know the Lord Mayor!

CARRIE: As crowds began to arrive, compared appearances and concluded that my dress held its own against all but the grandest, and was *not* too low-cut, despite what Charles may think.

CHARLES: I shall never forget the grand sight. My humble pen can never describe it.

CARRIE: Considered it a pity we didn't know anybody, and repeated this thought to Charlie. (*To CHARLES.*) Isn't it a pity we don't know anybody?

CHARLES: I wish you would stop saying that, Caroline! In any case, isn't that Mr Franching, from Peckham?

(*As CHARLES turns to greet MR FRANCHING, CARRIE grabs his coat-tails in a panic.*)

CARRIE: Don't leave me!

CHARLES: (*Taking her arm.*) Proceeded to the supper room, where Carrie ate most heartily, which pleased me, for I sometimes think she is not strong. There was scarcely a dish she did not taste. For myself, I was so thirsty I could not eat much.

(*CHARLES has taken up a glass, CARRIE a plate and a napkin, from the elaborate Mayoral buffet.*)

CARRIE: He drank one glass of champagne after another.

CHARLES: Receiving a sharp slap on the shoulder, I turned, and to my amazement, saw Farmerson, our ironmonger. He said in the most familiar way: 'This is better than Brickfield Terrace, eh?' I simply looked at him and said coolly: 'I never expected to see you here.' He said, with a loud, coarse laugh: 'I like that – if you, why not me?' To which I retorted: 'Certainly.' I wish I could have thought of something better to say.

(*With a sniff, CARRIE firmly removes his hand and puts it on a table.*)

Farmerson said: 'Can I get your good lady something?'

CARRIE: I thank you – no.

CHARLES: I said to him: You never sent to paint the bath, as
I requested.' Farmerson said: 'Pardon me, Pooter, no shop
when we're in company, please.' Before I could think of
a reply, one of the sheriffs, in full court costume, slapped
Farmerson on the back and hailed him as an old friend. To
think – that a man who mends our scraper should know a
member of the aristocracy.

CARRIE: The evening now began to deteriorate.

CHARLES: Introductions effected, the sheriff was so good as to
procure me a glass of champagne.

CARRIE: Averting my eyes for only a moment in order to deal
with a boiled custard, I addressed a word to Charles only
to discover he has deserted me and was chinking glasses
with Mr Farmerson. Stared at him until –

CHARLES: After a few moments' conversation I said: You must
excuse me now if I join Mrs Pooter.

(Bowing, he comes back to CARRIE.)

CARRIE: Don't let me take you away from your friends. I
am quite happy standing here alone in a crowd, knowing
nobody.

CHARLES: As it takes two to make a quarrel, and this was
neither the time nor the place for it, I gave my arm to
Carrie and –

CARRIE: – tried to make it up to me by asking me in the most
unctuous terms to dance.

CHARLES: *(To CARRIE.)* I hope my darling little wife will dance
the polka with me –

CARRIE: It's a waltz!

CHARLES: – if only for the sake of saying we have danced at
the Mansion House as guests of the Lord Mayor.

CARRIE: He could hardly see, let alone dance! None the less –

*(The dance music grows louder as CHARLES takes CARRIE in his
arms. They dance a few steps –)*

CHARLES: And one two three, one two three.

(– then fall over one another and sprawl to the floor. CHARLES sits up gingerly.)

Oh dear! A most unfortunate accident occurred.

CARRIE: *(Sitting up.)* In no time at all he had me over, grazing my elbow and breaking my priceless fan of Kachu eagle feathers belonging to –

CHARLES: Mrs James of Sutton. My head struck the floor with such violence that for a second or two I did not know what had happened.

CARRIE: There was a roar of laughter and I wished the floor would swallow me up. A gentleman named Mr Darwitts helped me up and escorted me for a restoring sip of wine, while Charles was brought back to his senses by his fine friends.

(CHARLES and CARRIE have risen and are turned in opposite directions.)

CHARLES: I expressed myself pretty strongly to Farmerson and others on the danger of having to dance on a plain polished floor.

CARRIE: Mr Darwitts was most polite and considerate, and talked easily of this and that as if the distressing incident had never happened. *(Dreamily.)* He used to own a book-bindery in Cornhill, but is now in the wholesale stationery line.

CHARLES: Farmerson said: 'Are you going? If so, you can give me a lift.'

CARRIE: *(Getting into a state.)* Of the journey home, what with the stench of tobacco smoke, Mr Farmerson knocking Annie's Kachu eagle-feather fan out of my hand as I tried to waft away the fumes, and Charles badgering him to come in for a nightcap of 'Lockanbar' whisky, despite the lateness of the hour – not to mention Mr Farmerson offering not a farthing towards his share of the cab, I shall say nothing! *(She goes into the house, slamming the door.)*

(The parlour tracks back in. It is morning.

SARAH enters and draws back the curtains. Barrel-organ sound from the street. Doing a little tidying, she goes out again.

Pause.

CHARLES, back in his day clothes, creeps slowly back into the room, clearly nursing a monumental hangover.)

CHARLES: *(Hollowly.)* Woke up with the most terrible headache. I could scarcely see, and the back of my neck was as if I had given it a crick. Went to Brownish's, the chemist, who gave me a draught, but was so bad at the office, I had to get leave to come home. Brownish's dose seems to have made me worse. Have eaten nothing all day.

(CARRIE flounces in.)

CARRIE: This evening, unable to eat the supper prepared for him – cold veal rolls with fat bacon and forcemeat – he came out with the cock-and-bull tale that –

CHARLES: I do believe I have been poisoned by the lobster mayonnaise at the Mansion House last night.

CARRIE: Champagne never did agree with you!

(CHARLES pursues her to the door as she sweeps out of the room.)

CHARLES: What nonsense you do talk, Caroline! I only had a glass and a half, and you know as well as I do –

(But she is gone. He turns back to his desk and studies a copy of the 'Blackfriars Bi-weekly News')

May ninth. Still a little shaky, with black specks. The *Blackfriars Bi-weekly News* contains a long list of the guests at the Mansion House Ball – including even that of Farmerson, our ironmonger. Disappointed to find our names omitted. More than vexed, because *(He dumps a bundle of newspapers into the wastepaper basket.)* we had ordered a dozen copies to send to our friends. Shall write to the editor.

CARRIE: *(Sweeping back into the room.)* *I* would have preferred to have let the subject of the Mansion House Ball drop, since no good ever came of protracted recriminations, but he was the one who had to bring it up at breakfast.

(They sit opposite one another at the parlour table.)

CHARLES: *(After reading his paper for a moment.)* Caroline –

CARRIE: Don't mention the Mansion House Ball to me!

CHARLES: I don't understand you, I'm sure.

CARRIE: Probably not – you were scarcely in a condition to understand anything.

CHARLES: Caroline – that will do!

CARRIE: Don't be so theatrical, it has no effect on me. Reserve that tone for your new friend *Mister* Farmerson, the ironmonger.

CHARLES: *(Rising stiffly.)* Will you excuse me, Caroline?

CARRIE: No, I will not, sir! Now *I'm* going to say something.

(Loud shunting noises as smoke billows into the room. The following speech by CARRIE is completely unheard as she pursues CHARLES about the room, wagging her finger and berating him.)

After professing to snub Mr Farmerson, you permit him to snub *you*, in my presence, and then accept his invitation to take a glass of champagne, and you don't limit yourself to one glass, oh no! You then offer this vulgar man a seat in our cab home…

(The train has gone by. We hear CARRIE loud and clear.)

Nor is that all!

CHARLES: Oh, but it is! *(He flees the room.)*

CARRIE: May tenth. Charles still sulking. He can be like a child sometimes. I told him as much: 'You can be like a child sometimes.' May eleventh. To the Fancy Bazaar, to look at new umbrella-covers. A tall, very straight-backed gentleman, standing by the stationery counter, raised his hat and hoped 'I was quite recovered'. It was none other than Mr Darwitts! We shook hands and talked for a moment, but then Mr Darwitts had to attend to his business – that of interesting the Fancy Bazaar in a new line of correspondence cards with rounded edges.

(During this, CHARLES has slunk back in, carrying a folded copy of the 'Blackfriars Bi-weekly News'. He sits.)

CARRIE: I told Charles of my encounter with Mr Darwitts, adding: 'I had not realized he was so tall. He has the bearing of a cavalry officer.'

CHARLES: A colour sergeant would be nearer the mark, from what I recall.

CARRIE: Which can be precious little, after what you had to drink that night.

CHARLES: I would rather not go into that again, *if* it's all the same to you, Caroline. *(He unfolds his paper.)*

CARRIE: I thought of more cutting remarks, but kept them to myself.

CHARLES: *(In exasperation.)* Oh, really! May twelfth! The *Blackfriars Bi-weekly News* has printed a short list of several names omitted from the guests at the Lord Mayor's Ball – but the stupid people have mentioned us as Mr and Mrs C. Porter!

CARRIE: I blame Charlie's illegible signature.

CHARLES: I will have you know Caroline, that Mr Perkupp considers my copperplate the best in the office.

CARRIE: We are not discussing your precious Mr Perkupp, or your precious copperplate, but your absurd signature.

CHARLES: The matter, Caroline, is closed. *(He turns away.)*

CARRIE: *(To her diary.)* We cannot go on like this. It will be better for both of us that I should go and stay for a spell with Annie Fullers –

(CHARLES, staring moodily out of the window, refuses to respond.)

Annie Fullers –

CHARLES: *(Sulkily.)* Now Mrs James.

CARRIE: Of-?

CHARLES: Sutton!

CARRIE: – until the storm clouds have blown over. I sent off a telegram and packed. Overhearing me instructing Sarah –

CHARLES: *(Brusquely.)* Her maid.

CARRIE: – on what to look for in a knuckle of veal, Charlie said –

CHARLES: Don't worry about me. I can always dine at the Club.

(CARRIE, putting on her bonnet, kisses him on the cheek.)

CARRIE: He will have to join one first.

(She picks up her hat box and goes off. CHARLES escorts her out. He returns, hidden behind an opened out copy of the 'Blackfriars Bi-weekly News' which he eventually screws into a ball and throws into the wastepaper basket.)

CHARLES: May sixteenth. Absolutely disgusted on opening today's *Blackfriars Bi-weekly News* to find the following paragraph. 'We have received two letters from Mrs and Mrs Charles Pewter, requesting us to announce the important fact that they were at the Mansion House Ball.' My time is far too valuable to bother about such trifles.

(At a loose end, CHARLES crosses and looks out of the window. He walks about the room and straightens a picture or two.)

May twentieth. The last few days terribly dull without Carrie.

(With his penholder, he taps out a little tune on his cheeks, then does some more pottering about, realigning the picture he has already straightened once.)

May twenty-first. Hoped Cummings or Gowing would call. Didn't. Called on them. Out.

(More pottering about. Then he brightens as SARAH brings in a postcard on a salver.)

May twenty-second. Welcome postcard from Carrie! 'Weather good. Annie' – now Mrs James of Sutton – 'and I just off to the Bon Marche to see demonstrated the new electro-plated self-pouring tea-pot. Forgot to mention that most of your collars are with the laundress. Your loving wife.' *(Kisses the postcard.)* Your *loving* wife. Forgiven at last! *(As he winds up the clock.)* May twenty-fourth. Thought of a joke. Question – how should one best buy a clock? Answer – on tick.

(He repeats it for the benefit of SARAH, who is clearing some things away.)

On tick!

(But SARAH goes out without reacting.)

(With a sigh.) No one to tell it to. *(Still listless, he brightens as he hears the sound of horse's hooves. Crossing to the window.)* May twenty-fifth. Carrie home again!

(As CARRIE enters, carrying some of her luggage, he welcomes her with open arms.)

Hurrah! She looks wonderfully well – except that the sun has caught her nose.

(She crossly detaches herself from his embrace, but then relents as she looks around the room.)

CARRIE: Home, sweet home, again! I would not change my dear little home for all the world – unless Charlie would agree to return to Peckham.

CHARLES: June first. This last week has been like old times, with Carrie being back, and Gowing and Cummings calling every evening. Played Consequences. It is a good game.

CARRIE: June second. Consequences yet again this evening. Mr Gowing several times overstepped the limits of good taste.

CHARLES: June fourth. To Mr and Mrs Cummings' to spend a quiet evening...

CARRIE: Away from Mr Gowing...

CHARLES: Gowing was there also. Mrs Cummings sang five or six songs, 'The Garden of Sleep' being best in my humble judgment. Then Carrie was persuaded to sing.

CARRIE: *(Promptly.)* 'Pretty Mocking Bird' by Sir Henry Bishop.

(She crosses to the piano.)

'Pretty Mocking Bird'

(Singing.) Living echo, living echo birds of eve,
Hush, hush thy wailing, cease, cease to grieve,
Pretty warbler wake the grove, pretty warbler wake the grove
To notes of joy, to songs of love,
To notes of joy, to songs of love, to songs of love, to songs of love,
Pretty mocking bird, pretty mocking bird,
Pretty pretty pretty mocking bird thy form I see,
Pretty mocking bird, pretty mocking bird,
Swinging with the breeze in the mangrove tree,
Swinging with the breeze in the mangrove tree,
Pretty pretty pretty pretty pretty pretty pretty mocking bird,
Thy form, form I see.

CHARLES: It was beautiful. If Carrie had been in better voice I don't think professionals could have sung it better.

CARRIE: July eighth. Brought some of the new fashionable correspondence cards, with rounded edges, at the Fancy Bazaar. Informed by the assistant that they are 'all the go'. Mr Darwitts must be well pleased.

(CHARLES scowls. Pause.)

July nineteenth. After an unusual silence, Charles said –

CHARLES: I have half a mind to keep Belgian hare rabbits.

CARRIE: Only a man with half a mind would think of such a stupid idea.

(Hurt, CHARLES disappears behind a copy of 'Exchange and Mart'.)

(To her diary.) He did not utter another word the whole evening.

(While CHARLES continues to read, CARRIE crosses and surreptitiously picks up his diary.)

July twentieth. His diary has become a succession of blank pages. What can he be about?

(Returning CHARLES's diary to its hiding-place, she sees him at work, now having removed his coat. She approaches on tiptoe. CHARLES, now sprawled on the floor working with a large sheet of graph paper and ruler, is startled as CARRIE looks over his shoulder.)

CARRIE: *(Reading.)* 'Elevation and plan for a hutch to house twelve Belgian hare rabbits…'

CHARLES: 'Scale – one quarter inch to one foot.'

CARRIE: On the day twelve rabbits enter this house, Charles, I shall leave it.

CHARLES: They will not be in the house, they will be in the garden.

CARRIE: Are you insane? What do you suppose the neighbours will think when they see the Pooters have turned their back garden into a poultry yard?

CHARLES: Rabbits are not poultry, dear. If only you would read the *Exchange and Mart,* Carrie, and see what Belgian hares are fetching these days. Quite apart from the money, and the little luxuries it would buy, every man should have his hobby.

CARRIE: I quite agree. Why do you not paint another brick?

(She whisks up the sheet of graph paper and crosses to the table where she uses it to wrap a book.)

July thirty-first. Posted to our dear son Willie, who is with the Bank at Oldham, the volume he has asked for especially, for his twentieth birthday…

CHARLES: Spink and Wicklow's *Principles of Banking*?

CARRIE: *On the Stage and Off,* by Mr Jerome K. Jerome… Used the only stiff wrapping paper I could find.

CHARLES: August fourth. The first post brought a nice letter from our dear son Willie, acknowledging a trifling birthday present from his mother.

CARRIE: No sooner had I read it for the eleventh or twelfth time, than a hackney carriage pulled up at the door –

CHARLES: – and to our utter amazement –

CARRIE: – who should step out of it but Willie himself!

CHARLES: He looks well.

CARRIE: He looks thin.

CHARLES: He seems taller.

CARRIE: Practically consumptive.

CHARLES: He said he had got leave from the Bank, and as Monday is a holiday he thought to give us a little surprise. What a fine young man he has grown.

CARRIE: He has begun to slouch, he wears his hair too long, and has been biting his nails, and his complexion is yellow, like parchment, from the sulphuric air of the north – but otherwise, what a fine young man he has grown!

CHARLES: One would scarcely believe he was Carrie's son. *(Hastily as she glares at him.)* More like a younger brother.

CARRIE: Eked out our usual leg of mutton with macaronis and cheese, followed by Welsh rarebits and apple fritters which I am sorry to say Willie hardly touched.

CHARLES: We had a bottle of port after dinner, and drank Willie's health.

(He has poured a large port for himself and a small one for CARRIE. They raise their glasses.)

CARRIE: The toast was the signal for Willie, unbuttoning his waistcoat, to announce –

CHARLES: *(As LUPIN.)* 'Oh, by-the-by, did I tell you I've cut my first name, "William", and taken the second name, "Lupin"? In fact, I'm only known at Oldham as Lupin

Pooter. If you were to "Willie" me there, they wouldn't know what you meant.'

CARRIE: I am delighted and honoured that my only son should wish to be known by his mother's maiden name. It is a proud and distinguished name, and one that goes back into the mists of history.

CHARLES: *(Who has been courteously waiting for her to finish.)* August sixth –

CARRIE: The Berkshire Lupins, as my branch is, have graves in Reading and district dating as far back as 1709. There may be earlier Lupins, but they are indecipherable.

CHARLES: August sixth –

CARRIE: The Essex Lupins, mainly smallholding stock, may be traced back to the seventeenth century, so I have been told.

CHARLES: *(With a yawn.)* August sixth –

CARRIE: There have been many outstanding Lupins. Edward Lupin was a member of the Metropolitan Board of Works, Alexander Lupin was at the University of Durham, later to become –

(CHARLES has heard this many times before. He joins in!)

BOTH: The general manager of the Mutual steam Boiler Insurance Company.

(Another pause, as CHARLES still waits. But CARRIE has now finished. With a sweet smile, she prompts him.)

CARRIE: *(Obligingly.)* August sixth...

CHARLES: Bank Holiday.

CARRIE: No sign of Willie – Lupin – at breakfast.

CHARLES: Or at dinner. *(Crossing to the door he shouts.)* Willie!

CARRIE: *(Correcting him.)* Lupin!

CHARLES: Sorry – Lupin! Reminded my son that little though we have seen him, if he was to catch the 5:30 train he must leave in an hour.

CARRIE: Lupin said –

CHARLES: *(As LUPIN.)* 'Look here, guvnor, it's no use beating about the bush. I've tendered my resignation at the Bank.'

CARRIE: Not before time.

CHARLES: I said: 'How dare you, sir? How dare you take such a serious step without consulting me? Don't answer me, sir! You will sit down immediately, and write a note at my dictation, withdrawing your resignation and amply apologizing!'

CARRIE: Now he is at liberty to offer his services to one of the Lombard Street banks –

CHARLES: Imagine my dismay when he replied with a loud guffaw: 'It's no use. If you want the good old truth, I've got the chuck.'

CARRIE: – or even the Bank of England. I care not, so long as he lives at home, where he belongs.

CHARLES: The ambition of my life would be to get him into Mr Perkupp's firm. But first – *(Throwing off his cares.)* August thirteenth. Our annual holidays. Hurrah for good old Broadstairs!

(The parlour trucks upstage. The minstrels' gallery reveals pianist and banjo-player in Christy Minstrel costumes. CHARLES dons a straw helmet and CARRIE acquires a sun bonnet and a parasol. A pair of bright deck-chairs are set up by the FACTOTUM, to the tune of a vigorous cakewalk.)

CARRIE: *(Less enthusiastic.)* To Broadstairs. Not our usual rooms, as Charlie left it too late to secure them, but clean apartments near the station. Lupin observed, as a passing train rattled the windows –

CHARLES: *(As LUPIN.)* 'Halloh! Quite the home from home!'

CARRIE: Our son has become something of a wit. I'm sure I don't know where he gets it from.

CHARLES: The landlady had a nice five o'clock meat-tea ready, which we all enjoyed, though Lupin seemed fastidious because there happened to be a fly in the butter... August fourteenth.

CARRIE: Rain. August fifteenth.

CHARLES: Rain. August sixteenth.

BOTH: Aah! *(They respond to the sun.)*

CARRIE: By train to Margate, where the first person we met was Mr Gowing. Charlie seemed surprised. I was not. *My* only surprise was not to find Mr Cummings there also. That omission, however, is soon to be remedied, for Mr Gowing said –

CHARLES: *(As GOWING.)* 'You know the Cummings are here too?'

CARRIE: If we went to the North Pole, we should bump into Mr Cummings and Mr Gowing and end up playing Consequences.

CHARLES: August twentieth. Gowing suggested we should play Cutlets, a game we never heard of. He sat on a chair, and invited Carrie –

CARRIE: As usual, overstepping the mark.

CHARLES: – to sit on his lap.

CARRIE: I think not, Mr Gowing.

CHARLES: After some species of wrangling, *I* sat on Gowing's knees and Carrie sat on the edge of mine. Lupin sat on the edge of Carrie's lap, then Cummings on Lupin's, et cetera, et cetera.

(He and CARRIE, playing the participants in the game, sit on one another's laps in a deck-chair in turn.)

We looked very ridiculous and laughed a good deal.

CARRIE: Mr Gowing then said –

CHARLES: *(As GOWING.)* 'Are you a believer in the Great Mogul?' We had to answer all together –

BOTH: Yes – oh yes. Yes – oh yes. Yes – oh yes.

CARRIE: *Then,* Mr Gowing said –

CHARLES: *(As GOWING.)* 'So am I' – and suddenly got up.

(CHARLES and CARRIE fall to the ground.)

The result of this stupid joke was that poor Carrie banged her head on the fender. Mrs Cummings put some vinegar on, but through this we didn't have anything to put on our fish supper.

(The parlour trucks back in as they return home.)

CHARLES: August twenty-first. Home, sweet home, again.

CARRIE: House fusty and beads not aired. *(She runs her finger along a piece of furniture.)*

CHARLES: *(Looking through his letters.)* Fripps, Tapster and Partners write to say they are sorry, but they have no vacancy among their staff of clerks for Lupin. August twenty-third. Bought a stag's head made of plaster of Paris and coloured brown. It will look just the thing for the parlour, and give it style.

(As he speaks CHARLES mounts a chair and hangs the stag's head over the door.)

CARRIE: September fifth. Despite his many influential acquaintanceships in the City, Charlie is having difficulty in finding a place for Lupin. Our son is not much at home these days.

CHARLES: He has to catch up on London life, as he puts it.

CARRIE: I wish he would tell us where he goes.

CHARLES: October thirtieth. I should very much like to know who has wilfully torn the last five or six weeks out of my diary. It is perfectly monstrous!

CARRIE: He at once suspected me. I should like to know why.

CHARLES: I asked Carrie if she knew anything about it.

(CARRIE sniffs.)

That is not an answer to my question!

CARRIE: Waving his arms in a grandiose manner, he knocked over a vase given to me for our wedding by Mrs Bursett, of Dalston. Oh Charlie.

CHARLES: Carrie was very upset.

CARRIE: I let him *believe* I was upset. In truth, I never liked Mrs Bursett, or her vase, and it is a relief to see the back of it.

CHARLES: November third. *(Opening a letter.)* Good news at last. Mr Perkupp has got an appointment for Lupin. Oh, how my mind is relieved. Went to Lupin's room to take the good news to him, but he was in bed, very seedy.

CARRIE: Declining breakfast, Lupin explained that he had last night been elected a member of an amateur dramatic club, called the Holloway Comedians, and though it was a pleasant evening, he had sat in a draught, and got neuralgia in the head.

CHARLES: Had up a special bottle of port in the evening.

CARRIE: We filled our glasses,

(CHARLES does so.)

and Charlie said –

CHARLES: Lupin, my boy, I have some good and unexpected news for you. Mr Perkupp has procured you an appointment!

CARRIE: Lupin said –

CHARLES: *(As LUPIN.)* 'Good biz!'

CARRIE: And we drained our glasses. Lupin then said –

CHARLES: *(As LUPIN.)* 'Fill up the glasses again, for I have some good and unexpected news for you.'

CARRIE: I hope we shall think it good news, Lupin.

CHARLES: *(As LUPIN.)* 'Oh, it's all right, mater. I'm engaged to be married!'

(CARRIE swoons. CHARLES, hastily putting down the decanter from which he is pouring, just manages to catch her in his arms.)

Act Two

CHARLES and CARRIE are discovered at the piano (with SARAH turning the pages of the music) singing a duet, 'When Other Lips'. This they do most sweetly, though one verse is spoiled by a train thundering past. The duet over, they bow and curtsey respectively.

CHARLES: When other lips and other hearts their tales of love shall tell

CARRIE: In language whose excess imparts, the power they feel so well

CHARLES: There may perhaps in such a scene some recollection be

CARRIE: Of days that have as happy been, and you'll remember me

CHARLES: And you'll remember, you'll remember me.

CARRIE: When coldness or deceit shall sleight, the beauty now they prize

CHARLES: And deem it but a faded light, which beams within your eyes

When hollow hearts shall wear a mask 'twill break your own to see

BOTH: In such a moment I but ask that you'll remember me

That you'll remember me, you'll remember me.

(CARRIE goes off.)

CHARLES: November fourth. Carrie and I troubled about that mere boy Lupin getting engaged to be married without consulting us or anything. He tells us that the lady's name is Daisy Mutlar, that she is the nicest, prettiest and most accomplished girl he ever met, and that he will wait fifty years for her if he must. Otherwise we know nothing about the young lady.

(CARRIE now returns wearing an outdoor coat and hat, of which she divests herself during the following extract from her diary.)

CARRIE: Miss Daisy Mutlar resides at Avoncrest, No. 17 Atha Grove, with her parents and brother. Chancing to pass along Atha Grove on my afternoon walk, I could not help but notice the house. It is a double-fronted residence with a porch and claret-glass surrounds to the bay windows, with engraved corner sunbursts.

(CHARLES tries to continue, but fails.)

Miss Mutlar is older than Lupin, although he will not say by how many summers. She is neither tall nor short – of the medium height, I gather.

(Again CHARLES tries to get a word in.)

She occupies herself with charitable works for unfortunates, at the North London Outcasts' Haven.

CHARLES: Lupin further said –

CARRIE: Lupin was introduced to Miss Mutlar by her brother Mr Frank Mutlar, of the Holloway Comedians amateur dramatic club.

CHARLES: Lupin further said –

CARRIE: Miss Mutlar herself does not indulge in amateur theatricals. Miss Mutlar speaks a little French fluently. She has not been engaged before that we are aware of. *(Removing her gloves and sitting.)* That is the sum of our knowledge of Miss Mutlar for the present.

CHARLES: Thank you, my dear. Lupin further said, with much warmth, that he lived with an object now – to make Daisy Mutlar Daisy Pooter, and he would guarantee she would not disgrace the family of Pooter.

CARRIE: *(With a sniffle.)* It seems only yesterday since I was pushing our little son in his bassinet across Peckham Rye.

CHARLES: November fifth. Lupin went with me to the office, and had a long conversation with Mr Perkupp, the result of which was that he accepted a clerkship in the firm of Job Cleanands and Co., Stock and Share Brokers. In the evening we went round to the Cummings', to have a few fireworks. It began to rain, and I thought it rather dull.

CARRIE: A damp squib. *(She waits expectantly, but in vain, for his laugh.)*

CHARLES: Yes – a complete waste of time and money.

CARRIE: He can be very dense sometimes.

CHARLES: November seventh. Lupin asked Carrie to call on Mrs Mutlar.

CARRIE: After consulting *(Doing so.)* my 'Lady Cartmell', I informed him that it was Mrs Mutlar's place to call on me. Lupin cried –

CHARLES: *(As LUPIN.)* 'Oh, pooh, mater!' The matter was settled by Carrie saying she could not find any visiting cards, and we must get another twenty-five printed.

CARRIE: I suggested Messrs Darwitts' –

(CHARLES looks suspicious.)

– the wholesale stationers, who advertise in the *Globe*, but Charles said coldly that –

CHARLES: You have Darwitts on the brain, Caroline. I shall go to Black's as usual.

CARRIE: Our last 'as usual' was four years ago. November ninth. The house next door standing empty, whom I see being escorted up the path by the agent but the Misses Tipper, acquaintances form our Peckham days. Presently they called. They are mindful to move to Holloway to be near their brother, Mr Oswald Tipper, who has a veterinary practice here, but next door does not suit.

CHARLES: November eleventh. Returned home to find the house in a most disgraceful uproar. Carrie appeared very frightened, while Sarah –

CARRIE: *(Tearfully.)* My maid.

CHARLES: – was excited and crying. The charwoman, Mrs Birrell, who had evidently been drinking –

CARRIE: She's been at the 'Lockanbar' whisky!

CHARLES: – was shouting at the top of her voice –

CARRIE: *(As MRS BIRRELL.)* 'I'm no thief – I'm a respectable married woman, I am, what has to work 'ard for 'er living, and I'll smack anyone's face what says different.

CHARLES: I ascertained that the cause of the row was that Sarah had accused Mrs Birrell of using the missing pages of my diary to wrap up some kitchen fat and leavings.

CARRIE: My Charlie took command of the situation.

CHARLES: Mrs Birrell had slapped Sarah's face saying –

CARRIE: *(As MRS BIRRELL.)* 'I've never took no leavings, never, 'cos there's never no leavings to take!'

CHARLES: I ordered Sarah back to her work, and requested Mrs Birrell to go home at once.

CARRIE: If only Mr Perkupp could have seen him! When occasion demands, my husband can be as masterful as the captain of any ship!

(CHARLES, preening himself at this compliment dons his hat. Sound of church music. Downstage, CHARLES and CARRIE are seen strolling home from church, arm-in-arm. They are bowed off by the FACTOTUM as the Vicar.)

CHARLES: November twelfth – Sunday. Coming home from church we met Lupin, Daisy Mutlar and her brother. *(Raising his hat.)* Daisy was introduced to us and we walked home together.

CARRIE: Miss Mutlar is *not*, after all, of the medium height. She is what I would call large, being big boned, as well as a good three inches taller than Lupin. Her dress, although by no means 'flash', was not, I thought, subdued enough for a Sunday. She is too old for him –

CHARLES: By at least eight years...

CARRIE: I should say ten. Her hair is no stranger to the automatic curler. However, I found her sensible and respectful in conversation, although given to giggling at the merest pleasantry. This is probably nerves. Taking one thing with another Miss Mutlar seems a nice young woman, who makes the best of a naturally plain appearance.

(They re-enter the parlour.)

CHARLES: Spent the afternoon writing invitations, as we have asked Miss Daisy Mutlar and her brother over on Wednesday to meet a few of our friends.

CARRIE: We may as well make it a nice affair. Why not ask Mr Perkupp?

CHARLES: I fear we are not quite grand enough for him.

CARRIE: There can be no offence in asking him.

CHARLES: Certainly not!

(SARAH enters with a tray of cards, looking at them excitedly.)

CARRIE: November fourteenth. Nearly all our friends have sent word that they take pleasure in –

CHARLES: Or in some cases have the honour –

CARRIE: Of accepting our invitation to a reception at The Laurels tomorrow. Mr Perkupp –

CHARLES: – if able to get away from a previous engagement in Kensington.

CARRIE: An unspecified number of the Holloway Comedians accepted orally, with the message conveyed by Lupin –

CHARLES: *(As LUPIN.)* 'Good biz. Lead us to it.'

CARRIE: Mr Darwitts greatly regrets his inability to attend... *(Disappointed.)* Mr Darwitts.

CHARLES: *(Smirking.)* Annual dinner of Master Stationers' Company – so he says.

CARRIE: Kept very busy making ladies' fingers, saucercakes, coconut buns, jam puffs, and glazing a ham, baking a stand-pie...

(The catalogue is drowned by the sound of a train going by.)

...and preparing a blancmange. Valuable time lost in picking cinder fragments out of an Indian trifle.

CHARLES: My dear Carrie – this is no time to concern yourself with *trifles.*

CARRIE: Charles Pooter, I am very busy with the preparations for our party. Indeed, I am distraught, from the effort of making everything just so, in case your precious Mr Perkupp should *deign* to drop in after visiting his fine friends in Kensington.

CHARLES: That is unfair, Caroline. You were the one who *would* invite Mr Perkupp.

CARRIE: *You* were the one who said he was too grand for us, and that is why I am slaving to make our home look like a palace.

CHARLES: It has always been a palace to me, Carrie.

CARRIE: *(Back to her diary.)* The compliment came just in time, for I chanced to be holding a jug of blancmange mixture, of a size approximating to his hat.

The entire evening spent rearranging the furniture and moving our Japanese screen.

(During this CHARLES and CARRIE are performing the tasks she is describing. They cross to a Japanese folding screen.)

CHARLES: If we moved the Japanese screen once we moved it a hundred times... After – ahhh! *(A piercing yell as they do so, trapping his hand.)* – trapping my hand badly, we decided to leave it be.

CARRIE: November fifteenth. Our first important party since we have been in this house.

(They move towards the door to receive their guests. SARAH pulls back the folding doors to reveal a splendid supper laid out in the back parlour.)

CHARLES: *(Handing a glass of champagne to CARRIE, he toasts her. To his diary.)* The supper room looked ever so nice, and Carrie truly said –

CARRIE: We need not be ashamed of its being seen by Mr Perkupp, should he honour us by coming.

CHARLES: Carrie looked a picture.

CARRIE: Miss Mutlar wore a dress of pillar-box'red sateen, which even Annie Fullers – now Mrs James, of Sutton – declared was cut too low, and without a shred of lace to cover her shoulders, which are very large, and freckled.

CHARLES: The first arrival was Gowing, who with his usual taste, greeted me with: 'Hulloh, Pooter; why, your trousers are too short.' I simply said: 'Very likely, and you will find my temper short also.'

CARRIE: We had some music...

(We hear light piano music – a ballad mixing into a comic song – over the following.)

CHARLES: Lupin, who never left Daisy's side for a moment, raved over her singing of 'Some Day'. It was pretty enough...

CARRIE: Out of tune... Supper was at ten. Messrs Cummings and Gowing ate as if they had not had a meal for a month.

CHARLES: I told Carrie to keep something back in case Mr Perkupp should honour us. Gowing annoyed me very much –

CARRIE: And me.

CHARLES: – by filling a large tumbler of champagne, and drinking it straight off. Tried to keep a bottle back, but Lupin got hold of it –

CARRIE: *(Disapproving.)* And took it to Daisy Mutlar.

CHARLES: Stillbrook then amused with a song, 'What have you done with your Cousin John?', during which Lupin and Frank disappeared. Asked where they were, Mr Watson, of the Holloway Comedians, said: 'It's a case of "Oh, what a surprise!" '

CARRIE: We were directed to form a circle, which we did. *(They join hands, as in a circle.)*

Mr Watson then said –

CHARLES: *(As WATSON.)* 'I have much pleasure in introducing the celebrated Blondin Donkey!' Frank and Lupin then bounded into the room, Lupin with his face whitened like a clown and Frank with a hearthrug tied around his waist!

CARRIE: How we howled!

(They roar with laughter and then stop abruptly, wheeling round and looking at the door.)

Why, Mr Perkupp!

CHARLES: He would not leave his hat. I apologized for the foolery, but Mr Perkupp said: 'Oh, it seems amusing.' I could see he was not a bit amused. There was no champagne left...

CARRIE: Mr Gowing saw to that.

CHARLES: Mr Perkupp said he required nothing but a glass of soda water. *(Pressing an empty siphon, he looks apologetic.)* Mr Perkupp said to Carrie, with a smile: 'I really require nothing, Mrs Pooter. I am most pleased to see you and your husband in your own home.'

CARRIE: There cannot be many clerks in the City, whose principals would bother to cross London, just to drink their health in soda water – had there been any to drink. It shows how my husband is regarded.

CHARLES: I took Mr Perkupp out to his carriage.

CARRIE: As they went out, I saw that Mr Perkupp had stepped on an open jam puff that must have dropped from somebody's plate. The encumbrance cannot have escaped his notice, his dress boots having thin soles, yet neither by word nor gesture did he intimate his awareness of treading cherry jam into my carpet. Whatever his deficiencies as a man of commerce, Mr Perkupp is a *gentleman.*

CHARLES: I felt despondent as I went back to the room and told Carrie: 'The party has been a failure.'

CARRIE: Nonsense. It was a great success.

CHARLES: I drank two glasses of port and felt much better.

(He kisses her.)

CARRIE: Oh, Charlie. What a spoony, old thing you are! *(To her diary.)* And so saying, I squeezed his hand –

(CHARLES lets out an almighty yell.)

– quite forgetting he had trapped it in the Japanese screen.

CHARLES: November sixteenth. Liverish.

CARRIE: *(Drily.)* Champagne poisoning again. Great excitement at what sounded like the First Life Guards clattering along Brickfield Terrace.

(She crosses excitedly to the window, where she is joined by CHARLES.)

Drew back the curtains to see no fewer than *three* pantechnicons outside – the house next door having been let at last.

CHARLES: Good quality furniture...

CARRIE: The *pièce de résistance* was one of the new Wenham Lake ice safes – I have seen them in Merryweather's. *(Returning to her worktable.)* November seventeenth. At breakfast, asked Charlie if he didn't think the blancmange, left over from our party, a little warm and sour to the taste.

(CHARLES, reading his newspaper, grunts.)

I said: 'I have been wondering about an ice safe. It would be a boon in hot weather, and would pay for itself in the end.'

CHARLES: Then when that day comes, we will order one, and let the ice safe settle up.

CARRIE: Mr Gowing came round this evening, ostensibly to thank us for the party but in reality to help us eat our supper. The blancmange being brought in, he cried –

CHARLES: *(As GOWING.)* 'Hulloh! The remains of Wednesday?'

CARRIE: What breeding!

CHARLES: November eighteenth. Woke up quite fresh at last, after two days of headaches, and feel quite myself again. At breakfast, told Sarah –

CARRIE: My maid.

CHARLES: – not to bring up the blancmange again. It seems to have been placed on our table at every meal since Wednesday.

CARRIE: It has to be eaten up, dear – unless you would like me to bottle it, which is the only means we have of preserving food in this house.

CHARLES: November nineteenth. At twelve minutes past nine of that evening, Lupin entered the house with a face that could have come down from a poster for a melodrama.

CARRIE: He drank off a good wineglassful of 'Lockanbar' whisky –

CHARLES: Neat.

CARRIE: – then threw himself into a chair and smoked moodily. Presently I asked lightly: 'I hope Daisy is well?' Lupin said –

CHARLES: *(As LUPIN.)* 'You mean Miss Mutlar? I don't know whether she is well or not – but please never to mention her name again in my presence!'

CARRIE: A mother's forebodings confirmed.

(During the following they hang up some Christmas decorations.)

CHARLES: Christmas Day. By train to Carrie's mother's. We were just ten at dinner, including dear old Reverend John Panzy Smith, who married us. I proposed his health and made, I think, a very good speech.

CARRIE: *(Simultaneously.)* Christmas Day. By train to mother's. We were just ten at dinner, including dear old Reverend John Panzy Smith, who married us. Charlie proposed his health and made a very long speech.

CHARLES: 'On an occasion like this we are all of one mind, and think only of love and friendship. Those who have quarrelled with absent friends should kiss and make up. Those who happily have *not* fallen out, can kiss all the same.'

(A moment of tenderness while CHARLES and CARRIE kiss.)

CARRIE: *(Briskly, as presents are exchanged.)* Charlie gave me another bangle. A charming little thing, but I shall soon have enough bangles to start a hoop-la stall. December twenty-sixth.

CHARLES: Boxing Day!

CARRIE: Mr Cummings and Mr Gowing to supper, again... To my surprise, Charlie allowed himself to be persuaded to sing.

(CHARLES clears his throat and whispers to her.)

I knew that I did not have the music. What I did not know was that Charlie did not have the words.

(They have crossed to the piano where CHARLES takes up a pompous recital posture and CARRIE plays.)

CHARLES: *(Singing.)* 'I am the very model of a modern Major General; I've rumpty tumpty vegetable, animal and mineral; I know the something something and tiddly idle rumpty-al; From Waterloo to somewhere else in order mathematical –

(CARRIE crashes down the lid of the piano.)

CARRIE: December thirty-first.

CHARLES: The last of the Old Year.

CARRIE: My New Year resolutions. One. To be less sharp with my dear husband. Two. To discourage the belief in some quarters that The Laurels is open house. Three. To acquire a Wenham Lake ice safe, even if I have to serve rancid mutton all summer long.

CHARLES: At a quarter to twelve, decanted a bottle of 'Lockanbar' in which to drink out the Old year – a custom we have always observed.

CARRIE: There was some brandy in the other decanter, provided by Lupin.

CHARLES: As the witching hour approached, I *(Doing so.)* poured two measures of whisky.

CARRIE: I knew very well it was brandy.

(The strokes of midnight punctuate the following.)

CHARLES: No – whisky.

CARRIE: No – it's brandy.

CHARLES: Be assured by your husband, Caroline – that is whisky.

CARRIE: Be assured by your wife, Charles – it is brandy.

CHARLES: Do you drink brandy?

CARRIE: Hardly ever.

CHARLES: Then how do you know?

CARRIE: By the smell.

CHARLES: The smell is of whisky.

CARRIE: Brandy.

CHARLES: Whisky! *(To his diary.)* The result of our silly and unnecessary argument was that for the first time in our married life we missed welcoming in the New Year.

CARRIE: Better late than never. Happy New Year, dearest. *(They toast one another.)* Brandy.

(CARRIE takes out the glasses on a tray.)

CHARLES: January first. The New Year commences with a most important event. Getting back to the office after my midday dinner, I was told that Mr Perkupp desired to see me at once. After I had waited for quite twenty minutes he laid down his pen and said: 'Mr Pooter. You have been with us nearly twenty-one years, and we intend making a special promotion in your favour.' I need not say how dear Carrie received the joyful news.

CARRIE: At last we can have a Wenham Lake ice safe.

CHARLES: Be assured, Caroline, I have set my face against ice safes. January third. Two days now, and still no word as to what my new position is to be.

(They dismantle the Christmas decorations.)

CARRIE: Mr Perkupp is keeping him on tenterhooks deliberately. In his place, I should shake Mr Perkupp until his teeth rattled. January fourth.

CHARLES: Mr Perkupp sent for me at last and told me that my position would be that of –

CARRIE: *(In disgust.)* One of the senior clerks!

CHARLES: I was overjoyed.

CARRIE: I thought you had been a senior clerk all along.

CHARLES: It would appear not.

CARRIE: He still doesn't know what his new salary is to be. Poor, dear Charlie!

CHARLES: January fifth. I can scarcely write the news. Mr Perkupp has told me my salary would be raised by –

BOTH: One hundred pounds!

CARRIE: He was expecting twenty at most!

CHARLES: I sent Sarah –

CARRIE: My maid.

CHARLES: – round to the grocer's for a bottle of 'Jackson Frères' champagne. Carrie said –

CARRIE: It is an inducement to prevent you throwing down your pen and taking your abilities elsewhere.

CHARLES: No, dear; it is the reward for twenty-one years' tireless and faithful service to a good master.

CARRIE: He makes himself sound like a dray-horse.

CHARLES: Lupin then rapped the table and said: 'My guvnor, as a reward to *me,* has allotted me five pounds' worth of shares in a really good thing. Result: today I have made two hundred pounds.'

CARRIE: One hundred pounds – two hundred pounds – where will it end?

CHARLES: *(Laconically.)* Shopping.

CARRIE: First to Merryweather's, where I ordered a new chimney-glass for the parlour, and obtained an illustrated price-list of the Wenham Lake prize-medal ice safes. Bought a pair of Armstrong's Jubilee braces for Charlie at Peter Robinson's where I took morning coffee and a macaroon –

CHARLES: *(Surveying his new braces.)* It is a hundred a year, not a thousand.

CARRIE: – then to Darwitts', wholesale stationers, to enquire the cost of binding up my completed set of 'Lady Cartmell' blue cloth with deckled edges. While I waited at the trade counter, Mr Darwitts came out, every bit as tall and straight-backed as I remembered him. He returned my bow but looked mystified. I said: 'I am sure you haven't forgotten the Lord Mayor's Ball, already, Mr Darwitts?'

CHARLES: *(As DARWITTS.)* 'Forgive me, dear lady – I was lost in a brown study. It's Mrs Twentyman is it not?'

CARRIE: Mrs Pooter.

CHARLES: *(As DARWITTS.)* 'Of course. How are you, Mrs Pooter?'

CARRIE: Unaccountably, I was seized by what Lupin would call 'a fit of the blues' on the bus home – bit cheered up when dear Charlie brought me back a little present.

(He gives it to her. She unwraps it.)

Oh Charlie! It's a bangle!

CHARLES: February twelfth. Frank Mutlar called this evening, bringing with him Mr Murray Posh of Posh's three-shilling hats.

CARRIE: *(Impressed.)* He wore a diamond pin, and talked a great deal about hats – but a great deal more about Daisy Mutlar, with whom he seems very intimate.

CHARLES: February seventeenth. My birthday, uneventful.

CARRIE: He never did like a fuss being made of it, but now that his hair is growing thinner he refuses to observe it at all. I did feel that the occasion should be marked in some small way, and so as a token gave him a bottle of 'Koko' hair tonic.

CHARLES: Hulloh – this is no good! You have bought me a ladies' preparation.

CARRIE: Hair is hair, Charlie. Koko is just as efficacious for me as for women.

CHARLES: That is where you show your ignorance, Carrie – men's hair is utterly different, otherwise all the ladies would have beards. We don't know what might happen if I try this concoction.

CARRIE: We know what will happen if you don't. You are losing enough each day to stuff a cushion.

CHARLES: February eighteenth.

CARRIE: The Misses Tipper paid a call, asking if they might look over the house. Miss Tipper senior seemed strangely interested in how we got our big wardrobe upstairs.

CHARLES: Sawed it in half, of course.

CARRIE: Of course.

CHARLES: February twentieth. *(Opening his paper.)* Bless my soul, Caroline. 'Great Failure of Stock and Share Dealers. Mr Job Cleanands absconded.'

CARRIE: What a blessing.

CHARLES: I fail to see what is good about the disappearance of Lupin's employer.

CARRIE: It is good for Lupin. Mr Cleanards was never a good influence.

CHARLES: March second. We see little of Lupin since the announcement of Daisy Mutlar's engagement.

CARRIE: To Mr Murray Posh, the three-shilling hats chap.

CHARLES: He sleeps all day and spends his evening at music halls.

CARRIE: Last night he came in very late, singing that he was –

CHARLES: *(As LUPIN, singing.)* 'Quite all right, and tight as a tick, on Esmeralda's elder brother's elderberry wine.'

CARRIE: He continued to sing long after he must have gone to bed. I do not like Lupin singing in bed – it is not healthy. March eighth. This mid-morning a railway train broke down at the bottom of our garden, and was there for a good half hour, belching steam at us until the house resembled a vapour bath.

CHARLES: Yes – it will almost certainly have been the nine twenty-five from Royston.

CARRIE: I do not care if it was the night mail from Glasgow! If this is how it is to be, I would sooner live in a tent on Farringdon station.

CHARLES: March twenty-first. My great dream has been realized. Today my good master Mr Perkupp sent for Lupin and took him into the firm.

CARRIE: I feel as the wives of colliers do, when their sons are obliged to follow their fathers into the pit cage.

CHARLES: What a generous master Mr Perkupp is. My cup runneth over. My boy in the same office as myself. We can go down together by bus, come home together and together put a nail in her or a nail in there, or in summer paint a plantpot. It is all I have ever wanted.

CARRIE: April eighth. Mr Oswarld Tipper, the brother of the Misses Tipper was good enough to call, though unexpectedly. He would take nothing but a cup of hot water, with which he swallowed a powder. Mr Tipper asked –

CHARLES: *(As MR TIPPER.)* 'In the most general terms, Mrs Pooter, what is the rateable value of the houses hereabouts?'

CARRIE: I know nothing about such things, Mr Tipper. You would have to ask my husband.

CHARLES: *(As MR TIPPER.)* 'It is too high, I'll warrant, Mrs Pooter. The poor Rate is a scandal. Do you realize how much we are paying for the maintenance of lunatics, when there is not an asylum for miles?'

CARRIE: This striking me as men's talk, I changed the subject by pressing Mr Tipper to more hot water. After taking a sip he said –

CHARLES: *(As MR TIPPER.)* 'I believe you have a fondness for Peckham, Mrs Pooter.'

CARRIE: I have happy memories of Peckham, Mr Tipper, and should like to live there again one day.

CHARLES: *(As MR TIPPER.)* 'Do you know, at all, where my sisters live, in Stonequarry Terrace? They have asked me to say that they would like to invite you there for luncheon one day.'

CARRIE: I should be honoured.

CHARLES: *(As MR TIPPER.)* 'I have what you may consider a curious proposal, Mrs Pooter. The fact is that my sisters have taken a great fancy to your house. Being deaf, the proximity of the railway troubles them not; but I am given to understand that it vexes you greatly. The proposition I wish to put to you is this, Mrs Pooter...

(CHARLES, as MR TIPPER, begins to talk and gesticulate earnestly, his words being drowned, however, by the sound of a passing train.)

... *(As the noises die down.)* All things being equal, how would it be if you were to exchange houses?'

CARRIE: *(To her diary.)* I was flabbergasted. Either the proposal was hare-brained, or it was a stroke of genius. *(As if to MR TIPPER.)* You must give me time to think. And of course, I shall have to consult my husband.

(Wringing her hands and clearing her throat, she steels herself to do so. But CHARLES, 'entering', is not in a receptive mood.)

CHARLES: May thirteenth. A day of terrible misfortune. Lupin is discharged from Mr Perkupp's office.

CARRIE: It appears he has been so remiss as to recommend to one of the firm's most valued clients, Mr Crowbillon, who was dissatisfied with the Perkupps, that he should take his business to the firm of Messrs Gylterson and Co.

CHARLES: The name of Pooter will be blackened from one end of the Square Mile to the other! *(To his diary.)* I am to spend tomorrow at home, composing a letter to Mr Crowbillon, apologizing for Lupin's ill advice.

CARRIE: Lupin himself seems quite unconcerned. He came home wearing one of Posh's three-shilling hats. I thought he would sooner walk the streets bareheaded – but no: he and Mr Posh are the greatest of friends again. May fourteenth.

CHARLES: *(Chewing his pen.)* 'Dear Mr Crowbillon...'

(During the above CARRIE has put her bonnet on. Now she sets off for Peckham, represented by a street sign downstage. CHARLES remains at his desk.)

CARRIE: I have not set foot in Peckham since we left our dear little house in Shanks Place over a year ago. The Misses Tipper's residence is quite charming. Bow windows back and front – and no railway! Instead, the garden slopes gently down to the mellow old wall of Ackthorpe, Hollyman and Smedleys 'Jamboree Ales' Brewery.

CHARLES: *(Screws up a sheet of notepaper and starts again)* 'My dear Mr Crowbillon...'

CARRIE: We were just four for luncheon – the Misses Tipper's other guest being their next-door neighbour, Mrs Batch.

CHARLES: 'Esteemed Sir...'

CARRIE: On the excuse to Mrs Batch that I was 'interested in rooms', Miss Tipper junior conducted me on a thorough tour of the establishment.

CHARLES: 'With my renewed respects and apologies, I remain, my dear Mr Crowbillon, ever your obedient servant.'

CARRIE: I noticed a tin of Sheen's 'Murderem' Cockroach Fumigating Fluid on a scullery shelf, but was otherwise favourably impressed. If only I dare tell Charlie of my expedition, I could be very happy in Stonequarry Terrace.

CHARLES: May eighteenth. Hulloh! See this letter, Carrie! It is from Mr Franching, of Peckham.

CARRIE: *(Taking the letter.)* Peckham? Four Gables. The big house on the corner of Stonequarry Terrace, but seven doors from the Misses Tipper!

CHARLES: Two intended guests having let him down, he wishes us to dine with him this evening.

CARRIE: We cannot possibly accept, at such short notice!

CHARLES: We *must* accept. It is to meet Mr Hardfur Huttle, the distinguished journalist, who has come all the way from America.

CARRIE: He has not come especially.

CHARLES: I will brook no argument, Caroline. I have written our telegram of acceptance. *(He flourishes it.)*

CARRIE: Very well. Then you must buy me a new dress. *(To her diary.)* Never have I derived so little enjoyment from buying a dress. It is in bottle-green surah, with puffed sleeves, pulled tight with smocking, and scalloped about the neck –

(Downstage is trucked part of Mr FRANCHING's elaborately set dinner table. The FACTOTUM acts as waiter.)

CHARLES: *(Interrupting – to his diary.)* Later. What a journey it is from Holloway to Peckham! Why do people live such a long way off?

CARRIE: *(To her diary.)* Fears that my clandestine visit to the Misses Tipper should be exposed proved to be groundless. The company – which was attended by a hired waiter – was drawn not from the mere confines of Peckham but from the entire Metropolis. Mr Hardfur Huttle, the guest of honour, seized command of Mr Franching's table at once.

CHARLES: How I wish I could remember even a quarter of his brilliant conversation. I made a few little reminding notes on my menu card –

(Producing the menu card, he clears his throat. CARRIE gets in ahead of him.)

CARRIE: Here are two examples of Mr Hardfur Huttle's table talk. I ventured to ask: 'And what, Mr Huttle, is our opinion of the ice safe, which I have been told is the coming thing?'

CHARLES: *(As HUTTLE.)* 'Anyone who is told that the ice safe is the coming thing, ma'am, has the right to ask: "If it is only now coming, why was it not here before?" '

CARRIE: By and by, I shall remind Charlie of that speech. Later on, I had the opportunity to ask Mr Huttle his opinion of Peckham, as a place to live. Mr Huttle replied as follows:

CHARLES: *(As HUTTLE.)* 'Peckham is, ma'am, as ancient Athens was. In Peckham we have all that civilized man requires. Peckham is not across the river from London, ma'am – London is across the river from Peckham.'

CARRIE: I shall remind Charlie of that also.

(As they set off home.) Mr Hardfur Huttle spoke very warmly of ice safes, dear.

CHARLES: You have ice on the brain, Caroline.

CARRIE: So will you, dear, in the morning!

(The dinner table trucks off as they return to Brickfield Terrace.)

CARRIE: May nineteenth...

(She looks expectantly towards the door, but CHARLES does not appear.)

(Louder.) May nineteenth.

(CHARLES now groggily re-enters with an ice-bag on his head, and carrying two letters.)

CHARLES: *(In a croak.)* Lobster poisoning.

CARRIE: Champagne poisoning.

CHARLES: I drank very little of Mr Franching's champagne!

CARRIE: Then the lobster must have drunk it.

CHARLES: A letter from Mr Crowbillon. 'Sir, I totally disagree with you. Your son, in the course of five minutes' conversation, displayed more intelligence than your firm has done during the last five years.' What will Mr Perkupp say?

CARRIE: And a letter for Lupin from Gylterson and Co –

CHARLES: – enclosing a cheque for twenty-five pounds commission for introducing Mr Crowbillon, and offering him a position at two hundred pounds a year!

CARRIE: He is a second Hardfur Huttle! NB – he is also using bay rum again, and when he goes out at night, sports a button-hole. I expect we shall be vouchsafed the lady's name, in due course. *(A loud knock on the door. Answering it CARRIE becomes agitated.)* Mr Oswald Tipper! He said he had ventured to call, seeing as he had been in the next street attending to a grey parrot. I said in a low voice: 'I am sorry, but I cannot receive you, Mr Tipper, as my husband and son are in the house, and they know nothing of our business yet.' Mr Tipper asked, had I formed a favourable impression of his sisters' house? I told him 'We cannot discuss it on the doorstep. You must go.'

CHARLES: Who was that at the door?

CARRIE: Only the knife-grinder.

CHARLES: At the front? What are we coming to? May twenty-fifth. Wrote a satirical letter to the laundress. I said: 'You have returned the handkerchiefs without the colour. Perhaps you will return either the colour or the value of the handkerchiefs.'

CARRIE: I had not the heart to tell him that the laundress cannot read. June twelfth. The Misses Tipper called. While Miss Tipper senior was attending to her toilette, Miss Tipper junior asked if she could speak in confidence on a delicate matter. Miss Tipper junior then said: 'Oh, Mrs Pooter, it has become vital that we exchange houses for without my knowledge, my dear sister has already sawn the wardrobe in half.'

CHARLES: *(Entering.)* June twenty-ninth. Lupin has taken furnished apartments at Bayswater, to be near his friends, the newlyweds Mr and Mrs Murray Posh.

CARRIE: Making his fond farewells, our dear boy reeked of bay rum.

CHARLES: July third. We were invited to eight o'clock dinner at Lupin's rooms. Mr and Mrs Murray Posh, and Mr Posh's sister, Miss Lilian Posh –

CARRIE: Whom he has never previously mentioned.

CHARLES: – are to be the other guests. We were introduced to Miss Posh, whom Lupin called 'Lillie Girl' as if he had known her all his life. It is the way of young people nowadays.

CARRIE: Lupin and Miss Posh are in love. She was forever pushing him, and giggling, and giving him playful slaps. I must say, however, that I do *not* approve of young women smoking.

CHARLES: On arriving home at a quarter-past eleven, we found a hansom cab waiting with a letter. 'Dear Mr Pooter, Come down to the Victoria Hotel without delay, whatever the hour. Important. Yours truly, Hardfur Huttle.'

CARRIE: He came staggering back at two o'clock, having had goodness knows what to drink on top of all that champagne he was swilling down at Lupin's, and babbling about some friend of Mr Huttle's being able to put a large amount of business in Mr Perkupp's way. I made Charlie drink a pint of warm water, to help his liver.

CHARLES: July eleventh. One of the happiest days of my life.

(CARRIE's following speech is punctuated by spectacular shunting noises and billows of steam and smoke.)

CARRIE: July eleventh. It is the last straw. Today, while I was taking tea in the garden, an excursion train steamed into view, and with a hissing and a grinding of brakes and a shuddering of couplings, came to a halt in obedience to a new semaphore signal. It was packed with East End hobbledehoys and their donahs, who commenced to lean out of windows, cupping their hands and shouting –

(CHARLES, off to the City, turns and calls.)

CHARLES: *(As a cockney.)* 'Oh, my, ain't we the one!'

CARRIE: *(As a cockney.)* 'Wotcher, your lidyship!'

CHARLES: *(As a cockney.)* 'Hy sy, shell we hev arternoon tea wiv 'er nibs'?

CARRIE: My mind is made up. This very evening I shall sit down calmly with Charlie and inform him that I am positively desirous of removing to Stonequarry Terrace, Peckham. Should he demur, he will find a rat in his nightshirt.

CHARLES: This afternoon Mr Perkupp sent for me. Referring to my business with Hardfur Huttle, he said: 'My faithful servant, I will not dwell on the important service you have done our firm. I propose to purchase the freehold of your house and present it to the most honest and most worthy man it has ever been my lot to meet.' I could not speak. I sent a telegram to Carrie – a thing I have never done before – advising her of our good fortune.

CARRIE: *(Weeping, reads the telegram.)* Thus I am doomed to live out my days in Brickfield Terrace!

CHARLES: On arriving home I found Carrie crying with joy.

CARRIE: *(Sniffling.)* Dear, good, Charlie. I shall make the best of this misfortune and make The Laurels as pretty a little home as it can be.

CHARLES: I sent Sarah round to the grocer's for two bottles of 'Jackson Frères'.

CARRIE: It is a pity, on such a hot day, that it will not be chilled – it never is.

CHARLES: Carrie, my dear, I have a confession. I did not come straight home with my news – I made a diversion to Merryweather's.

(Crossing the room, he pulls on the mended bell which rings through the household in a prolonged and jangling peal.)

CARRIE: Charlie, your never – !

CHARLES: That I did – with what in our former circumstances would have been the next quarter's rent!

(And the FACTOTUM trundles in a gleaming, blackleaded kitchenstovelike contraption – the Wenham Lake ice safe.)

CARRIE: A Wenham Lake ice safe!

(From one of its cabinets CHARLES produces a bottle of 'Jackson Frères'.)

CHARLES: A proviso! In the limited space available, 'Jackson Frères' must always take precedence over blancmange.

CARRIE: It will! It will! Dearest Charlie.

(He is prising off the champagne cork. Both he and CARRIE look expectantly up to the ceiling – then down at the floor as the cork pops unexuberantly out of the bottle on to the carpet. As CHARLIE is about to pour champagne, SARAH hands him a letter which he opens, handing her the bottle.)

(To her diary.) The last post brought Charlie a letter from Lupin. He read it in silence, then said –

CHARLES: Hulloh! Here's one more reason for us to celebrate. Lupin writes that he is engaged to be married to Lillie Girl – and the wedding is to be next month!

(Expecting CARRIE to faint again, he holds out his arms.)

CARRIE: I know, dear. I know.

(They embrace each other, CARRIE weeping again as the CURTAIN falls.)

WWW.OBERONBOOKS.COM

Follow us on www.twitter.com/@oberonbooks
& www.facebook.com/oberonbook

www.ingramcontent.com/pod-product-compliance
Ingram Content Group UK Ltd.
Pitfield, Milton Keynes, MK11 3LW, UK
UKHW020720280225
455688UK00012B/439